LeeWards *Illustrated Library of*

Arts and Crafts

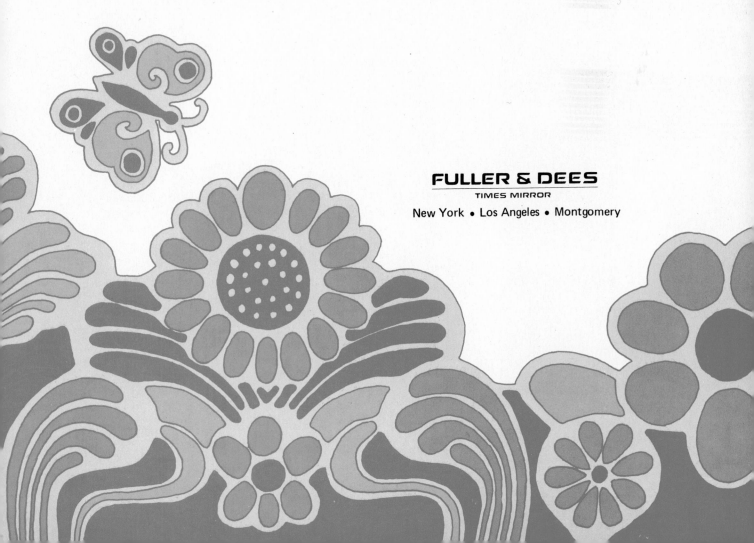

FULLER & DEES
TIMES MIRROR
New York • Los Angeles • Montgomery

Table Of Contents

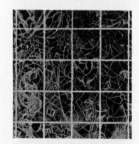

© FULLER & DEES MCMLXXIV
3734 Atlanta Highway, Montgomery, Alabama 36109
Library of Congress Cataloging in Publication Data
Main entry under title:

The Illustrated Library of Creative Arts and Crafts

1. Handicraft.
TT157.I43   745.5   74-22068
Complete Set ISBN 0-87197-076-7
Volume II ISBN 0-87197-078-3

From the time of the early cave dwellers to the present, rugs have been created to fill man's needs for warmth, comfort and beauty.

Plaster is an inexpensive, readily available and versatile material which may be used in traditional or innovative ways.

A revolutionary art medium, the science of plastics has merged with the fine arts to create an endless variety of art forms.

Decoupage became popular in the eighteenth century. Today this technique is used to create many beautifully finished items which include furniture, gift items and trinkets.

Because of its versatility and adaptability, paper can be used by all ages to create attractive, decorative objects.

FULLER AND DEES

PRESIDENT
James Lueck

PROJECT EDITORS
Pat Warner
Nell McInnish

THOMAS A. CHACHARON & ASSOCIATES AND SYNTHEGRAPHICS CORPORATION

EXECUTIVE EDITOR
Richard G. Young

CONSULTING EDITORS
Thomas A. Chacharon
Sidney Lewis

PROJECT EDITOR
Bonnie Oberman

ART DIRECTOR
Will Gallagher

PICTURE EDITOR
Holly Harrington

ASSOCIATE PICTURE EDITOR
Barbara Metzger

LAYOUT STAFF
John Mahoney
Deloras Nicholas
Joseph Petek

COPY RECORDERS
Nancy Bonfield
Linda Noel

ASSIGNMENT PHOTOGRAPHY
Larry Gregory
Wayne Lennenbach

ILLUSTRATIONS

Joanna Adamski-Koperska
Victor Brecher
Joe Chmura
John Draves
Ken Hirte
Margalit Matso
Will Norman
Joe Petek
Gabriel
David Meyer

LEE WARDS

CONSULTANTS
Ward Beck
Ken Bieschke

CONTRIBUTING AUTHORS

Alicia Anderson (Rug Making)
Consultant, Author
Dundee, Illinois

Lucille Bealmer (Doll Making; Patchwork, Quilting, and Appliqué)
Instructor in Art Education
Art Department
Northern Illinois University

Barbara R. Cohen (Crewel)
Vice President, The Yarn Shop, Inc.
Latham, New York

Douglas Eric Fuchs, f.s.c. (String and Wire Art)
Coordinator, Art Department
LaSalle School
Albany, New York

K. Riccio Guerin (Paper Crafts)
Teaching Assistant
Northern Illinois University

Jeannette Hart (Decoupage)
Crafts Instructor
Albany Institute of History and Art
Albany, New York

Terry Mullady (Stained Glass)
Instructor
Albany Institute of History and Art
Albany, New York

Dr. Philip S. Wells (Plaster Crafts)
Assistant Dean
College of Visual and Performing Arts
Northern Illinois University

Lizbeth Clark Wolf (Plastic Craft)
Graduate Assistant
Northern Illinois University

Pages 406, 407 Craft Course Publishers, Inc.

This lovely example of crewel work, from a picture worked by Lynne Knoll, uses a traditional design, the "tree of life."

Crewel

An ancient worsted embroidery technique, created out of a need for warmth and a desire to imitate Oriental styles, crewel work has once again become a popular craft.

The earliest embroidery styles originated in England and were determined by the preferences of the court. In the latter part of the sixteenth century, Queen Elizabeth I displayed a preference for embroidered roses and other typical English flowering plants, thus establishing the subject matter for the needlework of the day. When Oriental styles became the desire of the court — as during the reign of James I, who followed Elizabeth I — a new embroidery trend was set. And, if the court wished to emphasize religious or mythological motifs, these were created for needlework designs.

Because flax was commonly grown, spun, and woven into linen cloth in many English households, crewel was originally worked on linen used mainly for bed furnishings. In fact, linen was primarily used until 1764, when James Hargreaves, inventor of the Spinning Jenny, discovered a method for spinning cotton that yielded a thread strong enough to provide the warp for English weavers.

Figure 1. This attractive folding screen (opposite) displays three panels which have been embroidered with crewel yarns and silk threads. Oriental motifs were used to create the different designs.

The crewel stitches first used were plain tent stitches — short stitches slanting to the right forming solid backgrounds. These were worked to cover the cloth completely, assuring the thickness necessary for warmth.

Often, certain stitches were preferred because they used less wool. Surface embellishing stitches became popular and the solid background was only intended to show amidst the different flat, looped, and knotted stitches.

Figure 2. This eighteenth-century Queen Anne sidechair is a fine example of early upholstered furniture. The fabric design is typical of this period. (Courtesy, Victoria and Albert Museum.)

In the latter part of the seventeenth century, there was a drastic change in the style of needlework. Embroiderers began using silk and, simultaneously, crewel work began to lose its heavy look. Popularity for this type of needlework lagged a bit in England until the early eighteenth century when, during the reign of Queen Anne, upholstered furniture became more commonly used. Indeed, at this time, crewel work seemed to

reach its pinnacle: it acquired a delicate look, highlighted with touches of silk threads.

Shortly thereafter, crewel work in England subsided and was not revived until Victorian times. Unquestionably, the masterful English pieces which have survived to this day were often the result of the work of several people under the close supervision of one British gentlewoman. Eventually, the popularity of crewel spread across the Atlantic to America, but patterns, oddly enough, contained a great deal of Oriental influence. Typical motifs were of herons and other waterfowl as well as water plants.

Figure 3. American colonists continued the English tradition of crewel embroidery, as shown in the wing chair above, but they modified the technique by using different stitches and a less formal design. (Courtesy, Mission House, Stockbridge, Mass.)

The early American colonists, remembering how fashionable crewel work had been in England, continued the craft long after their ancestors had tired of it. Furthermore, the crewel of American women developed its own light style, involving less work and the use of fewer kinds of stitches.

Along with renewed interest in such colonial communities as Williamsburg, Virginia, came a revived interest in early-American styles. It is the restoration of colonial customs and practices that accounts for much of the recent attention being given to crewel work.

Figure 4. These early American embroidered bed coverings provided privacy for the sleeper and helped to protect against the cold. (Courtesy, The Henry Francis du Pont Winterthur Museum.)

Common Terms Used In Crewel

Couching: a method for tacking threads to a fabric's surface: first, long stitches are sewn or placed on the area to be covered and then short stitches, generally of another color and/or fiber, are used to tack the longer ones in place.

Crewel Work: embroidery worked with fine, 2-ply yarns.

Double Threading: a technique for embellishing stitches already embroidered into the fabric; accomplished by working first in one direction and then back in the opposite direction. Embellishing stitches are sewn through the fabric only when beginning and ending the technique; the contrasting or secondary thread is brought under and over those stitches already sewn.

Interlacing: another embellishing technique which gives a circular lacy effect. (See also Double Threading.)

Laid Work: similar to couching, this work is generally used to create a pattern such as cross-hatching within an outline..

Tapestry Needle: a needle with a smooth rounded tip used in canvas work.

Tent Stitch: a common short stitch worked at a diagonal.

Threading: an embellishing stitch worked in one direction. See also Double Threading.

Warp: the series of vertical threads on a loom which run the full length of the material to be woven.

Whipping: an embellishing stitch in which the secondary yarn wraps the first by sliding under each stitch. The effect is like a fine rope. See also Double Threading.

Working Yarn: yarn being used to make stitches; not the yarn already worked.

Figure 5. The Long and Short Stitch was used to fill in the flower petals. This stitch is most attractive when different shades of one color thread are worked in the shape.

Basic Equipment And Supplies

Materials used in crewel work are easy to obtain and can usually be purchased in needlework shops and art/needlework sections of department stores. Kits are available, containing background material, yarn, needles, and instructions. Following is a list of basic items that may be used for a crewel project, including explanations about each. In addition to the following items, one will also need a staple gun, staples, and a sprinkler bottle.

BACKGROUND FABRICS

Linen is generally suggested as a background fabric because it is neutral in color and substantial in texture. A blend of cotton and linen, heavy cotton, and wool are also acceptable. There are also linen and synthetic blends, but unless used with a hoop or frame (explained below), these will not block well. British Satin, although a lovely fabric, is not as readily available as linen and is three or four times more costly. Because the right side has a sheen, it is quite formal.

If it is necessary to block the crewel work upon completion, the background fabric should be washable.

TRANSFER PATTERN AND TRANSFER PENCIL

These items, used to apply designs to the background fabric, are necessary because few companies provide background materials with patterns, unless in a kit. Transfer patterns and pencils are available in needlework shops and department stores. The former, which are easier to use, are drawn on a tissue-like paper in colored ink. The pattern is transferred by placing it, inked-side down, onto the right side of the fabric and pressing over it with a hot iron. Transfer pencils are used to draw original patterns and the result is the same as that achieved with a transfer pattern.

SHADOW BOX

A shadow box is an inexpensive method for transferring a design to fabric. It works on the same principle as placing a drawing against a bright window and then holding a plain piece of paper

Figure 6. A shadow box (above) is easily constructed from an ordinary cardboard box, glass, foil, and a lightbulb. The pattern and fabric are tacked against the box to transfer the design (opposite).

over it; the drawing is easily traced on the plain paper. The following items are necessary: a box (without cover) at least 4" deep and approximately 14" square; aluminum foil; a piece of clear glass to rest on top of the box; masking or freezer tape; a 60-watt bulb fitted into a socket and a cord long enough to reach an outlet so that it is at a comfortable height. (A "drop" or "lead" light is also appropriate.)

Line the box with the aluminum foil to avoid scorching. Place the light bulb in the box and cut a 1-inch wide vertical slot near one corner through which the light cord can pass. Tape all sides of the glass for safety.

In order to copy a design onto a background fabric, a non-running fine-point pen is needed. Also have handy a fine felt-tip pen. This will *not* be used on the background fabric, but rather to emphasize the pattern's lines, making them more easily seen for transferring.

HOOPS AND FRAMES

Hoops are oval or round; frames are square or

rectangular. The purpose of each is to hold the material taut. There are "lap" or "table" hoops and frames; others that stand on the floor give the embroiderer greater freedom. When shopping for a hoop or frame, the finished wooden types with a side tightening screw are preferable to those made of metal. Because it is not essential to work with a hoop or frame, the only way to decide if one will be useful is to experiment. However, using a hoop or frame is usually desirable for the Long and Short Stitch, French Knots, laid work, and couching. Moreover, when the embroidery is taut at all times, it is possible to have a better perspective of the entire piece. On the other hand, a project without a hoop or frame is easier to move around when it is worked other than at home.

STRETCHER BARS

These are wooden bars to which the fabric is stapled after it is blocked as part of the finishing process. They also can be used to hold the fabric taut during embroidering, but there must be sufficient fabric surrounding the design so that the bars are clear of the work area. When used, these bars become part of the finished piece and are placed in a recessed frame with the completed embroidery.

Figure 7. It is advisable to use a hoop or frame when working most crewel projects. This wooden lap hoop is one example of the many different types of hoops that are available.

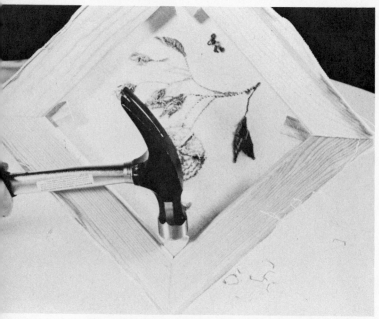

Figure 8. One method of holding the fabric taut is to staple the material to a stretcher bar. Wedges hammered into the corners keep the fabric from sagging while the embroidery is being worked.

CREWEL YARNS

Because the thickness or weight of crewel yarns varies, it is helpful to experiment with several different weights in choosing a satisfactory yarn. Generally speaking, a bolder, more contemporary piece looks best with a heavier yarn; fine detailing, as in a human figure or a dainty bird, is better worked with a finer yarn. In some shops, crewels may be purchased by the strand; however, it is more common to buy either a card of 30 yards or skeins of 1/4, 1/2, or 1 ounce.

NEEDLES

A crewel needle is sharp, has an elongated eye, and is available in packages sized 3 to 9 and 5 to 10. The smaller the number, the larger the needle. The needle should be large enough to bring the crewel yarn through the material easily. If the yarn has to be yanked through, a larger needle is needed to make a larger opening in the cloth. A tapestry needle may also be used, but only on the

Figure 9. Crewel equipment can be purchased wherever needlework materials are sold. Supplies include linen fabric, an assortment of yarns and needles, a hoop, and a pair of embroidery scissors.

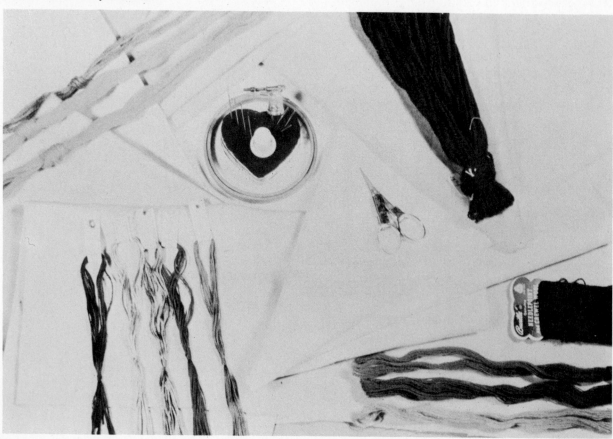

surface of the fabric, not to sew through it. These needles, which range in size from 18 to 22, are sold either in assorted sizes or all one size. Again, the smaller the number, the larger the needle. A size 18 will usually suffice unless the embroidery is very delicate.

BLOCKING BOARD

This should be a board to which either freezer paper, with the waxed side against the board, or waxed paper can be easily stapled. Freezer paper is preferred because it is easier to draw on and to see pencil lines for guiding the blocking of the embroidery.

Basic Procedures

No matter how anxious one is to begin a new project, certain precautionary measures will assure against unnecessary problems. Imagine how discouraging it would be to complete a lovely piece of crewel work, only to discover a nonfast color had been used, thus ruining the piece when it is washed. The following suggestions, therefore, are meant to help avoid such situations; their implementation takes only a little extra time.

THREADING THE NEEDLE

Hold the needle so that the narrow portion of the eye end is horizontal. *Fold* the yarn over the eye end; pinch it between the thumb and forefinger so tightly that the yarn is not visible. Slide the needle out without moving the thumb and forefinger, then turn the broad side of the eye end toward the thumb and forefinger. Gently push the eye between the thumb and forefinger and *slowly* open them. Because the yarn has been flattened, it will go into the eye as the eye is pushed into it. This procedure is relatively easy and takes only a minimal amount of practice.

PREPARING THE BACKGROUND FABRIC

It is not necessary to wash linen or British Satin, but do wash any blended material. Before applying the pattern to the fabric, be sure that the fabric is free of any creases and that all style numbers and other miscellaneous markings such as trademarks have been cut away.

If a hot iron transfer is to be used, place the inked or penciled side down on the right side of the fabric. After centering the transfer, pin it in each corner to prevent sliding when iron is applied. To see if the pattern has been transferred, after ironing, unpin one corner and gently lift the pattern.

Before beginning the embroidery, turn the edges of the fabric under about 1/2" and baste with running stitches, using regular cotton sewing thread. This keeps the fabric from ravelling. Then, place the fabric in a hoop or frame if desired. If using stretcher bars, stretch the material over the bars and staple it.

TESTING THE CREWELS

As with the background fabrics, it is necessary to be sure that the crewel colors will not run during blocking. To test the yarn, cut a 2-inch piece of each color; hold the pieces under lukewarm water for a few seconds; place them on a paper napkin; cover them with another napkin; let dry. If no dye is absorbed by the napkin, the crewels are fine to use.

TESTING THE PEN

Even a "waterproof" pen used to transfer a design onto fabric should be tested. Make a few marks on one corner of a paper napkin. Wet the opposite corner and fold the napkin so that the wet portion is over the markings. If the markings do not transfer, the pen is safe to use.

FLAT STITCHES

There are hundreds of embroidery stitches, some of which are particularly common to crewel work. Although each *variation* of every stitch has its own name, the list of basic stitches is not overwhelming. Furthermore, each crewel worker has favorite stitches and usually does not use every possible stitch. Keep a small piece of fabric nearby for experimenting with new stitches and for testing color combinations. Some of the more popular stitches are Satin, Surface Satin, Stem, Chain, Buttonhole, French Knot, Herringbone, Fly, Fishbone, Seed, and Feather. Each of these is discussed below. Some of the related diagrams show two different lines. These signify the use of more than one color or shades of one color.

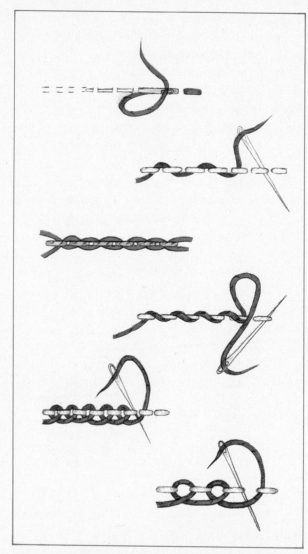

Figure 10. Pictured above are various kinds of Running Stitches: Running Stitch (A), Threaded Running Stitch (B), Double Threaded Running Stitch (C), Whipped Running Stitch (D), Pekinese Stitch (E), and Spaced Pekinese Stitch (F).

Running Stitch

Generally used for outlining, this simple stitch can also be used attractively in parallel rows to fill a shape. For a plain Running Stitch, use a crewel needle; for a whipped or threaded Running Stitch, also use a tapestry needle. The Pekinese Stitch shown here is simply another type of Running Stitch.

Back Stitch

The Back Stitch, like the Running Stitch, can also be threaded, double threaded, or whipped.

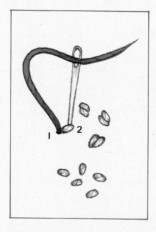

Figure 12. Bring the needle up at 1 and down at 2 to make a single Seed Stitch. To make a double Seed Stitch, make two stitches side by side.

Seed Stitch

This version of the Back Stitch is sewn in different directions, has an airy look, and appears smaller than a Back Stitch.

Satin Stitch

A familiar stitch used in monogramming linens, this stitch completely covers an area and uses as much yarn on the back as it does the front. It is prettiest when worked at an angle. Begin in from one end of the area to be worked and work to the

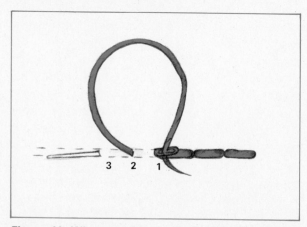

Figure 11. When sewing the Back Stitch, bring the needle up at 1, down at 2, and up at 3. Pull the thread through to complete the stitch.

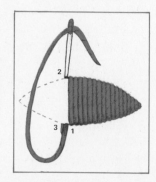

Figure 13. To do the Satin Stitch, bring the needle up at 1, down at 2, and up at 3. Pull the thread through, and continue working.

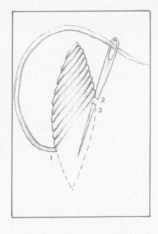

Figure 14. For the Surface Satin Stitch, bring the needle up at 1, down at 2, and up at 3. Pull the thread through and make a similar stitch on the opposite side. Continue working from right to left.

opposite end. Then turn the work around and complete the covering.

Long and Short Stitch

This effective stitch gives a sense of dimension but requires practice. It is a Satin Stitch worked in stitches of alternating lengths, with each succeeding row piercing the one above.

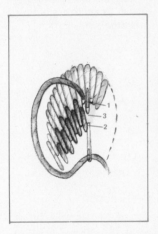

Figure 15. To begin the Long and Short Stitch, alternate long and short stitches in the first row. Work the second row with stitches of equal length by bringing the needle up at 1, down at 2, and up at 3.

Using a hard pencil, lightly draw broken lines on the fabric in the direction the stitches are to take. Then, starting at the center of this area, work to either the right or left, using the pencil lines to indicate the stitch direction. In the first row, bring the needle out at the bottom of the stitch and insert it just above the line to be covered. In succeeding rows, the needle is inserted just above the base of the stitch of the previous row. The first row of stitches is of alternating lengths, i.e., short, long, short, long. All succeeding rows until the last are of long stitches. The last row is again short and long.

When it is not possible to take a full-sized stitch because the pattern's shape narrows, make a smaller stitch or none at all. When a smaller stitch is used, it is referred to as a *compensating* stitch.

A suggested length for the Long Stitch is approximately 1/3"; the Short Stitch should be half that. However, the final determination of the size of the stitches really depends upon the size of the area to be filled and the preference of the embroiderer.

Fishbone Stitch

This is similar to the Satin Stitch. But, unlike the Satin Stitch, each Fishbone Stitch extends a bit beyond the center of the area to be filled so that the succeeding stitch crosses it, creating a depression in the center of the shape. Start with a vertical stitch at the top to cover any open space (see diagram) and then begin the Fishbone Stitches to the left of the first stitch.

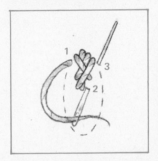

Figure 16. To make a Fishbone Stitch, bring the needle up at 1, down at 2, and up at 3. Pull the thread through and insert needle on opposite side. Continue working to the right and left of center until the shape is filled.

Stem, Crewel, or Outline Stitch

With the working yarn held above *or* below the needle, a very fine line is created by the use of this stitch. For an Alternating Stem, the position of the yarn is changed for each stitch.

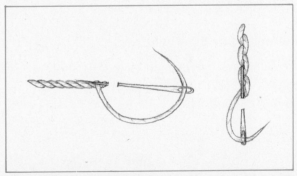

Figure 17. For the Stem Stitch (left), bring the needle up at 1, down at 2, and up at 3. Pull thread through and repeat. For the Alternating Stem Stitch (right), bring the needle up at 1, holding thread to the left of the needle, then, down at 2 and 3. Now, holding thread to the right, insert needle down at 4 and up at 5. Repeat, alternating thread from left to right.

Herringbone Stitch

This is a very fast stitch to work and has many variations. The needle is always moved horizontally across the back of the fabric.

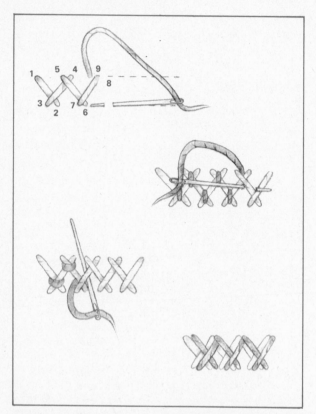

Figure 18. To sew a Herringbone Stitch (A), bring the needle up at 1, down at 2, and up at 3. Pull thread through, and repeat at 4 and 5. Continue, following the numbered sequence. Variations of the stitch include the Tied Herringbone (B), Interlaced Herringbone (C), and Double Herringbone (D).

LOOPED STITCHES

Buttonhole or Blanket Stitch

Hold the needle vertically and bring it up to the left of the yarn at numbers (3), (5), (7), etc., as shown. The stitches may be spaced far apart

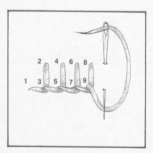

Figure 19. To do the Buttonhole Stitch, bring the needle up at 1, down at 2, and up at 3. Holding the thread under the point of the needle, pull the thread through and follow the numbered sequence.

(Open Buttonhole) or close together (Closed Buttonhole).

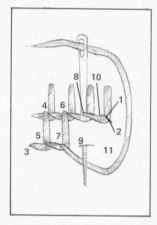

Figure 20. Make a row of Buttonhold Stitches to begin the Attached Buttonhole Stitch; tack the last stitch down at 1 and 2. Bring the needle up at 3, down at 4, and up at 5. Holding the thread under the needle point, pull the thread through and follow the numbered sequence.

Fly Stitch

Separate Fly Stitches resemble birds on the wing. When worked closely (Closed Fly), a center vein is created. This is a particularly good stitch for depicting feathers, pine tree boughs, or leaves.

Figure 21. For the Fly Stitch (left), bring the needle up at 1, and, holding the thread under the thumb, down at 2 and up at 3. Pull thread through and make a stitch to 4. A row of Closed Fly Stitches (right) is made by shortening the stitch between 3 and 4.

Feather Stitch

This is a slanted Buttonhole Stitch. It may be regularly spaced or the fabric may be turned alternately to the left or to the right to effect a look of openwork.

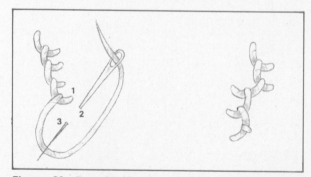

Figure 22. For the Feather Stitch (left), bring the needle up at 1, down at 2, and up at 3. Pull the thread through and follow the numbered sequence. To vary the stitch (right), make two Feather Stitches to the right and turn the fabric to make two to the left.

Closed Feather Stitch

This stitch is a one-sided Fly Stitch with the needle always held vertically across the back. A tricky stitch when ending and restarting, it is worked first to the right and then to the left.

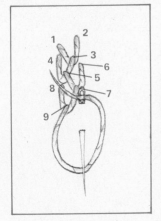

Figure 23. To begin the Closed Feather Stitch, bring the needle up at 1, and, holding the thread under the thumb, down at 2 and up at 3. Pull the thread and follow the numbered sequence.

Cretan Stitch

This is similar to the Feather Stitch except that the needle always takes the same size stitch across the back of the fabric. As the shape to be covered widens and narrows, an inner design is created. Start with a tiny stitch in order to cover the tip (see illustration) and always place the yarn under the needle.

Figure 24. To make the Cretan Stitch, bring the needle up at 1, and, holding the thread under the point of the needle, down at 2 and up at 3. Pull the thread through and make a stitch on the opposite side. Continue working until the shape is filled.

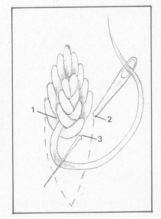

CHAINED STITCHES

Chain Stitch

Also known as the "Lazy Daisy," this stitch may be whipped, interlaced, or woven. When the needle is put down at number (2), it is a hair away from number (1). Before the loop disappears, catch it

by bringing the needle up at (3). Go down at (4) and the loop is held secure.

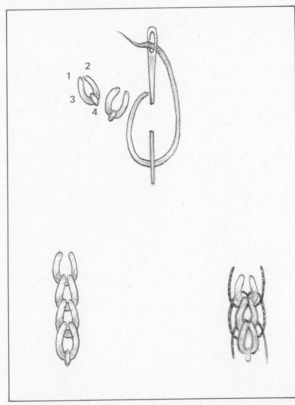

Figure 25. For the Chain Stitch, or Lazy Daisy (A), bring the needle up at 1, down at 2, and up at 3. Pull the thread through and make a stitch to 4. For the Attached Chain Stitch (B), bring the needle up at 1, and, holding the thread in a loop under the thumb, insert the needle at 2. Bring the needle up at 3, and, holding the thread, insert the needle at 4. Follow the numbered sequence, attaching the last loop of the chain by making a stitch from 9 to 10. An Interlaced Chain Stitch (C) is made by interlacing thread through the chain, as shown.

Split Stitch

This resembles a Chain Stitch but is much more delicate. It is a short straight stitch, pierced by the next stitch. At number (3) in the diagram, the needle is brought up through the stitch just above the number (2) position.

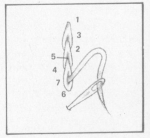

Figure 26. The Split Stitch is begun by making a stitch between 1 and 2. Bring the needle up at 3, and pull the thread through, splitting the stitch in half. Make a stitch from 3 to 4, and follow the numbered sequence.

Cable Chain Stitch

This is a fast and effective stitch. Bring the needle up, place it on the fabric horizontally under the yarn, slide the needle down, and take a vertical stitch, catching the loop of yarn as it comes up.

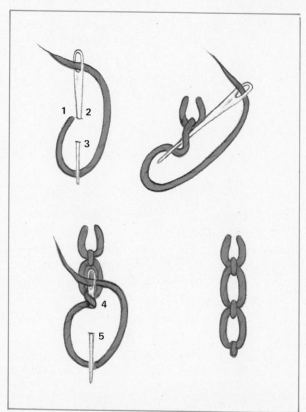

Figure 27. To make a Cable Chain Stitch, bring the needle up at 1, down at 2, and up at 3 (A). Wind the thread around the needle as shown (B). Insert the needle down at 4 and up at 5 (C), and pull the thread through to make the finished stitch (D).

Tête de Boeuf (Steer's Head) Stitch

Start with a Fly Stitch and complete with a Chain Stitch.

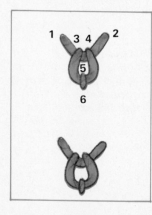

Figure 28. To make a Tête de Boeuf Stitch, bring the needle up at 1, and, holding the thread under the thumb, down at 2 and up at 3. Pull the thread through, then insert the needle at 4 and bring it up at 5, holding the thread in a loop under the thumb. Pull the thread through and make a stitch to 6.

KNOTTED STITCHES

Coral Knot

This is a dainty textured stitch. The yarn is held horizontally under the left thumb. The needle is inserted above the line and exits beneath it in the loop that is formed.

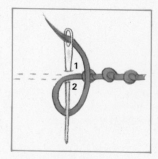

Figure 29. For the Coral Knot, insert the needle through the fabric at 1 and up at 2, holding the thread in a loop under the needle. Pull the thread through, and re-insert the needle at the instructed distance from the knot.

Palestrina Knot

This is similar to the Coral Knot in texture but involves a bit more work. Work from left to right, tugging gently on the yarn as each stitch is completed.

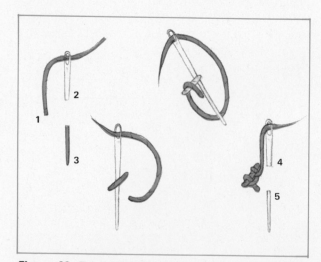

Figure 30. To begin the Palestrina Knot, bring the needle up at 1, and insert down at 2 and up at 3. Pull the thread through, and run the needle under the stitch as shown. Run the needle under the stitch a second time, as shown, and pull the thread. Insert the needle through the fabric down at 4 and up at 5. Pull the thread through, and continue working.

French Knot

Bring the needle up and position it horizontally. With the yarn at back of needle, wind it once around the needle. Tightly holding the yarn that is around the needle, put the needle back through the canvas as close as possible to its original position and pull it slowly.

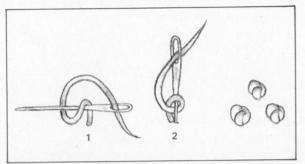

Figure 31. To do a French Knot, bring the needle up, and wind the thread around it as shown. Place the needle down just next to the point at which the thread emerges, and pull the thread through.

Bullion Knot

Bring the needle up at number (1). Determine the length of the completed knot (see illustration). Place the needle down at (2), where the knot is to end, but leave a loop long enough to wrap several times around the needle. Bring the needle up at (3), one thread away from (1), and wrap the yarn of the loop around the needle as many times as necessary to give the length desired. Gently hold loops in place on the needle while bringing the needle and yarn through them; put the needle down at (4), one thread from (2).

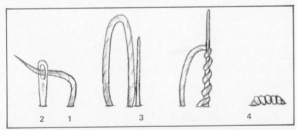

Figure 32. Begin the Bullion Stitch by bringing the needle up at 1, down at 2, and up at 3; leave enough thread to wind around the needle as shown. Place the needle down at 4 and, while holding the wound thread in position with the thumb, pull the thread through.

COUCHING OR LAID STITCHES

Couching

As mentioned earlier, couching is a method of tacking threads to the fabric surface. One must be careful not to disturb the longer threads when tacking them down. Tiny straight stitches can be used for couching. Open spaces may be worked

in varied stitches; long stitches may be whipped or laced.

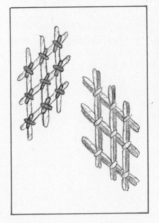

Figure 33. An area of horizontal and vertical threads can be couched, or tacked, to the fabric by making Cross Stitches (left) or Whip Stitches (right) at the points at which the threads intersect.

New England Economy Stitch

This covers well and has a very slight texture to it. Always work the stitch at an angle. Bring the needle up at number (1), down at (2), up and over at (3), and down again at (4). Notice that stitches (3)/(4) and (7)/(8) lie across long stitches, keeping the latter securely in place. This adds to the wearing quality of the stitch.

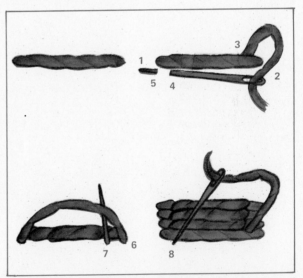

Figure 34. To do the New England Economy Stitch, make a stitch from 1 to 2, and bring the needle up at 3. Put it through at 4 and 5, and pull the thread through. Then bring the needle down at 6 and up at 7. Pull the thread through, and bring the needle down at 8.

Romanian Laid Stitch

This stitch is a variation of the New England Economy Stitch. By making longer stitches across the back of the fabric, the overlapping stitch in the center is shortened.

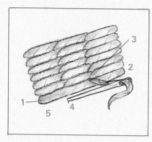

Figure 35. For the Romanian Stitch, take one stitch from 1 to 2. Bring the needle up at 3, and insert it through the fabric down at 4 and up at 5. Pull the thread through, and continue working.

Spider Webs

Either whipped or woven, these stitches are decorative and easy. While a whipped Spider Web may contain any number of spokes, a woven Spider Web must consist of an odd number.

Figure 36. For the Spider Web, bring the needle up at 1, down at 2, and follow the numbered sequence.

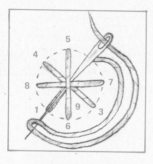

In working the whipped Spider Web, the needle is brought out at the center, close to the intersection of the threads. Slide the eye end under the threads and, before pulling the yarn all the way through, place the needle into the loop, forming a slip knot.

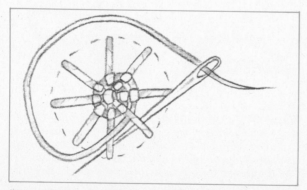

Figure 37. To do a Whipped Spider Web, first make a Spider Web, then bring the needle up at the center. Whip the thread under one spoke, bring the thread back under the same spoke, and whip it under the next spoke, as shown. Pull the thread, and continue working.

Because the remainder of the stitch is done on the surface except for the end, it may be preferable to use a tapestry needle at this point. Place the needle over one spoke to the right and pass it under two spokes to the left; pull gently; repeat until the web is as full as desired. It is fine to use one color for the spokes and another for the whipping, but leave the ends of the spokes partially exposed. To end, insert the needle down over the last spoke it went under and secure the yarn to the wrong side.

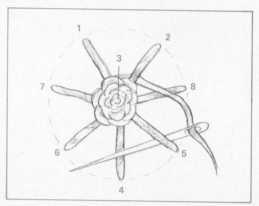

Figure 38. For a Woven Spider Web, first make a Spider Web, then bring the thread up at the center. Weave the thread under one spoke and over the next spoke, as shown, and continue working.

The woven Spider Web is easy to work and gives a very different look. Begin with a large Fly Stitch —(1) through (4)—for an uneven number of spokes. Bring the needle out at (5) and put it in at (3), out at (6) and in again at (3). Repeat the procedure for additional spokes. Then bring the needle out close to (3) and immediately begin weaving either with the eye end of the needle or with a tapestry needle. Work under and over, repeating until the area is as filled as desired. To finish off, insert the needle and secure well on the wrong side.

BLOCKING

It is necessary to block all crewel work except that which has been worked on stretcher bars. After the embroidery has been completed and basting stitches have been removed, wash the embroidered piece in lukewarm water and a mild soap (not a laundry detergent). Do not soak the fabric. Instead, move it gently back and forth through the water. When the fabric is clean, squeeze out the excess soap and water — *do not wring the fabric*

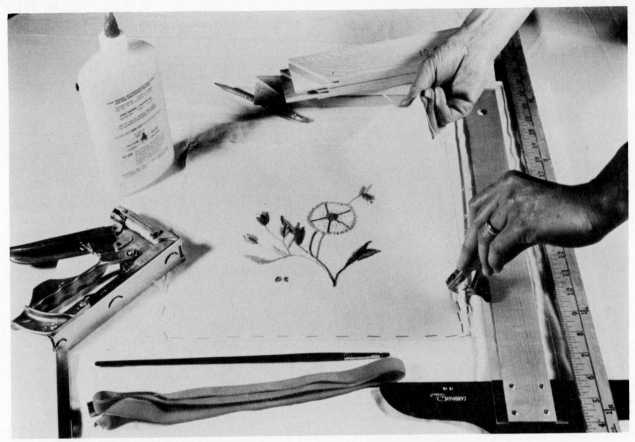

Figure 39. The embroidered fabric must be blocked unless it has been worked on stretcher bars. Remember to pull the material taut before fastening it to the blocking board.

— then rinse it gently in clear lukewarm or cool water.

Place the embroidery on a bath towel, fold part of the towel over it, then pat to absorb excess water. Remove the embroidery from the towel and place it on top of any clean nonabsorbent surface, such as a countertop or washing machine. It will take no more than a day to dry. As it is drying, pull (with clean hands) the fabric, first in one direction then in the other. Do this three or four times.

When the fabric is dry, it is ready to be blocked on the blocking board. Using a yardstick as a guide, draw lines at a right angle at least as high and as long as the finished piece. With right side up, start at the corner just drawn; align one side of the fabric to one of the pencil lines and staple it with a staple gun. Do the same along the other pencil line with the second side of the fabric. Draw a third pencil line at a right angle to the second and staple the third side. Finally, draw the fourth line at a right angle to the third and staple the last side. Sides one and two will be easy to attach to the blocking board. However, the third and fourth sides will be a bit more difficult because the material has to be pulled taut.

For the next step, saturate the entire embroidered fabric with water from a sprinkler bottle. (It takes a while for water to permeate wool because of its lanolin content.) To assure saturation, place a dampened open facecloth on the embroidery and pat it — this forces water into the piece and also absorbs the excess. Wring the cloth out and repeat the procedure twice. Be certain that there are no puddles on the board. Also avoid any dry spots — these will appear as stains when the piece dries. If at this point the fabric has stretched and is no longer smooth on the blocking board, remove the staples; repull the fabric; restaple. Lay the board flat while the piece is drying; make sure the embroidery stays taut. Once again, allow a day for drying, after which the piece will be ready for mounting. If immediate mounting is not planned, remove the piece from the board and keep it in a dry place.

Projects You Can Do

The following projects are designed not only to teach stitches but also to appeal to various tastes in styles. One is traditional; another is modern, but with ancient motifs; and the third is traditional, but a bit more complicated. None is costly or requires an inordinate amount of time.

EMBROIDERED FLOWER

When deciding whether to undertake this project, keep in mind that if the flower, which is rather large, were to be completely covered with closely worked stitches, it would not only be too heavy for the size of the piece but would also detract from the rest of the design. Because the Spider Web Stitch called for in the center of the flower is quite heavy, use of the Seed Stitch is also suggested to give the flower a lighter feeling. Notice too that different shades of green and a variety of stitches add more interest to the remainder of the piece. It would be dull if only one or two stitches were used. However, the color and stitches in-

cluded here are offered only as suggestions. Feel free to improvise in any way.

Materials

The following materials are needed for this project: (1) a 12-inch square piece of bleached or natural linen; (2) tracing paper and a transfer pencil; (3) a package of assorted crewel needles; (4) one tapestry needle; (5) one 30-yard card (or 1/4 ounce) of each of the following colors of crewel yarn: dark turquoise (t1), medium turquoise (t2), light turquoise (t3), yellow (y), coral (c), dark green (g1), medium green (g2), and light green (g3); (6) four 8-inch stretcher bars; (7) 1¼ yards of 1/2-inch trimming (velvet) for finishing; (8) white glue and a small 1/4-inch brush for applying; (9) brown wrapping paper (12" x 12"); and (10) eyelets and picture wire.

Directions

For the testing of the yarn and the size of the needle, refer to the information in the section on

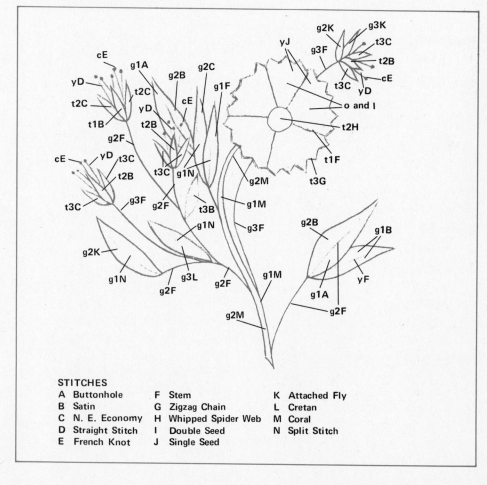

Figure 40. Trace and enlarge this flower pattern, then transfer the design to the embroidery material. Use the color guide (see text) and stitch key to work the "embroidered flower" project.

STITCHES

A	Buttonhole	F	Stem	K	Attached Fly
B	Satin	G	Zigzag Chain	L	Cretan
C	N. E. Economy	H	Whipped Spider Web	M	Coral
D	Straight Stitch	I	Double Seed	N	Split Stitch
E	French Knot	J	Single Seed		

"Basic Procedures."

1. Trace the pattern from the page onto tracing paper with the transfer pencil. (Remember, when using a hot iron transfer pencil, the design must be retraced on the other side of the paper so that the design will not be reversed when the pattern is ironed on.)

2. Center the design on the background fabric. The four dots in the diagram mark an 8-inch square outline. There should be 2" of excess material. Place a straight pin at each corner to keep the pattern from slipping.

3. Transfer the design to the fabric, using whichever method is preferred.

4. Baste the fabric on all raw sides.

5. The letters and numbers in the illustration denote colors and kinds of stitches. The color code is indicated in item 5 under "Materials" above. Because some shapes seem to overlap, the following is a suggested order for working the piece: (1) the largest leaf to the left of the large flower; (2) the small flower overlapping the largest leaf; (3) the leaf directly under the first leaf and its overlapping leaf in Satin Stitch; (4) the spokes of the large flower; and (5) the circumference of the large flower. The remainder can be worked in any order. When working sections that have more than one stitch or color, it is generally easier to work the center first and then the outer area.

6. After all embroidery is completed (add initials if desired), remove the basting threads and block as described under "Basic Procedures."

Mounting on Stretcher Bars

The most inexpensive way of finishing this piece is as a picture to be hung on the wall (directions are given below). However, there is enough excess material for seams for a pillow; add backing and stuffing.

Figure 41. To begin finishing the embroidered flower project for hanging, staple the fabric to the marked stretcher bars (A), trim off excess fabric (B), apply glue to the back of the stretcher bars (C), and place the project, glued side down, on brown wrapping paper (D) to dry overnight.

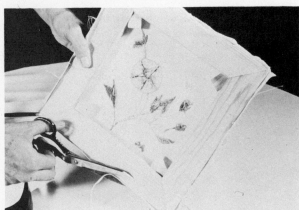

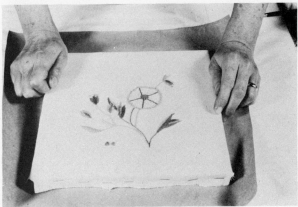

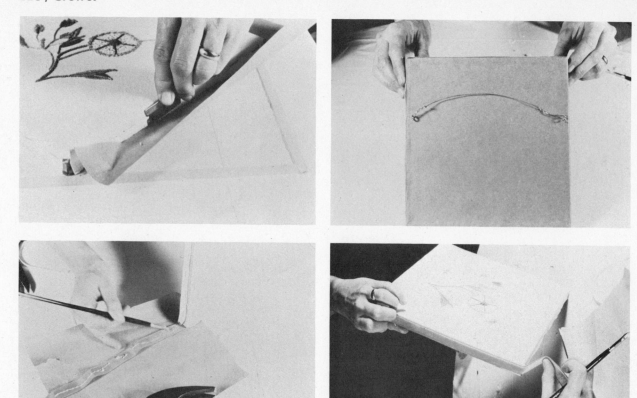

Figure 42. To complete the frame, trim the brown paper with a razor blade (A). Dampen the paper backing to smooth it, then attach eyelets and wire to the boards, as shown (B). Apply glue to the sides of the boards and the back of the ribbon (C). Place the ribbon around the edges of the bars to hide the staples and give the project a neat, finished look (D).

Figure 43. Finished and mounted, the embroidered flower is ready to hang. This design could also be worked on a hoop and used to make a pillow.

1. Assemble the stretcher bars into a frame.

2. Mark the center of each side of the frame and of each side of the embroidery. Use pencil on the frame; a running stitch of cotton thread, unknotted, on the fabric.

3. Staple the fabric sides at the marked center to the marked centers of the frame. Work slowly on each side and staple the remainder of the fabric sides to the frame sides. Allow space to insert scissors and cut a square of excess fabric at each corner. The fabric should be taut; if not, insert a wedge (which comes with the stretcher bars) in each of the four corners from the back of the frame. Tap gently with a hammer at each wedge. This will push the stretcher bars outward and pull at the fabric, making it tight. Add more staples to the sides if necessary.

4. Cut off excess fabric.

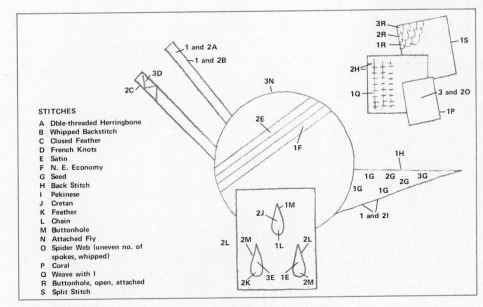

Figure 44. Trace and enlarge this pattern, then transfer the design to the embroidery material. Use the color guide (see text) and the stitch key to work the "modern picture" project.

5. Spread out the wrapping paper. Apply white glue with a brush to the inclined edge of the back of the frame and place this side down on the paper. Allow it to dry overnight. Then cut through the paper with a razor blade directly next to the frame and all around it.

6. With a damp washcloth wipe the brown paper backing. Let dry. This will shrink the paper, causing it to be smooth and taut across the back of the frame.

7. Screw the eyelets to the back of the frame and attach the wire.

8. With the brush apply glue to the entire back of the 1/2-inch trimming. Starting at the bottom, slowly and carefully place the trim all the way around. Join the two ends carefully.

A MODERN PICTURE

For those with less traditional tastes, this project is fun to do. Turned one way, it may resemble a cartoon-like bird; turned another, it may recall a utensil from a chemistry lab. Actually, it is abstract.

The Pekinese Stitch used on the lower edge of the rather long triangle is a stitch used on mandarin robes in the nineteenth century. The three oval shapes to the left of the center are one of the most ancient symbols in the world: they are known in Greece as the "seed of life"; in India as the "peacock's eye"; and in England as the "pine cone."

The suggested colors are red, blue, and purple. Equally attractive are the combinations red/orange/yellow or green/turquoise/blue. This project, like the preceding one, is planned for stretcher bars. Required materials are also the same except that the crewels needed are one 3-yard card (or 1/4 ounce) each of blue (1), purple (2), and red (3).

Directions

Test the yarns and size of the needle as described under "Basic Procedures." Follow steps 1 through the first part of step 5 as described for the previous project. Because some stitches are worked over others, use the following order for working: (1) the two narrow rectangles coming from the large

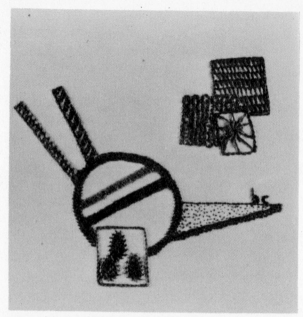

Figure 45. The finished modern picture, mounted or framed, may be hung in either of two ways. Turned one way (above) it resembles a bird; turned upside down, the design is more abstract.

circle; (2) the two bands in the circle; (3) the long triangle coming from the right of the circle; (4) the box to the left of the circle's center; (5) the circumference of the circle; and (6) the three boxes from front to back. Complete as for the first project.

A BOUQUET

This pattern uses the Long and Short Stitch, probably the most effective stitch in all embroidery. British Satin is suggested for a more formal look, but any suitable fabric is acceptable, of course. If this is to be a picture, use 12-inch stretcher bars. It may also be a pillow with backing and welting of British Satin.

Materials

For this project you will need: (1) 1/2 yard of British Satin; (2) one card each (or 1/4 ounce) of crewel yarns as follows: dark green (g1), medium green (g2), light green (g3), dark yellow (y1), medium yellow (y2), light yellow (y3), dark blue (b1), medium blue (b2), light blue (b3), and red (r); (3) crewel needle; and (4) hoop.

Directions

Test the materials as described under "Basic Pro-

cedures" and then proceed as follows:

1. Transfer the two halves of the pattern to one sheet of tracing paper. In doing this, be certain that the arrows meet, forming Xs. The pattern will match. Remember, if using a hot iron transfer pencil, retrace the complete design before placing it on the fabric.

2. Follow the color and stitch code as given. A hoop will be helpful, particularly for the French Knot, Long and Short Stitch, and Bullion Knot areas.

3. Complete as for the previous projects or make into a pillow.

Figure 46. The bouquet design was embroidered on British satin, backed with the same material, then stuffed. Although satin is recommended, any fabric may be used for this project.

For Additional Reading

Bucher, Jo, **Embroidery Stitches and Crewel,** Meredith Corporation, 1971.

Davis, Mildred J., **The Art of Crewel Embroidery,** Crown, 1962.

Lane, Rose Wilder, "The Story of American Needlework, #1: Crewel," **Woman's Day,** March, 1961.

McBride, Regina, **Creative Crewel Embroidery,** Doubleday, 1974.

Wilson, Erica, **Crewel Embroidery,** Scribner, 1973.

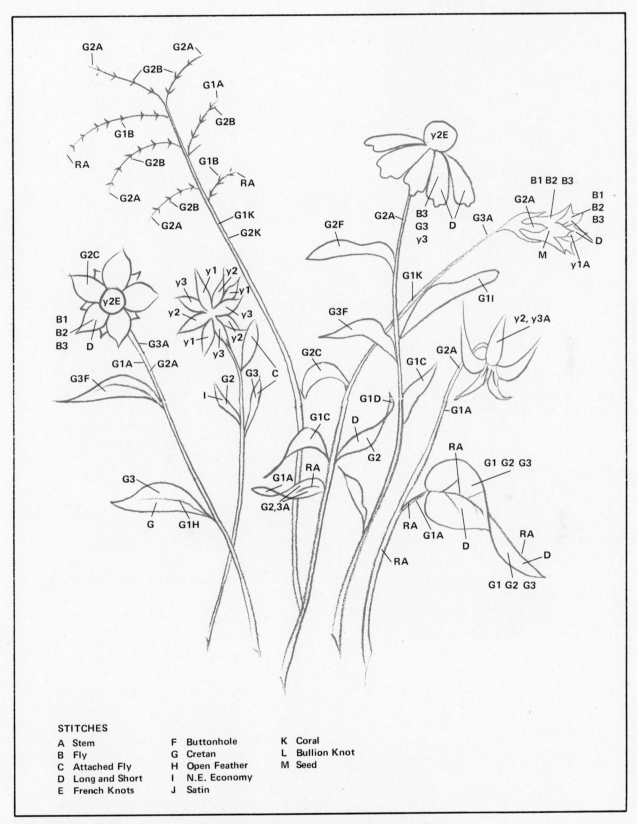

STITCHES

A	Stem	F Buttonhole	K Coral
B	Fly	G Cretan	L Bullion Knot
C	Attached Fly	H Open Feather	M Seed
D	Long and Short	I N.E. Economy	
E	French Knots	J Satin	

Figure 47. Trace and enlarge the above pattern, then transfer the design to the embroidery material. Use the color guide (see text) and stitch key to work the "bouquet" project.

Patchwork, Quilting, and Appliqué

Patchwork, quilting, and appliqué are ancient crafts which have been revived at various times throughout history.

Patchwork, truly a folk art craft, was invented by American pioneer women, who saved every tiny piece of fabric from their sewing projects. Then they planned designs and created patched or pieced mosaics of cloth which were used as the top layer of quilts. The patchwork designs were either geometrically shaped or patterned at random, thus the name "crazy quilt" for the latter.

The geometric designs depicted early pioneer days, travels, possessions, children, events, and feelings. They were all original and imaginative, and they represented true patchwork because each piece and design had special meaning. Many of the better known pattern names tell a history of the country: Lemon Star, Pine Tree, Duck's Foot-in-the-Mud, Crown of Thorns, Kansas Trouble, Rising Sun, Bear's Paw, Indian Hatchet, Folded Love-Letter, Tippecanoe and Tyler Too, and Log Cabin.

The crazy quilt was the earliest of the pieced type of quilt — it has existed as long as people have worn clothes. It was used in ancient Egypt, pre-Hispanic Peru, India, France, England, and the United States. In the Victorian age, these beautiful old quilts were made of haphazardly cut pieces of silk, velvet, damask, moire, brocade, and ribbons. Colors and fabric textures were carefully planned. The pieces were cut into irregular shapes, sewn together, and then decorated with intricate, elaborate embroidery. Some were edged with lace. The embroidery stitches followed and outlined the patterns of the cut pieces of fabric.

Quilting has been known in Europe, Asia, Africa, and South America for centuries. People in ancient Asia wore quilted and padded clothes. Byzantine and Persian silks were often quilted to give added weight to fabric so that jewels might be sewn on for embellishment. Quilted fabrics were also worn under chain mail or armor for protection and strength. Quilting was used in wall hangings to add warmth to homes and in floor coverings for comfort as well as warmth.

Figure 1. Cuna Indians created this striking "mola" (right) by cutting designs from four or five layers of stacked fabric. (Courtesy, Collection of Mr. and Mrs. William Bealmer.)

Figure 2. These appliqued panels, using an Egyptian motif, illustrate the variety of design possibilities in applique. (Courtesy, Collection of Mr. and Mrs. Jack Arends.)

Figure 3. The pattern of this patchwork quilt was created by individually pieced designs, precisely planned and sewn. (Courtesy, Collection of Mr. and Mrs. William Bealmer.)

Quilting was brought to colonial America by English and Dutch settlers, who made it a popular folk art. American women have continued to develop the art of quilting, still inventing new methods today. Contemporary quilting techniques have no limits.

Appliqué means "applied work" in French. Applying cloth, leather, or fur to a background surface has been an important creative art since early history. Appliqué has been used in America since colonial times, throughout the pioneer days of the westward movement, and to the present. Because craftsmen wanted to experiment with the use of curvilinear shapes, the appliqué technique, which allows much freedom in design, quickly became popular. Designs using plants, flowers, animals, and birds were developed. These were cut out of cloth, the edges were turned under, and the designs were sewn to the background material. Some were embellished with intricate stitches of contrasting colors. Craftsmanship quality of the appliqué quilts surpassed that of the earlier true patchwork quilts.

Another important technique in appliqué work is the reverse appliqué or cut work, such as that created by the Cuna Indians of San Blas Islands off Panama. These magnificent works, which are called *molas,* are made by using four or five colors of fabric stacked in layers. Designs are cut from several brightly colored layers.

Art created from fabrics is part of the contemporary museum and gallery scene. Soft sculpture has become a medium for many important artists and

Figure 4. A satisfying design and careful work are characteristic of traditional patchwork quilts. (Courtesy, Collection of Mr. and Mrs. William Bealmer.)

craftsmen. Many artists have used appliqué in creating cloth banners and wall hangings. Others use appliqué in combination with other stitchery methods. Imaginative sculptural forms by many contemporary designers incorporate the quilting methods of the past. Claus Oldenburg has used fabric in many of his three-dimensional works. Norman Laliberte uses cloth in his wall hangings and banners, many of which are stuffed, padded, and quilted. Alma Lesch, Marilyn Pappas, Sarita Rainey, Jean Ray Laury, Nell Sonnemann, Linda Vetter, Anna Sunnergren, and Elsa Brown are just a few of the contemporary designers using relief techniques and three-dimensional fabric forms.

Figure 5. The crazy quilt (above), one of the earliest types of pieced quilts, is designed with randomly shaped cloth pieces. (Courtesy, Collection of Mr. and Mrs. Edward Holcomb.)

Figure 6. Imaginative sculptural forms were used by Lucille Bealmer in this contemporary design (right) to emphasize the three-dimensional qualities of quilted fabric.

Common Terms Used In Patchwork, Quilting, and Appliqué

Appliqué: the fastening of a cut cloth design onto a background fabric by sewing or gluing.

Banner: a cloth poster depicting an idea in a simple design.

Padded Work: quilting in which cotton or dacron batting, foam rubber, or urethane foam may be stuffed between two layers of cloth.

Patchwork: a technique in which small cut pieces of cloth are sewn together to make a large fabric mosaic.

Quilting: three layers of cloth held together by hand or machine stitching; the top layer is the design fabric, the middle layer is the batting or filler, and the bottom layer is the backing.

Reverse Appliqué: a fabric design made by layering several colors of cloth and cutting through the layers to expose the desired color.

Sculptural Appliqué: three-dimensional designs made of stuffed forms or shapes of fabric.

Stitchery: an art form using expressive designs for decorating fabric.

Trapunto: a form of Italian quilting resulting in a high relief; two layers of cloth are quilted, the undercloth is cut open, stuffing is added, and the cloth is stitched together.

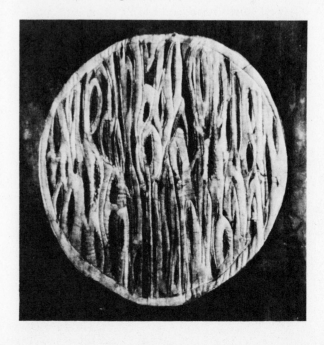

Figure 7. Quilting supplies are inexpensive and may be found in the household. Cotton batting, fabric, and sewing equipment are necessities, and a sewing machine can be very helpful.

Cotton

Cotton is excellent for both hand and machine appliqué. It is durable, does not fade readily, is inexpensive, and easily available.

Duck

Duck is a heavy fabric, made of cotton fibers. It is excellent for backgrounds and is best for machine appliqué.

Linen

Linen is an excellent fabric for stitchery on appliqué and also makes a wonderful background material for wall hangings. However, it is expensive and not abundantly available. Some fabric shops and upholstery shops may sell linen. It can also be purchased in various weights from some distributors of art materials.

Wool

Woolen fabrics are excellent for background and design pieces, and remnants often can be purchased inexpensively. However, remember that wool must be mothproofed.

Felt

Felt, available in a wide range of colors, can be easily used in hand appliqué. The beginner might have difficulty in working with felt in machine appliqué, because it tends to stretch. Felt is expensive for large areas.

OTHER MATERIALS

Excellent for appliqué are such materials as beads, buttons, lace, shells, pieces of wood, cord, yarns and threads, antique fabrics, and ribbons. These items are available in fabric shops, variety stores, antique shops, attics, and flea markets.

General supplies that one should have include the following: fabrics for cut designs, background, and backing; sharp needles; straight pins or silk pins; No. 50 mercerized cotton thread; small, pointed, sharp scissors; white glue; cotton or dacron batting for use in quilting; tailor's chalk; a ruler; and a sewing machine (optional).

Basic Equipment And Supplies

Supplies needed for any of these crafts are easy to obtain and reasonable in cost. Except for selecting a fabric, many of the items are probably already on hand.

FABRICS

The following fabrics may be purchased in fabric shops, department stores, and occasionally in upholstery stores. In addition to those described, many man-made fabrics — e.g., rayon, nylon, polyester, dacron, and acetate — can be used for applique if they are durable, fadeproof, and washable.

Basic Procedures

Patchwork, quilting, and appliqué are textile arts created with a minimum of materials. Patchwork is the sewing together of fabric pieces. Quilting is stitching through two layers of fabric with batting or filling in between. And, appliqué is applying fabric designs to a background. Each is basically easy to do. However, the beginner does need to consider quality and originality in design and imagination in color.

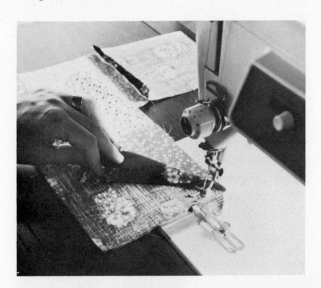

PATCHWORK

Patchwork is done by cutting out pieces of cloth and sewing them together at the edges. Some designs can be created in geometric patterns; others can be a variety of odd and random shapes of cloth sewn together into a "crazy quilt" pattern. These are the more traditional ways of designing patchwork. The contemporary designer of patchwork uses a mixture of shapes, fabrics, hand stitching, machine stitching, and adhesives. To

Figure 8. Stacks of colored fabric squares are sewn together at the edges to create patchwork. The squares are pinned with right sides facing each other, then stitched along the edges.

Figure 9. This pieced patchwork is a good beginning project with only three different fabrics and a simple design. It may be used for a quilt, or as fabric for a larger piece of patchwork.

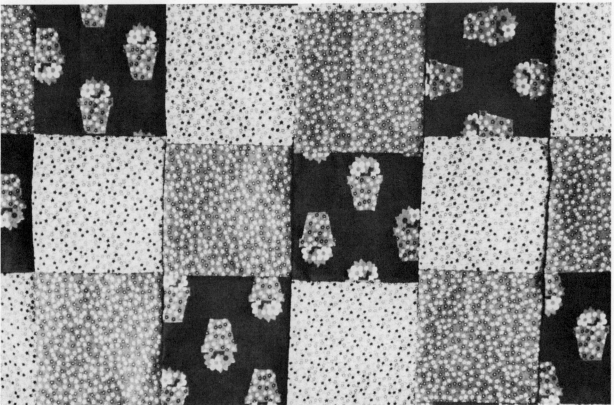

Figure 10. A crazy quilt design grows from the random shapes of cloth stitched together. Elaborate hand stitches or fancy machine stitches may be added for decoration.

create patchwork in traditional patterns, choose a design; cut out the pieces, using a cardboard template; keep pieces in stacks by color; then sew them together. The pieces can be stitched into squares and the squares can be sewn together either by hand or by machine. If a sewing machine is used, the squares, rectangles, or triangles should be cut about 1/4 inch larger on all sides than the final shapes. Pin the shapes with right sides facing each other and stitch along the edges on the 1/4-inch margin.

One of the simplest ways to learn how to do patchwork is to start with one yard each of three colors of cotton fabric. Cut each piece into 6-inch squares and place them in stacks. Start stitching the squares together in a sequence, alternating the colors. As the beginner gains more experience in patchwork, succeeding designs can be made

more complex. It is fun to create unusual patterns from one's own imagination.

Crazy quilt patchwork is more random in concept. The wonderful free shapes, when sewn together, become a large mosaic of colors, patterns, and textures. Today, the textile designer can create a beautiful "crazy quilt" because of the availability of a tremendous range of colors and fabrics. Random piecing of the fabrics makes a pattern unnecessary. All the designer needs is a needle, thread, scissors, and patches of fabrics totalling 2½ to 3 yards.

Use satin, brocade, damask, velvet, taffeta, silk, printed cottons, wools, or ribbons. Old trunks and chests in attics or shopping at a flea market can yield a fantastic quantity of interesting fabrics. Old ties can be opened out and cut up. Make 8- or 9-inch blocks of shapes by laying pieces out on paper. Overlap the edges of each piece and baste or pin them together. Connect them with decorative embroidery stitches by hand or with interesting machine stitches. Thirty-two to 36 blocks will make a throw. Another way of sewing these

Figure 11. This traditional quilt uses piecing on the top fabric to create a distinctive design. (Courtesy, Collection of Mrs. Florence Welch.)

kaleidoscopes of color and texture together is to connect the edges of the blocks with ribbons. The ribbon-decorated blocks can be stitched together to create a beautiful long skirt. Obviously, there are many ways to create "crazy quilt" mosaics.

Contemporary crazy quilts can be designed with a combination of shapes — geometric and free, precise and random. The stitches that are added can be beautifully manipulated to become part of the expression. Experimentation can extend to use of various weights of fabric, transparent against transparent or textured against bright, smooth cloth. Designing means making choices, being selective and individualistic, and always being concerned with the integrity of the materials. The beginner should experiment with materials and techniques just as the experienced craftsman does. Indeed, the beginner should try some designs other than the traditional geometrics or Victorian "crazy quilt" mosaics.

One simple way to start is to cut 1 yard each of several colors of fabric into 2- or 3-inch widths of strips or bands. Make the strips 2, 4, 6, and 8 inches long. Stitch them end to end into ribbons or bands that are 6 feet long. Be sure to alternate colors. The next step is to sew bands together into a rectangle. The way color works and creates a visual impact is apparent in the easily designed patchwork fabric.

Machine stitching can be used to outline the various areas of color. The fabric can be quilted. Designs can be cut from the patchwork and appliquéd to another background. Hand embroidery can be used to enhance sections. Printed borders can be added to the width of the fabric. The ways in which the fabric can be used are limitless. With a little experience, training, and confidence, the beginner can become involved in the creation of beautiful patchwork designs.

Quilting is the stitching together of the quilt top, the filler, and the backing. The three layers are sewn together either by hand with fine quilting stitches (small, evenly spaced running stitches) or with machine stitching. Lines are drawn on fabric with tailor's chalk and a ruler. The threaded needle is pushed down through three layers and then up — usually there are five to nine stitches to

an inch. Knots are pulled into the batting. Before quilting on a large scale is attempted, the textile designer should always practice on a small sampler.

Machine quilting works best on diagonal lines because the fabric does not pucker as much as it would if it were stitched on horizontal or vertical lines. When using cotton batting, the quilting lines should be quite close because the batting tends to wad up. The quilting should be done with straight stitching set at six to ten stitches per inch.

Both hand quilting and machine quilting should be started at the center and worked out to the edges. Fabrics for both the top and the backing should always be of the highest quality; the batting can be of cotton or dacron. Some people prefer a very thin, well-washed cotton sheet blanket for the filler. The needle should be short and sharp. There are special quilting threads;

Figure 12. The edge of a quilt (below) is pulled apart to show the three layers which make it up: the backing fabric, the cotton batting, and the top fabric.

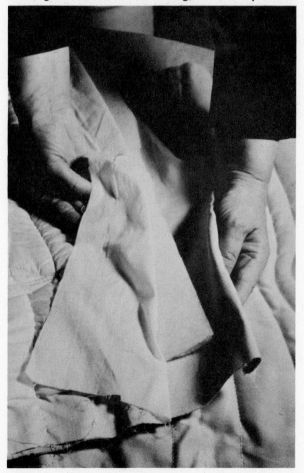

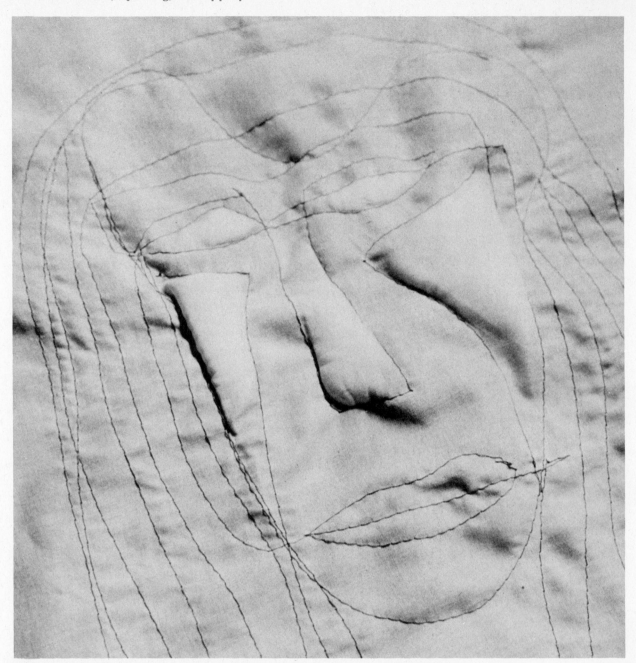

Figure 13. The eyes, nose, and cheeks of this figure have been padded in trapunto, a quilting technique that creates a relief effect.

however, mercerized thread between No. 50 and 70 is excellent. In hand quilting, the needle often is pushed through the cloth with the thumb. For this reason, it is sometimes a good idea to tape the thumb. Pins should be used to hold the three layers together. After quilting is completed, be sure to trim the edges so that fabrics and batting are even. The edges are bound with double fold bias tape. The beginner should start with a small quilted project and then advance to larger quilts only after gaining some expertise.

Trapunto

Trapunto quilting is sewn through two layers of cloth, after which areas are padded or stuffed. A relief effect is achieved by slitting the backing cloth in an area enclosed by stitching, inserting the stuffing, and then sewing the slit together.

The top fabric in trapunto often is a sheer off-white material, such as organdy, dacron, or voile. The backing for the top fabric can be a dark material, brown or black, of a loose weave, such as netting. The two fabrics should be pinned together. Then, using beige thread, machine stitch the outline of any light pencil drawing on the top cloth. Machine sewing also can be used to enclose various areas of the design. After these areas have been outlined with machine stitching, they are ready to be stuffed. The trapunto piece is turned over, dark side up. The enclosed areas are slit and stuffed, then the slits are hand sewn together.

Another way to work trapunto is to stitch partly around a design area, leaving a small opening. Stuffing is pushed into the opening, after which stitching is completed. In this way stitching and stuffing are done concurrently. Trapunto is a beautiful way to work with relief and sculptural surfaces in creating lights and shadows. The machine stitching resembles a line drawing.

Even the beginner can explore possibilities of using different fabrics, various colors of cloth and thread, and unlimited design ideas. Moreover, trapunto can be combined with stitchery and applique. One should experiment with new techniques before undertaking a major project.

Stuffed, padded, and quilted forms are exciting sculptural ideas for a beginner to try. First a design should be planned and drawn. Then the kinds of fabrics should be selected, taking into consideration color, weight, and texture. Decisions should be made as to which areas are to be built up or stuffed and which are to be flat. Any of the previously described methods can be used, either individually or in combination. Prestuffed pieces can be made by cutting out two identical shapes for each unit. Turn these with right sides facing each other. Pin the fabric pieces together. Hand or machine stitch around the shape but leave a small opening. Stuff the shape with cotton or dacron batting and sew up the opening. When the individual shapes are ready, they can be appliquéd to a background fabric, or attached in such a way that the design is in the round and can be seen from all sides.

APPLIQUÉ

Appliqué is the redesigning of cut pieces of fabric and applying or fastening them to a background of cloth. A relatively simple process, it requires few materials: cloth, needle, thread, and scissors. However, it is the artist's imagination that influ-

Figure 14. This beautiful example of stitchery and appliqué, called ''Bathsheba's Bedspread,'' was made by Alma W. Lesch. (Courtesy, Museum of Contemporary Crafts, New York City.)

ences his own productivity and uniqueness. It is the combination of ideas, kinds of fabric, colors, variety of stitches, textures, and design implementation which can lead to an endless number of appliqué ideas.

Appliqué is an excellent way of adding shapes to cloth. Hand stitching can be used to hold pieces to the background. Fanciful stitches of embroidery can also enhance or accent parts of the appliqué. Traditional appliqué was often finished with very small precise stitches. The contemporary designer uses both fine stitching and bold stitches to strengthen the design of the appliqué.

As with all crafts, the quality of the design and the workmanship is important. The beginning artist in applique should plan simple shapes in interesting color combinations. To create an original design is far more satisfying than to copy something created by another person. The use of simple free shapes in nature, geometric shapes, or letters and numbers can be developed into limitless design ideas. Designs sewn on small squares of cloth can be joined together into a large piece or they may be worked directly onto a large background fabric. To hold appliquéd pieces, select a background fabric that is heavy enough, such as felt, heavy cotton, or canvas. Linens and wools are also fine, but they are expensive. The best fabrics for cutting out the pieces of the design are felt, cotton, and synthetic fabrics which keep an even edge and will not ravel or fray.

After the pieces are planned and cut out, they can be arranged on the background fabric and pasted or pinned into place. Fabric shops sell a web-like fabric, called Stitch Witchery, which fuses to cloth with heat. The appliqué designer can cut pieces of the fusible cloth in the same designs as the cloth pieces. The fusing material should be placed between the appliqué piece and the background fabric. A hot iron is applied to the appliqué, causing the fabrics to fuse.

To hand stitch, the appliqué piece is pinned to background fabric. The edge is turned under and stitched with small running stitches. The thread used should be mercerized cotton of the same color as the appliqué. The needle should be sharp enough to go through appliqué and background easily. Additional embroidery stitchery can be used to enhance the design.

Figure 15. A fabric shape and a fusible web are placed on background fabric and then ironed. The fabrics will adhere to one another and keep the appliquéd piece on the background.

The sewing machine has become standard equipment in so many homes today that the beginner may choose to use it. The machine can be used simply to stitch design pieces to the background or it can be used for very decorative stitchery on the appliqué.

Part of the fun in creating appliqué with a sewing machine is to experiment with various lengths and thicknesses of stitches. The beginner should use a variety of pattern shapes to explore available possibilities of various sewing machine stitches. These stitches can be used to overlap the edges of the appliqué or to create decorative patterns on the design pieces. The best fabric for these purposes is a heavy cotton such as duck, canvas, or denim. The small pieces will not slide around and the fabric will not pucker under the machine stitching.

There is beauty in letting raw edges show. Edges of appliqué are often frayed deliberately by craftsmen who like the contrast between a hard, clean-cut edge and a soft, uneven, raw edge. Raw edges of the appliqué can be decorated with zigzag sewing: close zigzag stitching will cover the edges with a band that looks like a satin stitch. (This can be done by hand but the sewing machine is faster.)

Most innovative craftsmen use both hand and machine work in their appliqué wall hangings and banners. The beginner in appliqué designing should explore many different possibilities and be open minded enough to incorporate unique, unusual effects with traditional patterns.

Reverse Appliqué

Reverse appliqué is a highly decorative way of designing with fabric. Often five or more layers of brightly colored cloth of the same size are tacked together; various layers of cloth are then cut through, folded back, and stitched down.

Working in reverse appliqué is fairly easy to do. However, it takes time, care, and patience. The beginner can use felt effectively because it does not need any hemming. Until one learns, it is best to work a sample with 6-inch by 6-inch squares of cloth; colors should be bright and contrasting — for example: orange, bright blue, red, and black. The beginner should avoid patterned, printed cloth.

The basic steps in reverse appliqué are: (1) stack or layer four pieces of cloth which have been cut to exactly the same size; (2) baste or pin the piece together along the edges; (3) draw the design to

Figure 16. In reverse appliqué, drawn shapes are cut away from felt. They are then folded back and stitched down. Different layers will reveal different colored designs.

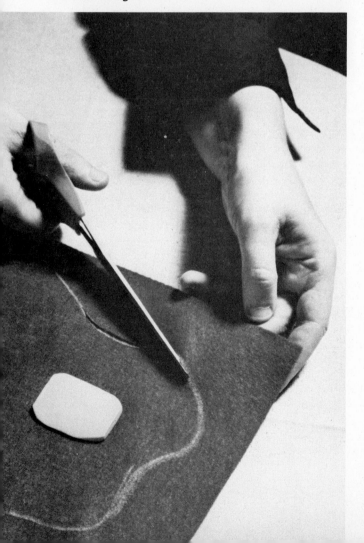

be cut out on the top square; (4) cut the design out of the top layer to show the second color; (5) draw and cut the design out of the second layer to reveal the third color; and (6) draw and cut the design out of the third color to reveal the fourth layer. If felt has been used, white glue can be put under the edge of each cut layer. If the felt is to be sewn, then hand stitch or machine stitch the edge of each cut design to the layer below with tiny stitches.

If cotton cloth is to be used for reverse appliqué, the colored fabrics should be cut the same size and stacked one on top of the other. Baste the cloth pieces together at the edges so the cloth will not slip. Again outline the design on the first or top layer. Cut out the design carefully so that the second fabric color shows. Repeat the process for each layer until all colors show as desired. As each color is cut, leave a narrow line about 1/4-inch wide around and inside of the design. Turn this edge of fabric under and sew it with tiny stitches.

Relief Appliqué

Appliqué can be padded; stuffed to raise the surface as in a relief; or, the design can be stuffed or more heavily padded for a three-dimensional effect. One of the simplest ways to create appliqué in the round is to create small patterns in flat appliqué. When completed, these can be rolled into a cylindrical or tubular shape with stitched designs on the outside. The cylindrical appliqué can be suspended as a sculptural hanging. Fine strong thread, cord, or fish line can be used.

There are two other simple methods of relief appliqué. One is to sew an appliqué design to a background, leaving a small opening. Insert a stuffing of cotton or dacron and close the opening by hand stitching. The other way is to cut two pieces of the same design and sew them together except for a small opening for stuffing. After the opening is stuffed and stitched closed, the appliqué can be attached to the background fabric.

Combinations of patchwork, quilting, and appliqué can be used effectively and aesthetically by the imaginative, innovative textile designer. The beginner can start with simple techniques and add ideas as expertise is gained.

Figure 17. Cloth pieces for a crazy quilt pillow are machine stitched into two squares, the top piece slightly larger than the bottom.

Figure 18. The two squares are sewn together, right side to right side, along three sides.

Projects You Can Do

These are simple projects that involve each of the procedures previously discussed. It is up to the individual craftsman to choose the one he prefers.

CRAZY QUILT PILLOW COVER

1. Gather together some fabric remnants, cut them into small geometric or random shapes with straight edges, and stack the shapes according to color.

2. Measure and cut a sheet of newspaper into two squares, each 4 inches wider on each side than the pillow size desired. For a 14-inch pillow, cut the newspaper into an 18-inch square.

3. Lay out the pieces of fabric on the newspaper squares, straight edges to straight edges.

4. Arrange and rearrange pieces so that colors and shapes are distributed in interesting patterns.

5. Pieces can be hand sewn or machine stitched together. They can be pinned with right sides together first and then sewn. Turn seams back and press.

6. After pieces have been sewn together into the two squares, additional decorative embroidery stitches can be used to outline each shape (the

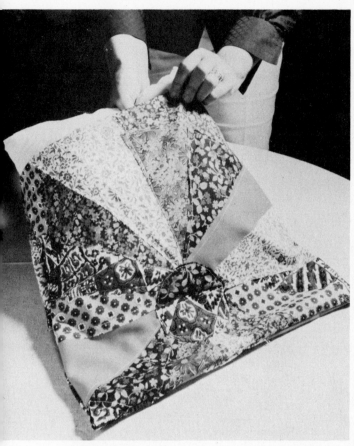

Figure 19. The pillow form is inserted between the stitched sections, and the fourth side is sewn.

embroidery may be added as a last step) or the squares may be quilted. This is left to personal preference.

7. After the two squares have been pieced, place them right side to right side and sew along three sides. Leave the fourth side open.

8. Turn right side out after pressing seams and insert pillow.

9. Turn in the edges of the open side, pin, and close with hand stitching.

10. If desired, decorative embroidery or ribbons can be hand stitched at this point instead of at step 6.

Figure 20. Decorative hand embroidery or ribbon work may be added to finish the crazy quilt pillow, a bright and attractive accent piece that may be proudly displayed on a chair, a couch, a bed, or near a bright window.

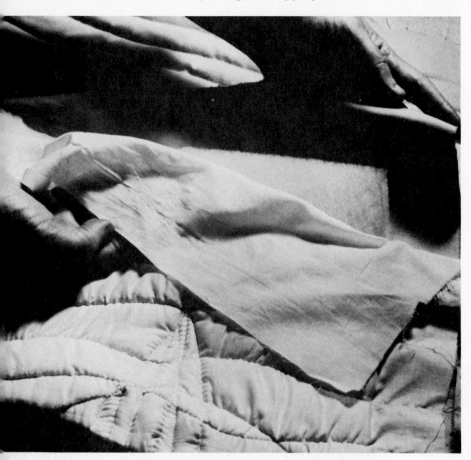

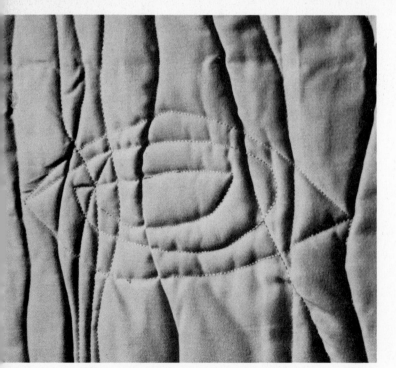

Figure 21. In making a framed quilted panel, layers of top fabric, filler, and backing are tacked together (top left). The design is then quilted with a sewing machine (top right), and the finished panel (bottom) is ready to be stretched and framed.

FRAMED QUILTED PANEL

1. Plan a design, estimate the size of panel to be framed, and select suitable fabrics and filler.

2. Cut fabric 2 inches larger than the frame dimensions. Using pencil or tailor's chalk, draw the design on the top cloth.

3. Place top fabric, filler, and backing together. Then, pin or baste the three layers together at central points to keep them from slipping.

4. Thread a sharp needle or machine needle with matching or contrasting thread. Always hand or machine quilt from center, working out to the edges. Machine quilting works especially well on diagonal lines because there is less puckering of fabric. If cotton filler or batting is used, quilt lines should be closer together.

5. Hand or machine quilt on the design outlines, using evenly spaced running stitches through the three layers.

6. After the panel of cloth is completely quilted, it is ready to be stretched and framed. This can be done at a frame shop.

Figure 22. Detail (above) of the traditional quilt shown on page 238 reveals sewing techniques of the pieced work as well as the intricate stitched pattern on the quilt itself.

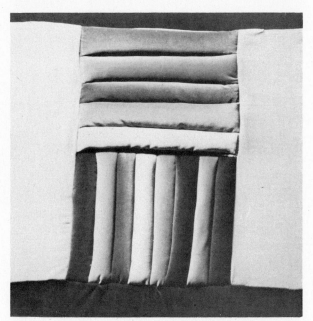

Figure 23. This design (above) incorporates the traditional quilting methods of stuffing and padding and a modern pattern. The texture of the velvet fabric accents the sculptured effect of the quilting.

Figure 24. A contemporary quilted panel (above) designed by Lucille Bealmer features an intricate geometric pattern of many separate but interrelated forms.

BORDER APPLIQUÉ ON FABRIC LENGTH

1. Plan a simple geometric or floral design suitable for a repeat pattern along a border. Draw the design on cardboard to the exact size needed. Draw the design again with edges extended 1/4 inch. Cut them out. These are templates.

2. Select fabrics for appliqué designs and for background length. Fold appliqué design fabric so that four thicknesses are pinned together.

3. Place larger template on lengthwise grain of fabric to be used for appliqué designs. Draw around the template with a pencil or tailor's chalk. Draw as many designs as needed.

4. Cut drawn designs out of fabric with sharp scissors. Four thicknesses can be cut at a time.

5. Place appliqué piece right side down. Center smaller template on the piece and turn edge of design piece over edge of smaller template.

6. Press edges back with hot iron.

7. Arrange appliqué designs on background fabric along one long edge or selvage. When arrangement is satisfactory, pin appliqué pieces to background fabric.

8. Thread hand or machine needle with matching thread. Using a simple tiny stitch, sew appliqué designs to background fabric. An alternative to stitching the appliqué pieces is to use fusible web.

9. Appliqué can be further enhanced through use of quilting and decorative embroidery stitches.

Figure 25. Fabric and fusible web are cut out on the cardboard template pattern.

Figure 26. The printed fabric pieces with fusible web beneath are arranged on the background fabric.

Figure 27. After printed fabric edges are turned under, they are appliquéd to the background with an iron.

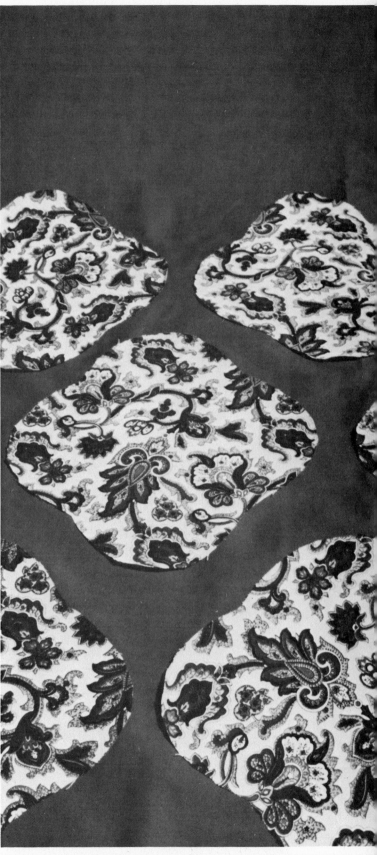

Figure 28. The finished appliquéd piece may finally be decorated with fancy stitching or embroidery.

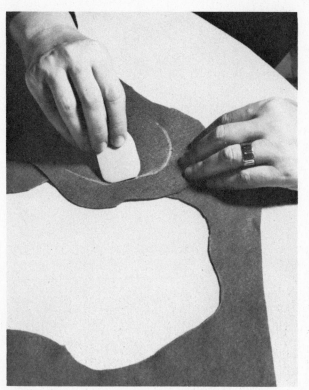

Figure 29. Tailor's chalk is used to draw designs for a reverse appliqué banner.

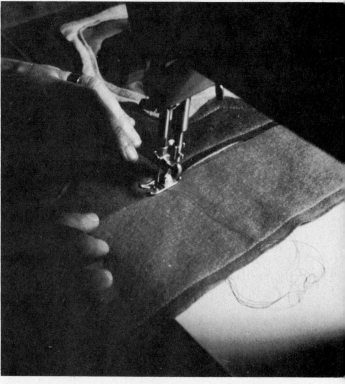

Figure 30. The cut-out designs are layered, arranged on the banner, and appliquéd.

REVERSE APPLIQUÉ FELT BANNERS

1. Plan a simple cut-out design on 9" x 12" paper.

2. Select 12 pieces of 9" x 12" felt. Use various shades of bright colors in a similar color range, such as the warm range of oranges, reds, and red-violets or the cool range of blues and greens. (Note: Instead of felt, cotton broadcloth of bright colors can be used.) As each piece is cut, turn in and stitch down the hem or edges of the shape. Edges can be left raw and machine stitched after all cutting is completed.

3. For background, select a color of felt in the same color range. It should be 1½ yards in length and 1 yard in width. Fold the felt cloth in half lengthwise, cut along the fold, and stitch together for banner.

4. Layer three different colors in each of four stacks, place cut-out paper designs on top felt piece of each stack, and draw design on each of these pieces.

5. Cut out shapes drawn on top felt pieces and lay these down on second felt colors in each of the four stacks.

6. Draw smaller shapes inside of cut spaces, letting an edge of the second color show.

7. Cut shapes from second felt layers.

8. Repeat process with third or bottom layers to let background color show through.

9. Glue, hand, or machine stitch layers together.

10. Arrange each of the four layered designs on banner backing and appliqué.

11. Attach felt loops at top of banner and hang on a dowel rod.

Figure 31. Machine stitching of the appliquéd pieces is nearly completed.

For Additional Reading

Anders, Nedda, **Appliqué Old and New,** Hearthside Press, 1967.

Belfer, Nancy, **Designing in Stitching and Appliqué,** Davis, 1972.

Laliberte, Norman and McIlhany, Sterling, **Banners and Hangings,** Reinhold, 1966.

Laury, Jean Ray, **Quilts and Coverlets,** Van Nostrand, 1970.

Meilach, Dona L., **Creating Art From Fibers and Fabrics,** Regnery, 1972.

Rainey, Sarita R., **Wall Hangings: Designing with Fabric and Threads,** Davis, 1971.

Safford, Carlton L. and Bishop, Robert, **America's Quilts and Coverlets,** Dutton, 1972.

Van Dommelen, David B., **Decorative Wall Hangings,** Funk and Wagnalls, 1962.

Wilson, Erica, **Embroidery Book,** Scribners, 1973.

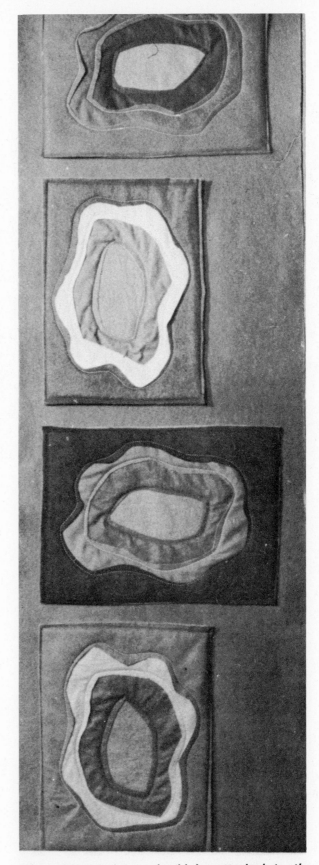

Figure 32. Felt loops should be attached to the finished banner so it can be hung on a dowel rod.

Doll Making

The doll and doll making have existed as long as humankind and flourish as a creative and collector's art today.

The doll — plaything, toy, fetish, talisman, puppet, sculpture, figurine, idol, ancestor figure, spirit figure, ephemeral figure, totem, amulet, or effigy — has become an important image in the history of visual and spiritual expression. Dolls have been made of common, sophisticated, and unusual materials — e.g., wood, twigs, bone, clay, fur, leather, cloth, metal, beads, and bread dough.

Wooden dolls made as long as 4,000 years ago have been found in Egypt. The arms and legs were defined and often movable. The bodies or torsos curved out and, in some instances, resembled hourglass shapes. Geometric clothing designs were often painted on these figures. The hair was made of strings of clay beads secured to the top of the wood shape with wax. In addition to wood, some of these dolls were made of terra cotta (burnt earth), bone, stone, or ivory.

The earliest soft, stuffed dolls also were found in Egypt. Evidently, the fabric has survived because of the arid desert. These early dolls were of Coptic origin and presumed to date from the sixth century A.D. The heads of these dolls were made of painted wood; the bodies were made of cloth — often woolens and linens — and the clothing was painted, colored, or dyed. Early fabric designs were created by using the wax-resist technique of batik (the use of hot wax and dyes for design motifs). Because they have been found in early Egyptian and Coptic graves, it can be assumed that there was a need and demand for interesting, aesthetically created dolls.

Ancient dolls have also been found in Greece. Whether these human images were children's playthings or amulets for sacrifice to the gods is speculative. The dolls were made by sculptors and craftsmen, as were the ancient Egyptian and Coptic dolls. They were usually made of terra cotta, with limbs jointed by wire which had been inserted into the clay. They were clothed with linen or woolen fabric decorated with geometric designs or bird and animal motifs. The faces were painted. Jewelry made of leather, beads, and even gold was added to the doll forms for further embellishment. Sometimes, real-hair wigs were glued onto the clay figures.

Dolls found in Roman graves were made of ivory, wood, bone, clay, or stuffed cloth. Cosmetics for these dolls were also found, as well as beautiful gold jewelry.

Elegant terra cotta dolls with jointed limbs have been found in Etruscan graves. The incised de-

Figure 1. Two well-loved favorites, Raggedy Ann and Raggedy Andy (opposite), are descendants of the soft stuffed dolls that have been cherished by children throughout the world since ancient times.

Figure 2. This terra-cotta doll figure dates back to the Pre-Columbian era. Dolls have been used for religious and decorative purposes as well as for play. (Collection, Mr. and Mrs. William Bealmer.)

signs of the hair styles suggest that the dolls belonged to patrician women and children.

Medieval Europe did not produce a wealth of dolls. However, clay dolls, horses, and knights reflecting the age of chivalry have been described in writings of the thirteenth century. Wooden figures which were jointed and clothed in fabric were enjoyed by the children of the aristocracy.

With the resurgence of the arts in Renaissance Europe, doll making became a very important industry and art as craftsmen became involved in the making of dolls and toys. Dolls were made of wood, alabaster, gold, silver, brass, pewter, wax, paper pulp, cloth, and even edible sweets. Bavarian wooden dolls with movable parts were exported to the rest of the world. German and Austrian dolls found an especially good market in America.

In the nineteenth century, after doll making became an industry, dolls became increasingly more plentiful. Dolls were manufactured in En-gland, France, Germany, Austria, and Holland. The heads were made with glazed stoneware or heavy wax and had eyes which that closed. As the inventiveness of the designers increased, dolls were made that could cry and walk.

In the Americas, folk-art craftsmen have created highly treasured dolls, some of which have found their way into museums and private collections. These include the Kachina dolls, rag dolls, and buckskin dolls of the North American Indians; the rag dolls of the mountain artisans; clay and bread dough dolls of South and Central America; as well as dolls of contemporary artists. Eva Aeppli, Manfred Schmale, and Niki de Saint Phalle are three artists who have received international recognition for their people figures.

Today, doll making has become an individual and expressive art medium. The materials are quite ordinary and easily available; methods are relatively simple. The imagination of the artist reflects individuality.

Figure 3. These nineteenth-century dolls have stuffed bodies with heads of wax, bisque, or china. Doll making became a thriving industry in Europe during this time. (Collection, Mr. and Mrs. William Bealmer.)

Figure 4. Navajo blue-faced dancers and Hopi Kachina figures are decoratively painted American Indian dolls carved from cottonwood root. (Collection, Mr. and Mrs. William Bealmer.)

Common Terms Used In Doll Making

Appliqué: a cut-out cloth design fastened onto a background fabric by sewing or adhesion.

Arch-Shaped Doll: a doll made of a simple, rounded shape without arms or legs.

Batik: a process of fabric dyeing in which waxes, resins, and flour pastes are used as *resists* wherever coloring is not desired.

Batting: cotton or dacron pressed into sheets and used for padding, stuffing, or quilting.

Bisque: clay which has been fired and is white to light tan in color.

Body: the torso, trunk, or main part of the doll, as distinguished from the head and limbs.

Bound Doll: a doll which has been made by binding or wrapping strips of cloth, ribbon, or leather around twigs, straw, or wire.

China Head: Used on dolls of the eighteenth and nineteenth centuries and made of porcelain which has been glazed and fired; the facial features are painted on with glazes.

Clothespin Doll: doll made with a wooden clothespin, which provides the basic shape for the head and body.

Cylinder Forms: forms made of rectangles rolled into a tube and stuffed; used for doll bodies and limbs.

Embroidery: stitchery or needlework using threads, flosses, or yarns.

Felt: a non-woven material made of matted wool fibers or hair which has been pressed flat; available in a wide range of colors.

Fiber Fill or Kapok: masses of fibers used for filling or stuffing cloth.

Fusible Web: fibrous material, such as Stitch Witchery or Pellon Fusible Web, which has adhesive on both sides; placed between two pieces of cloth and pressed with a hot iron to form the bond.

Gesso: coating made of plaster of Paris or gypsum and used on cloth or canvas doll faces so that features may be easily painted on.

Jointed Doll: doll with head and limbs that are attached to the body.

Knitted or Woven Dolls: dolls made of such materials as knit socks, stockings, or loosely woven cloth.

Papier-Mâché: a strong, hard substance made of paper pulp mixed with paste, glue, size, or resin.

Pillow Doll: a doll made from an existing pillow

or cushion; or made for use as a pillow or cushion.

Rag Doll: a soft fabric doll, usually stuffed.

Silk Screen or Stencil: art processes in which images are created by pushing ink through silk, parchment, paper, metal, or the like.

Single-Shape Doll: a doll made of one shape which has been cut out twice and sewn together — one piece for the front and the other for the back.

Stuffing: any material which can be used to give cloth a three-dimensional form; stuffing for dolls can be straw, hay, sawdust, cotton, old stockings, fiber-fill, kapok, or cotton or dacron batting.

Terra Cotta: a fired clay which ranges in color from yellow-red to reddish-brown.

Stocking Face Doll: a doll whose head is made of stuffed cloth and covered with a silk or nylon stocking. This gives a soft, unified appearance to the head.

Figure 5. Dolls of the early 1900s (right) had china or bisque heads and bodies of cloth, wood, or leather. (Collection, Mr. and Mrs. William Bealmer.)

Figure 6. Twentieth-century folk art craftsmen of Africa and North and South America created these dolls. (Collection, Mr. and Mrs. William Bealmer.)

Basic Equipment And Supplies

Most of the materials used for doll making are already available in many homes. Other supplies can be purchased in department stores, fabric shops, sewing centers, yarn shops, variety stores, or craft shops.

The following equipment and supplies can be supplemented as the beginner gains experience. For equipment you will need: (1) an electric iron for pressing fabric, for applying iron-on tape, or for bonding fusible web; (2) a sewing machine (optional); and (3) a table or working surface.

Basic supplies include: (1) batting; (2) beads, buttons, and other ornamentation; (3) clothes pins; (4) cotton; (5) felt; (6) fiber-fill or kapok; (7) fusible web; (8) glue (white or fabric glue); (9) iron-on tape; (10) needles; (11) paper of various kinds; (12) pencil, crayon, charcoal, marking pen, or tailor's chalk; (13) pipe cleaners; (14) pillows; (15) ribbons, tape, or other binding materials; (16) ruler and tape measure; (17) scissors; (18) socks and stockings; (19) stuffing; (20) thread; and (21) yarns and flosses of various weights which can be used for hair and for embellishment.

Basic Procedures

Doll making consists of just a few basic steps. The doll maker must plan and draw the doll design, cut it out of fabric, sew the parts together, stuff it, and finish sewing. Dressing and embellishment of the doll are the final steps. The dolls can be made by hand sewing or by machine sewing. The more imagination the doll maker has, the more exciting and fun the dolls will be.

The kind of fabric will dictate the type of doll to be designed. For example, checked gingham would suggest a simple rag doll, while velvet and lace might suggest a more elegant doll. Doll shapes should be quite simple and the doll maker must decide how the shapes will hold together. The type and amount of stuffing also require consideration — the beginner should be open minded enough to change the concept of the doll image as it starts to develop. As a doll takes shape, it becomes a personal image which reflects the individuality of the designer. Children as well as adults can become experienced doll makers. Children have a wonderful spontaneity and ex-

Figure 7. Doll-making supplies can be purchased at any fabric or variety store. Ornamental items such as beads, ribbons, and buttons are common household items.

citement which affects the personality of the dolls they create.

DESIGNING THE DOLL

Drawing a doll shape is easy if the beginner remembers to keep it simple. The head should be rounded or circular and the body should be oval or rectangular with curved edges. The neck should be thick enough to support the head. After stuffing, the head, neck, and body will be smaller in appearance, so the doll design should allow for the final size as well as for sewing. If limbs are part of the single doll shape, the doll maker should remember that the arms should be longer than the body and the legs should be longer than the arms. Arms and legs can be shaped, rounded, tapered and have hands, fingers, or feet. A doll can be made to look short and stocky or tall and thin by the structure of the limbs. Fingers can be depicted

Figure 8. The materials used in this collection of folk art dolls include straw, leather, cloth, and corn husks. The home dollmaker has an equally wide choice of materials. (Collection, Mr. and Mrs. William Bealmer.)

by sewing. The beginner should draw and cut several doll shapes out of newspaper or newsprint. A seam allowance of approximately 5/8 to 1 inch may be drawn inside the cut outline of the doll shape. This will help the doll maker visualize the necessity for making the doll design or pattern quite a bit larger than the final product.

Another way to plan the doll design is to draw around a satisfactory shape on newsprint. Draw a second line about one inch larger around the figure. This will allow for the seam and the thickness created by stuffing. When the design seems satisfactory, transfer it onto lightweight cardboard and cut it out very carefully. This can then be a durable pattern for making many dolls.

STUFFING AND FABRIC

The stuffing material can be fiber-fill, old nylons, scrap rags, cotton, kapok (which is hard to find), foam chips, or dacron or cotton batting. There are always new materials available, and fabric or upholstery shops carry a variety of stuffing material. The individual designer must select the type of filling needed. This will depend on whether the doll is to be very soft, tightly stuffed, or padded. As he gains experience, the doll maker will acquire a list of favorite kinds of cloth and stuffing material.

Fabric for the dolls is, again, the personal choice of the designer. Felt is an excellent material for the beginner. Muslin and knit sock material is also excellent for simple basic dolls. Cotton thread is best for hand or machine sewing: use mercerized No. 50 in a suitable color. A sharp, medium-length needle is best for hand sewing.

After the doll shape has been planned and cut out of cardboard; fabric selected; and stuffing, needle, thread, and scissors made ready, the designer can proceed with the making of the doll.

MAKING THE DOLL

The cardboard pattern or template should be placed on cloth which has been folded with right sides together. Pin the two layers of cloth together, and then use a pencil to draw around the cardboard shape on the cloth. After drawing around the cardboard shape, carefully lift it away from the cloth. Next, sew the two fabric pieces together along the drawn line. Leave openings at the top of the head and at the left side of the body — the body opening should be about 1½ to 2 inches in length. Whether hand stitching or machine stitching, the stitches should be short and tight. After the sewing is completed, cut out the doll shapes: cutting should be 5/8 inch to 1 inch outside of the sewing line. After the shape is cut, turn it inside out. (Felt dolls can be stuffed without turning inside out.)

Insert the stuffing carefully and in small quantities. Work it into the doll with a pencil, popsicle stick, or thin dowel, pushing it into corners and edges. The neck, especially, needs to be firmly padded or stuffed to support the head. After the doll feels firmly stuffed, stitch the openings in the head and body. Turn the raw edges in at the openings and stitch them together with close, small, almost invisible stitches.

Add hair and facial features to the doll. Yarn embroidery is excellent for defining features. Draw the hair line lightly with pencil, and stitch individual lengths of yarn to the head using a simple running stitch. The hair can be made of cloth, strips of cloth, felt, yarn, jute, beads, ribbon, ball fringe, chenille, or whatever else one wishes to use. The hair can be sewn on, glued on, ironed on, painted on, or even printed on the head.

Also mark the facial features lightly with pencil: the eyes are about halfway on the oval of the head; the bottom of the nose is marked just above the halfway point of the lower half of the oval; the mouth is just above the bottom one-fourth mark of the oval. Features can be embroidered, sewn, ironed, or painted on. Further decoration, dressing, or embellishment of the doll depend entirely on the creativity and imagination of the doll maker.

HANDKERCHIEF DOLL

A simple and easy-to-make soft doll can be made from handkerchiefs, fabric squares, scarves, old sheets, flannel, bandanas, or blankets. To make the head, put a wad of stuffing into the exact center of a handkerchief. Then, to form the head, tie a string or ribbon around the cloth at the base of the wad. Paint or stitch features on the head. This simple doll can be wrapped like a baby in another piece of cloth.

To make a doll with limbs tied into it, first fold a square of fabric diagonally in half to make a triangle. Then put a wad of stuffing into the center and tie as before to form the head. Tie each end of the folded side close to the tip to make hands. Tie the tips at the bottom triangle to make feet. Tie a ribbon around the waistline. Add yarn hair to the head.

Larger dolls can be made of larger pieces of cloth with more stuffing added into the body and head. Making these handkerchief dolls is a basic, easy, and excellent way to begin — for both a young child and an adult.

Figure 9. A handkerchief doll is easily made: push up the handkerchief in the center (top) and stuff it. Form the limbs by folding the cloth and tying the ends (center). The finished doll (bottom) has yarn for hair; her face is painted.

Figure 10. A clothespin, pipecleaners, and stuffing are the basic supplies needed for a simple doll (above). The addition of clothing, yarn hair, and a painted face make a charming little toy.

CLOTHESPIN DOLL

A wooden clothespin is the basic form for another kind of simple doll. The top or rounded part of the clothespin is the head, the middle can be padded to serve as the body, and the split part of the wood is an adequate shape for the legs. Arms can be structured from pipe cleaners. Twist three pipe cleaners together at the ends and glue them to make one very long piece. Wrap the middle of the extra-long pipe cleaner around the top of the clothespin just below the indentation. The extended pipe-cleaner lengths make up the arms, which can also be slightly padded. The head can have facial features painted on it, yarn can be glued to the top of the clothespin for hair, and simple clothing can be made.

STOCKING DOLL

The stocking doll can be very crude or it can be quite attractive, depending on the kind of sock or stocking used. Turn the sock inside out — the opening or cuff should be at the top. The heel of the sock should be left as is — it will form the seat or rear of the doll. Push the point of the scissors into the sock an inch below the heel, and cut along the fold line of the sock. Keep cutting around this line, past the toe, until you reach the point opposite where you began cutting. The two equal halves will become the doll's legs. Sew each half together down the entire length of each leg.

After the halves are sewn, turn the sock right side out and stuff it to 2 or 3 inches from the open end. Tie the top of the sock. Indicate the neckline a few inches below the tied part by tying or stitching. Use the loose end of the cuff as part of a cap for the doll. Embroider facial features on the head. Small, stuffed tubular shapes can be attached for arms. Some doll makers use nylon stockings with stitched features to make charming stocking face dolls.

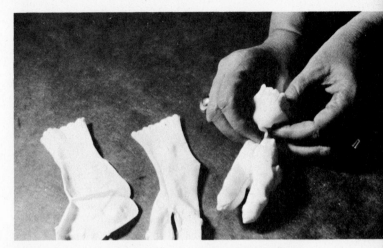

Figure 11. A sock turned inside out (above) is the form for a small, soft doll. The heel is left as is, the toe portion is split and stitched up for legs, and the sock is turned to the right side and stuffed. Yarn is used to indicate the neckline and cap, and felt markers are used for the face.

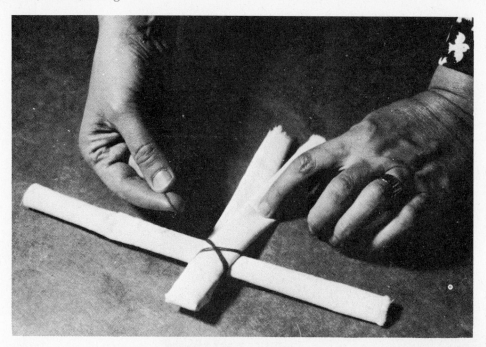

WRAPPED OR BOUND DOLL

The bound or wrapped doll has been popular in several countries in the world. Common in Asia and Europe, the bound doll is also a favorite among the American Indians.

The doll maker can make bound or wrapped dolls quite easily. Instead of using a sheaf of straw, as the Indians do, roll a square of fabric into a solid form. Double it over and tie it together about an inch below the fold. Roll another fabric square into a thinner form and push it through the opening of the doubled-over long roll to make the arms. Bind the head with ribbons. Extend the binding or wrapping over the body and each of the legs. Bind the arms and top of the body with a single color of ribbon. Paint or stitch features on the head, and add clothing and hair to complete the doll.

Figure 12. Fabric is rolled into solid forms, doubled over, and tied together to form the body of a bound doll (opposite). The arms are wrapped with cloth tape and sewn. Stitching may be used for the doll's face, yarn for the hair, and remnants for clothing (above). Popular the world over, this technique created this straw-wrapped doll from Bali (right).

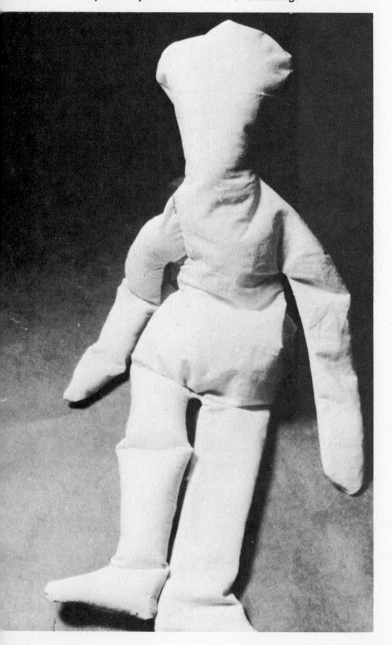

Figure 13. Sewing across the arms and legs of a stuffed doll is an easy way to indicate the joints of the arms, legs, and body. The flexibility of the doll depends upon the amount of stitching.

JOINTED DOLL

A soft fabric doll is designed in the same way as a single-shape doll except that stitching is used to emphasize the joints. Design the doll, draw it on cloth using a template or pattern, and stitch it. Leave openings at the side of the body and the top of the head. Turn the doll right side out. While stuffing, stitch lines across at each joint. For example, push stuffing into the foot of the doll. Stitch a line across at the ankle, above the stuffed area. Stuff the leg — stitch a line across the top of the leg, above the stuffed area. Follow the same procedure for the arm by adding a line of stitching at the wrist. This is an easy method for creating jointing of the limbs.

The basic single shape doll is made more complex by actually joining stuffed limbs to the body. This is the type of figure that is called a jointed doll. The various parts are individually made and then combined into a doll form. There are several ways to create jointed dolls. Some doll forms utilize simple shapes; others use many-pieced complex structural designs. The head, neck, body, arms, hands, legs, and feet can be made and stuffed separately and then joined together. Body contours can be made by structuring pieces to build convex and concave areas before stuffing. Muslin and felt are used by many doll makers for the doll forms. Other cotton fabrics, woolens, velvets, kid, suede, and fur have also been used successfully, exhibiting imagination.

The doll maker can give vital personalities to dolls through individual designs, choice of materials for structure and embellishment, care in finishing hair and faces, and decoration or dressing. The beginner can try some simple shapes and then develop a flair for ornamentation.

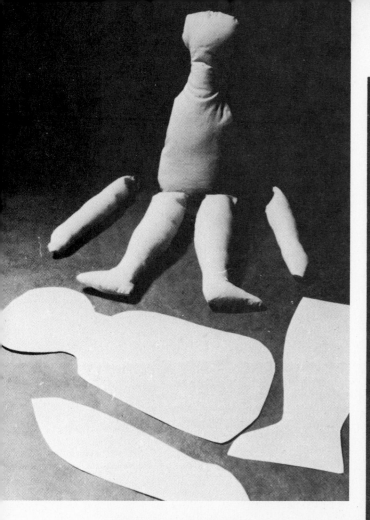

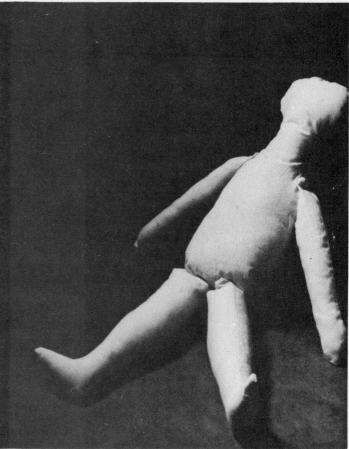

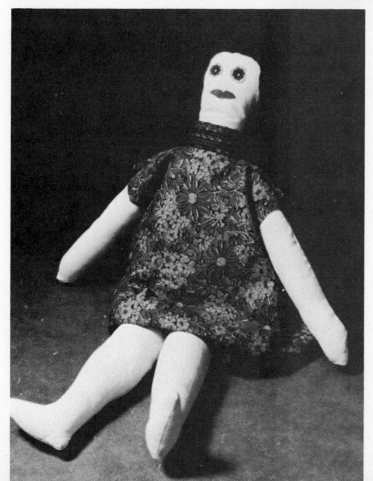

Figure 14. A more complex jointed doll is made by individually cutting patterns (above left) and stuffing and sewing them. The joints are sewn together (above). The resulting basic doll form can be clothed and decorated to the doll maker's individual taste (left).

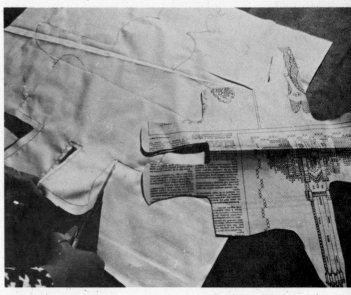

Figure 15. To make a one-shape doll, begin with a simple outline drawn on newspaper (above); transfer the outline to the material, stitch, and cut out. The doll form is turned right side out and stuffed. After the doll is stuffed, the openings are closed by turning in the edges of fabric and hand sewing with tiny stitches (opposite). The finished doll can be decorated as the artist chooses (opposite, below).

Projects You Can Do

Here are three simple projects. The beginning doll maker will probably want to try each one.

ONE-SHAPE DOLL

Using a one-shape design for the front and back of a doll is an easy method of doll production. The shape has a head, a body, and limbs.

1. Draw a simple outline for a doll shape on newsprint or newspaper. The head, body, arms, and legs can be included in the pattern without details. The shape should allow from 5/8″ to 1″ for sewing seams and expansion from stuffing.

2. Place the cut-out doll shape on a piece of cardboard, draw around the outline, and cut it out. The cardboard shape becomes a pattern or template which can be used and saved for future doll making.

3. Select a fabric — muslin, cotton broadcloth, poplin, or velveteen are excellent choices. For stuffing, use fiber-fill, kapok, or foam chips for a soft, loose doll. For a tighter, more solid doll, use batting or clean old rags. Old, clean nylon stockings also make excellent stuffing. Estimate the fabric length needed by measuring the pattern doll at its longest and widest points. Make an allowance for a little extra fabric. Remember that two of the shapes will need to be cut, one for the front and one for the back of the doll. For example, to make a doll which is 12 inches tall and 10 inches wide, a half yard of 36-inch fabric will be sufficient.

4. Press the fabric smooth and fold it in half lengthwise with right sides inside. Lay it on a flat surface, smooth it again, and pin the layers together at the outside edges.

5. Lay the cardboard template on the fabric and draw around the outline. Use a pencil or tailor's chalk.

6. Hand sew with fine, close stitches or machine stitch around the outline of the doll shape drawn on the fabric. Leave a 2-inch opening in the side of the body and an opening at the top of the head.

7. Using pencil or tailor's chalk, draw a line around the shape 1/4 inch outside the stitched line. Cut along the newly drawn line with sharp scissors.

8. Turn the doll shape right side out.

9. Stuff the doll. Use a thin dowel or pencil to push stuffing into limbs and curved areas. Be careful not to poke through the fabric.

10. After the doll is stuffed, close the openings by turning in edges of fabric and hand sewing with tiny, close stitches.

11. Draw hairline and facial features on the head. Stitch yarn or cloth hair on the head. Embroider, appliqué, or paint on facial features.

12. Embroider or appliqué clothing on the doll form.

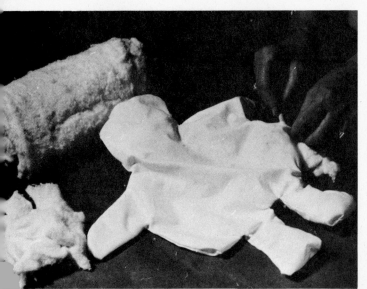
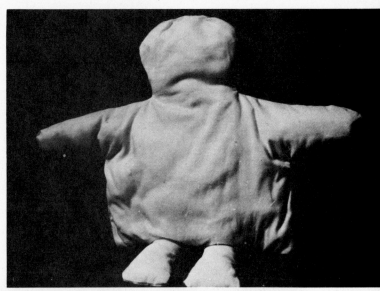

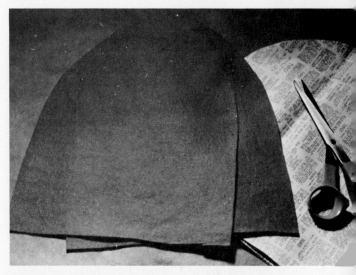

SIMPLE-SHAPE FELT DOLL

The simple-shape doll form is an arch or rectangle which is rounded and tapered at the head or top. Felt is the best fabric for the beginner.

1. Draw a simple arch outline for a doll on newsprint or newspaper and cut it out.

2. Draw simple arm and leg shapes on newsprint or newspaper and cut them out.

3. Place the doll and limb shapes on cardboard. Draw around the shapes and cut them out.

4. Select felt colors for the doll. The arch and limbs can be from one color or from contrasting colors. Cotton or dacron batting or fiber-fill can be used for the stuffing. Felt usually is sold by the yard in widths of 60 or 72 inches. One-half yard of felt will be sufficient for a doll that is 15 inches high and 10 inches at the widest part. Ribbons, felt, or fabric scraps, iron-on tape, and yarn can be used for decoration.

5. Fold the felt in half lengthwise and pin it at the folds to prevent slipping.

6. Lay the cardboard template on the felt and draw around the outlines, using pencil or tailor's chalk. Draw one outline of the arch shape; draw two outlines each of the arm and leg shapes.

7. With very sharp scissors, cut the outlines out of the folded and pinned felt. There will be two arch shapes, four arm shapes, and four leg shapes.

8. By hand or machine, sew each arm and leg separately, using two of the cut felt pieces for each limb. A second row of stitching may be added 1/4 inch inside the first stitching for decoration.

Figure 16. Arch shapes cut from felt (above) will make a simple-shape felt doll. The body and limbs are sewn together with stuffing in between the large arch areas (opposite). Felt appliques may be added for the face (opposite, below).

9. Place the two arch shapes together. Insert the tops of the arms between the felt at about the middle of the arch on each side. Pin. Repeat procedure for legs at base of arch shape. Be sure that at least 1/2 inch of the limbs shapes are inserted into the body shape.

10. Leave an opening for stuffing the body. Hand or machine stitch around the body outline except for the opening.

11. Stuff the body and close the opening by hand or machine stitching. The arms and legs are not stuffed.

12. Cut facial features out of felt and glue or sew them onto a felt circle. (Iron-on Tape may also be used for facial features.)

13. Appliqué the felt circle onto the doll.

14. Cut a hair-do shape out of felt, and glue or appliqué it around the doll's face.

A flatter, padded arch doll can be made by placing dacron or cotton batting between simple cut-felt shapes. Cut the batting 1/2 inch smaller than the doll shape. Add arms and legs. Sew the outside line of stitching. Facial features and decorative ribbons, laces, or cloth can be adhered with glue or stitched on to decorate the doll or, as an alternative, the doll can be covered with embroidery.

PILLOW DOLL

Pillow dolls can be simply designed or intricately embellished. Beginners, children, and advanced doll makers can all utilize the pillow forms for dolls that are fun to make.

1. Select a sofa throw pillow — it can be ready-made and square, rectangular, round, or triangular. The doll form is determined by the size and shape of the pillow.

2. Plan the doll design, which is, or course, limited by the size and shape of the pillow.

3. Cut two head shapes out of cloth. Stitch the pieces together leaving the neck open.

4. Draw on the facial features.

5. Stuff the head with dacron or cotton batting.

6. Cut out four arm pieces (two for each arm). Stitch together and stuff.

7. Hand sew head and arms onto the pillow, which is the body of the doll.

8. Decorate the body of the pillow doll with lace, ribbons, tape, buttons, or beads to resemble clothing.

9. Make hair of yarn or felt strips which are sewn into place or use embroidery.

Another way of making a pillow doll is by using any kind of pillow, such as a sofa pillow, bed pillow, or child's crib pillow, for the inside. Appliqué the head, body, and limbs onto the pillow case or cover, either by hand sewing, machine sewing, or ironing on fusible web. Cut fusible web exactly the same size as the appliqué designs and put it between the appliqué pieces and the pillow casing. Seal the fabrics together with a hot iron. The doll also can be made of a combination of appliqué, embroidery, and attached stuffed pieces. As the doll maker gains experience in craftsmanship and in design quality, the dolls will become more diversified.

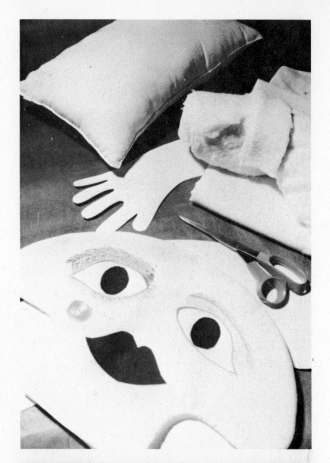

Figure 17. Pillow dolls are easily created from ready-made pillows. The stuffed forms (opposite) are assembled and sewn and then imaginatively decorated with yarn, jewelry, fancy stitches, and felt (above).

For Additional Reading

Bachman, Manfred, and Claus, Hansmann, **Dolls the Wide World Over,** Crown, 1973.

Culff, Robert, **The World of Toys,** Paul Hamlyn, 1968.

Christopher, Catherine, **Doll Making and Collecting,** Dover, 1971.

Coleman, Dorothy S., Elizabeth A., and Evelyn J., **The Collector's Encyclopedia of Dolls,** Crown, 1968.

Fawcett, Clara Hallard, **On Making, Mending, and Dressing Dolls,** Hobby House, 1963.

Fox, Carl, **The Doll,** Harry Abrams, 1972.

Laury, Jean Ray, **Doll Making,** Van Nostrand, 1970.

Lind, Vibeke, and Albrectsen, Lis, **Dolls and Toy Animals,** Van Nostrand, 1971.

Stained Glass Crafts

Nothing quite matches the beauty of stained glass, which provides ever-changing features depending upon the time of day, the season, and the mood of the viewer.

Although some consider stained glass to be one of the newest of the art forms sweeping the country, it is actually an ancient craft. Its history dates back to approximately 7000 B. C., when stained glass was worn in the Near East primarily as a jeweled body adornment. Moslem designers made intricate mosaics by fitting tiny pieces of stained glass into wood, stone, and plaster.

Later, as massive Romanesque walls were eliminated from buildings, stained glass became accepted as an integral part of building structures, its function being basically that of illumination. Then, with the invention of the blowpipe, which enabled the craftsman to control size, shape, and thickness, stained glass increased in availability. Nevertheless, because it was still scarce and expensive, stained glass was a luxury which was limited chiefly to religious buildings.

Christianity had the most profound effect on stained glass windows. As early as the fifth century, stained glass was thought to be a symbolic manifestation of divine light. By the tenth century, glass stained to depict biblical history and dogma became the trend as skilled craftsmen were heavily influenced by the church fathers.

Church adornment and architectural development reached its peak during the twelfth and thirteenth centuries, with great Gothic windows exemplifying the era. To create these windows, metallic oxides were fused with glass right in the melting pot, with the resulting glass varying in color, thickness, and texture. This glass would be crude by today's standards, but the beauty of many of the resulting light refractions has seldom been duplicated. The glass master would set up his kiln at the site of the church and would seldom create windows for more than one church in his lifetime. In fact, he was so highly regarded, that he was the only artisan permitted to marry royalty.

With the gradual coming of the Renaissance, stained-glass craftsmen began to copy the style used in oil painting. Scenes developed more realism than the idealism of the Gothic era; people looked more alive, with interesting facial expressions. At the height of this era, the Black Plague of 1347 and a subsequent epidemic swept Europe and killed the majority of the old, skilled glass masters. The remaining apprentices were novices and much of the talent was never recovered. A second blow came with the Reformation, and its opposition to church adornment. These fundamentalistic attitudes resulted in the willful destruction of many beautiful stained-glass windows.

There was a lull in stained-glass developments until the sixteenth century, when techniques involving enamel paints were introduced. Because these paints could be applied to the total piece before firing, the leading of glass declined.

During the seventeenth-century Baroque period and the eighteenth-century Rococo style, gaudiness overpowered the arts and garish, flowery,

Figure 2. The intricate design of this Peacock Window was the work of John LaFarge, a late 19th-century American artist and craftsman. (Courtesy, Worcester Art Museum.)

During the seventeenth-century Baroque period and the eighteenth-century Rococo style, gaudiness overpowered the arts and garish, flowery, overdecorated windows flourished. The nineteenth century brought the Art Nouveau style with many artists trying to recapture the lost arts. In America, this movement had many leaders. One was Charles Connick (1875-1945), whose vigorous efforts helped revive the ancient stained-glass methods. His "rose window" in St. John the Divine Church in New York City is said to be the finest example of the art anywhere. John LaFarge (1835-1910) popularized the use of opalescent glass in windows. His murals in the chapels of

Harvard and Columbia universities, Trinity Church, and the Church of the Ascension in New York City set a standard unsurpassed in the United States. Louis Comfort Tiffany (1848-1933) felt that glass should beautify every average American home. He created elegant windows for the home and used the scraps to design glassware and lampshades. Modern artists such as Chagall, Matisse, Leger, Braque, and Rouault were also fascinated with the unique qualities of stained glass.

Stained glass has even reappeared in modern architecture: one of the largest examples, designed by Robert Sowers, is the front of the American Airlines Terminal at Kennedy International Airport in New York City. Now, almost every city in the United States has its own example of stained glass.

Figure 3. Designer Louis Comfort Tiffany created the pattern for this Wisteria lamp; his work was highly sought after by collectors in the 1960s and 1970s. (Courtesy, Spinning Wheel Magazine.)

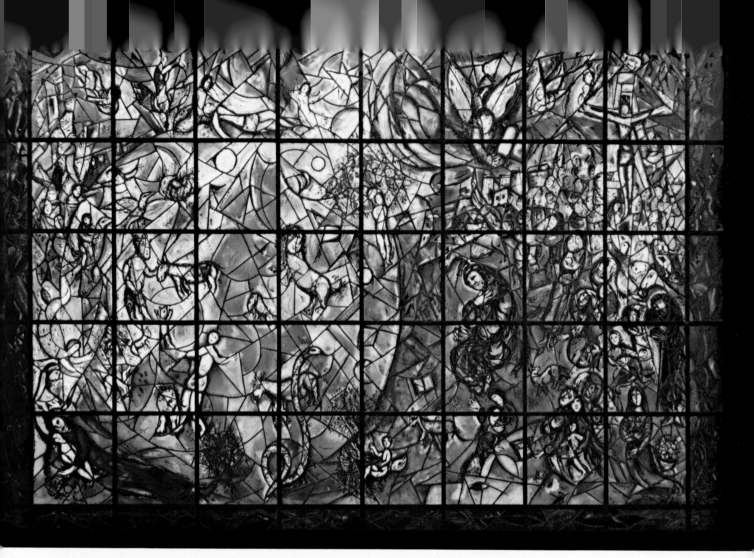

Figure 4. The contemporary French artist Marc Chagall designed this panel for the United Nations building in memory of the late UN Secretary General, Dag Hammarskjold. (Courtesy, United Nations.)

Common Terms Used In Stained-Glass Crafts

Abrasive: a substance which is used for grinding or polishing.

Abstract Design: a design which employs nonrepresentational or unnatural forms.

Aciding: the process of etching the surface coating of color from flashed glass (see below).

Alloy: a substance derived when different metals are fused together or completely mixed.

Banding: the process of soldering copper wires to lead cames so that they can be used to support large windows.

Cementing: the forcing of a special putty into the cames after soldering to make a window waterproof.

Cold Joint: a term used for a soldered metal seam on which the solder is melted but not actually fused.

Color Intensity: the degree of purity or brilliance of a color.

Color Value: the relationship of a color to lightness or darkness.

Copper Foiling: the process of using copper foil in place of lead came.

Compatible Glasses: glasses which expand and contract at the same ratio during heating and cooling cycles and can be fused together in a kiln.

Craze: the random cracks that are sometimes found in glass.

Dalle-De-Verre: the French term for "slab glass," which is 3/4" to 1½" thick.

Etching; the eating away of glass, usually by an acid.

Faceted Glass: slab glass which is cut and set in concrete or other material.

Flashed Glass: pale glass that has a surface coating of color and is used for etching.

Flow Point: the temperature at which heated solder liquefies.

Flux: the substance used to promote fusion in soldering.

Foil: a paper-thin sheet of metal.

Glaze: a thin coating of glass used in flashed glass.

Glazing: the process of setting the glass in the lead.

Grout: a mixture of cement and fine sand or marble dust used to fill in the crevices in mosaics.

Grozing: the nibbling of a small piece of glass with the teeth of cutter or pliers.

Kiln: a high-temperature furnace used for firing glass and other materials.

Laminate: to unite successive layers of glass with epoxy.

Lead Came: a grooved strip of lead that holds pieces of glass together.

Leaded Glass: either colored or uncolored pieces of glass bound together with lead cames. Stained-glass work is usually "leaded"; leaded glass, however, can be used in many applications other than stained-glass work.

Leading: the process of framing with lead.

Opaque: the quality of being impervious to light.

Oxidation: surface deterioration caused by exposure to oxygen in the air.

Patina: a colored film caused by natural aging or exposure to chemicals.

Refraction: the diffusion or bending of light rays as they are transmitted through a transparent material.

Rheostat: an instrument used to control the strength of electric current by controlling the amount of resistance.

Seeds: the bubbles which add sparkle to hand-blown glass.

Score: the cutting line made on glass.

Scribe: the score or cut made on glass.

Solder: an alloy made of tin and lead.

Soldering: the technique of using heat and solder to join pieces of metal.

Stained Glass: strictly speaking, either colored or uncolored glass upon which designs, pictures, or scenes have been painted. The glass is then heated in a kiln until the special paint has been fused and becomes part of the glass. The separate pieces are then assembled and "leaded" together to form a stained-glass window.

Support Bars: iron or steel bars with copper wires around them which are soldered to the lead came to support the window.

Tinning: the action of coating the tip of the soldering iron copper with the tin.

Translucent: that quality which permits the diffused transmission of light.

Transparent: that quality which permits unobscured transmission of light.

Basic Equipment And Supplies

Stained glass is a craft which is well suited to the home, with most of the equipment already available at home. If not, the investment in the necessary equipment is very modest. Not everything listed is necessary: one can improvise on many of the implements.

GLASS

There are two major types of glass: (1) cathedral, which is made by machine and has a uniform thickness; and (2) antique, which is made by blowing a bubble and slicing it down and which can vary in thickness. Cathedral is the easiest to work with, the most readily available, and therefore, the glass with which to begin. Start looking for glass in hobby and craft stores and glass supply houses. The following are the more common types of glass which one is likely to find:

1. Hammered cathedral glass: a bubbly, hammered-type of glass which is quite soft

Figure 5. The two broad categories of decorative glass are cathedral (A through G) and antique (H, I). Cathedral glasses include hammered cathedral (A), moss cathedral (B), and rippled cathedral (C). Opal glass (H), an antique variety, is used for lampshades because of its translucence.

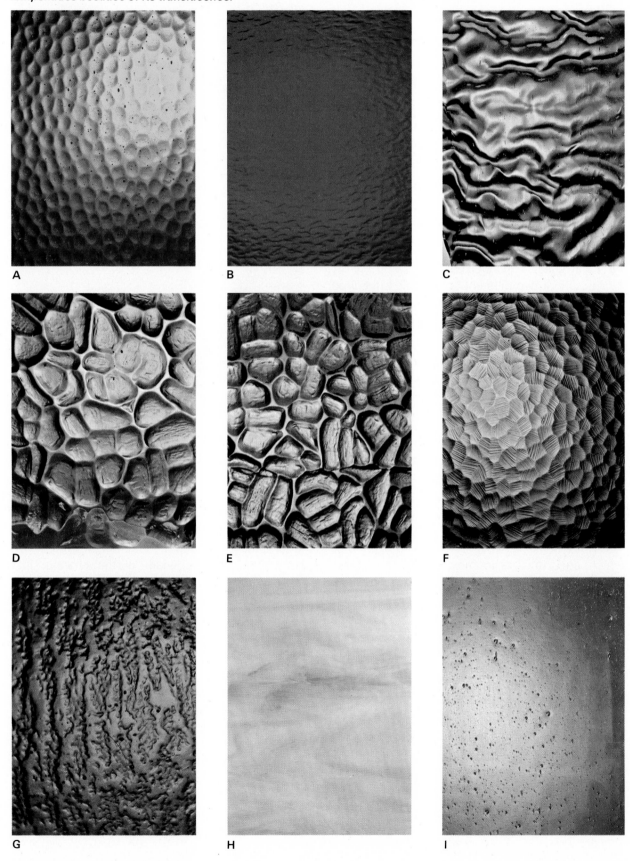

A

B

C

D

E

F

G

H

I

and usually found in hobby shops.

2. Moss cathedral glass: a rough hi-lo textured glass.

3. Rippled cathedral glass: a smooth, wide-spaced hi-lo textured glass.

4. Florentine cathedral glass: a glass textured with a star-like pattern.

5. Satin cathedral glass: a glass with a satin finish.

6. Sheet antique glass: an even-thickness antique glass which is thinner than most cathedral glass.

7. Full antique glass: a beautiful glass of varying thickness and type most often stained.

8. Opal glass: a marbleized, semiopaque glass, usually of two different colors (this is the type used for lampshades because it is more translucent than cathedral glass and will obscure the source of the light).

9. Opalescent glass: a semi-iridescent glass which is not as dense as opal glass and which glows more brightly when it is used in lampshades.

10. Milk glass: a pure white glass.

11. Flashed glass: a pale glass which has a surface coating of color and is used for etching.

LEAD CAMES

These are lengths of lead, roughly 6 feet long which are available in most hobby stores and from any glass supply house. Used to hold the glass together, lead cames are essentially the same today as those which were used for leading glass in the Middle Ages. They can be gently "stretched" or straightened to toughen or lengthen them. Sometimes the lead needs to have the channels or grooves opened with a pointed, blunt instrument before working with it. If the lead has been stored for a long period of time, oxidation will take place and the lead will darken. The dark surface must then be removed with a wire brush, sandpaper, or the edge of a knife, otherwise the lead will not solder.

U-channel or single-channel lead is used for the outside edges of an ornament, giving a smooth,

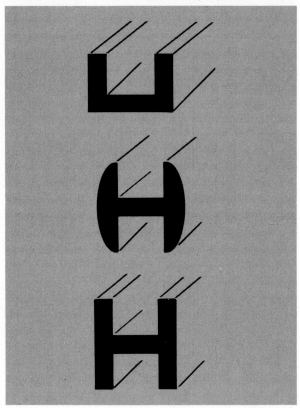

Figure 6. Lead cames, used to hold the glass together, are of two basic types: U-channel (top) and H-channel (center and bottom). The round "H" and the flat "H" are used for different purposes.

neat appearance. H-channel or double-channel lead is used wherever two pieces of glass are to come together. It can also be used around the edge of an ornament, adding some strength. The size by which the lead is sold indicates the height of the lead margin (the edge of the lead visible around the glass), although the height usually also corresponds to the width of the channel into which the glass fits. In ornament making, the 1/16", 1/8", and 1/4" lead will do well; the larger sizes are used in window and lampshade work.

SOLDERING IRON

There are many types of soldering irons available. The two most commonly used are the general, all-purpose, gun-type iron or the pencil-type iron. The latter is easier to handle and is available at most hardware and hobby stores. The 30-watt pencil-type iron is the best size; it radiates sufficient heat for a smooth, soldered joint, but not so much that the lead will be melted in the process. However, the 40-watt pencil-type iron is often more readily available. The problem with a pencil-type iron is that the heat at its tip is constant — a 40-watt iron can reach 850°F if left plugged in constantly. This will melt the lead and literally burn up the tip of the iron. This problem is easily remedied by either (1) unplugging the iron between uses, (2) installing a simple on/off switch on the cord to avoid all the unplugging, or (3) installing a rheostat on the cord. The last method is by far the best because it controls the exact amount of heat to the tip.

Both types of irons have replaceable tips: the conical or pencil-shaped tip gives the most satisfactory results for smaller projects. Remember: (1) fully insert the tip into the iron and be sure that the tip-holding screw is tight; (2) provide a safe place to lay the iron between solderings; (3) never replace the tip or clean the iron while it is still connected to the power source; and (4) keep the tip clean at all times to assure a clean, smooth soldered joint. This is done by frequently "swiping" off the black residue with a damp sponge or soft rag. Never hammer or strike the tip against an object. Never immerse the tip in water or flux. Never use sandpaper or a metal file on the tip as this will remove the tinning from the tip and ruin it.

SOLDER

Use the solid core, wire solder sold in 1/2- and 1-pound spools. For soldering lead, it is best to use the 60/40 solder which is available from glass or plumbing supply houses. The more readily available 50/50 solder is best for soldering copper foil. However, if 60/40 solder is not available, 50/50 solder may be used for lead soldering with satisfactory results.

FLUX

Available at any hardware store or supply house, flux is applied to the lead prior to soldering to prevent oxidation. Solder will not adhere to any metal if it is not fluxed beforehand.

UTILITY KNIFE

This is used for cutting the lead in place and for mitering the lead. This is the type with the replaceable blade that is available in any hardware store. An X-acto knife or any sharp blade will do.

GLASS PLIERS

These are used mainly for removal of excess glass. This is one of the more expensive extras ($8 to $12), but it is a good investment for anyone who is serious about working with glass. Most glass supply houses carry them. Regular workshop pliers will not do as they crush the glass. Glass pliers are wide-nosed and are designed so that the jaws are parallel when slightly open.

METAL FILE

A medium-grained file, available at any hardware store, is needed to file the edges of the glass and remove any sharp slivers. Coarse sandpaper may also be used, but with less satisfactory results.

GLASS GLOBS

Known as glass nuggets or flattened marbles, these are used for ornamentation and range in size from 3/8" to 1". Glass globs are available in a variety of colors at most hobby stores and glass supply houses.

COPPER FOIL

Copper foil should be used as a substitute for lead cames in all interior work. Fairly expensive, narrow strips of copper foil are wrapped around the edge of glass, thus taking the shape of U-channel lead. The adjacent pieces are then soldered together and all the foil is covered with solder. The result is a strong, rigid piece which is able to support a good deal of weight, making it ideal for panels and lampshades.

When copper foil is darkened, it has a rich appearance. Therefore, foil is a "must" when making jewelry. Buy copper foil adhesive-backed and on a roll — 1/4" is the standard size for most glass. Copper foil can be found in hobby stores which specialize in glass supplies and from glass supply houses.

COPPER SULFATE

Copper sulfate is used to darken the solder when using copper foil to give it an aged patina. The water-soluble, bluish crystals are available from glass supply houses and some chemical sources.

OTHER SUPPLIES

In addition to the items described above, other supplies needed include the following: (1) safety goggles to protect the eyes from flying slivers and chips of glass (regular eye glasses are inadequate because the glass can fly up under the lens); (2) a glass cutter with a ball at the end to aid in breaking the glass; (3) light lubricating oil in which the wheel end of the glass cutter is immersed to keep the cutting edge from becoming dull; (4) needle-nosed pliers; (5) copper or galvanized wire; (6) leather or rubber gloves; (7) a work surface; (8) glass paint (a special nonflammable paint for glass which is available for less than a dollar at most hobby stores); (9) a flat ruler for scoring straight lines and to lay under the glass to aid in breaking (do not use a ruler with a curved top); (10) clear glue — e.g., epoxys, special glass glue, and permanent-bonding glues; (11) small nails to hold the glass and lead in position on the work surface until they are soldered; and (12) old rags and alcohol to clean the lead and glass when soldering is finished.

Basic Procedures

This section gives step-by-step directions, including several "hints," to help develop the basic techniques. Cutting and leading the glass are not at all difficult once one acquires the knack, and this can only be developed by actually working with the glass.

DESIGNING A PATTERN

Designing one's own pattern is best postponed until experience is gained in this craft. However, a discussion of pattern design is essential to an over-all understanding.

It is best to work on a small scale at first. Work with sketches, refine and color them, and then transfer them to pattern paper. Various shapes convey various feelings: a square shape appears large and solid; a triangular shape is imposing; and a circle suggests a sensuous comfortable feeling, one of motion.

Keep the design simple. The success of a pattern depends upon the relationship of a component to all the other parts. A window or panel should have a main focal point, with the line of the design carrying the eye to this point.

Almost any idea or design can be transferred to glass, but keep two things in mind: (1) the shapes into which glass naturally breaks — a straight line, a curved line, or a wavy line; and (2) the effect the light will have on the design.

Remember to consider light — this is where the beauty of glass is unique. The light behind an object should always be greater than the inward light or the beauty of the glass is lost. Color is also a powerful tool when working with glass; interesting effects are developed when sections of glass are overlapped because the color changes.

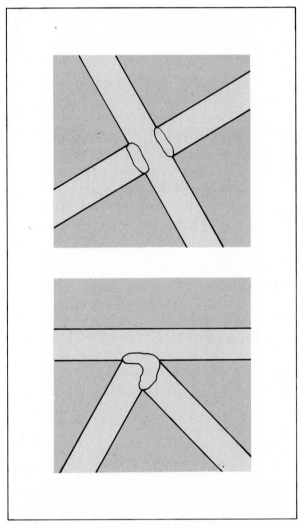

Figure 7. In designing any object, avoid weak structural points such as leads crossing (above) or leads meeting at the edge of a section (below). Also, avoid any structure too large to support itself.

The size of a composition, as well as the intended use, will determine what steps are necessary to avoid weak areas. There are three weak structural

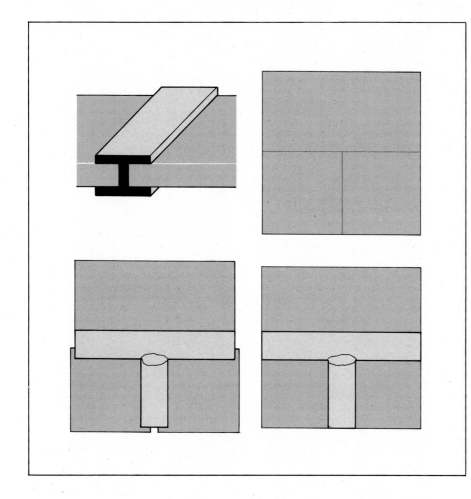

Figure 8. Another design "basic" is allowing 1/16" for leading between all glass pieces. Figure 8 shows (from top, left) H-channel leading between two pieces, glass marked for cutting, improper fitting due to lack of sufficient space, and proper fitting of glass and lead.

points to consider: (1) avoid points which would involve leads crossing; (2) avoid sections which would involve leads coming together at an edge; and (3) avoid designs which are too large to support themselves, unless bracing measures are taken.

When designing, remember that an allowance of 1/16" for the width of the inside wall of the lead is needed. This is especially important when two pieces fit together in a design. Also allow 1/16" for the lead which will hold the glass.

TRANSFERRING THE PATTERN

The pattern may be transferred to the glass in several different ways — practice will determine which method is best and most desirable for a particular glass. The pattern may be transferred (1) by placing the pattern beneath the glass and either scoring the glass directly or duplicating the lines on the glass with felt-tip marker and then scoring along the lines; or (2) by placing the pattern on top of the glass, tracing around it with a

felt-tip marker, and then scoring along the lines. In the case of very dark glass, merely place the pattern on the glass and score around it.

It is essential to allow the 1/16" in the pattern for the lead. Also, be sure to allow sufficient margins between the pattern and the edge of the glass so that there is enough leverage to break away the excess glass. Wherever possible, lay the straight edge of the pattern along a straight edge of the glass. This saves both glass and work.

CUTTING THE GLASS

Cutting the glass is probably the most difficult part of glass work. However, there is no reason to be frightened at the prospect of breaking glass as long as the correct cutting techniques are followed.

The protection of the eyes is of primary importance — wear safety glasses. A pair of well-fitting leather or plastic gloves will be needed to protect the hands. Another person should not be too near

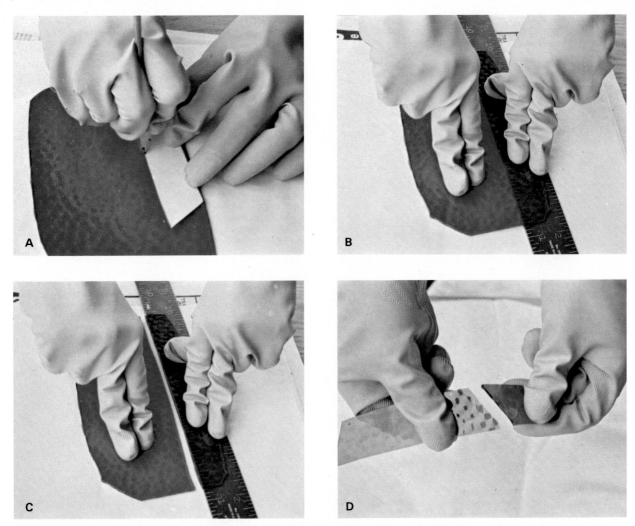

Figure 9. When working with dark glass, begin the cutting process by scoring along the edge of the pattern (A), snapping the scored straight line along a flat ruler (B, C), or — for a straight cut — snapping the glass by hand (D).

Figure 11. Final trimming may include these steps (from left): cutting a small margin of excess glass with the teeth of a cutter (I, J), breaking away a small excess with glass pliers (K), and filing edges (L).

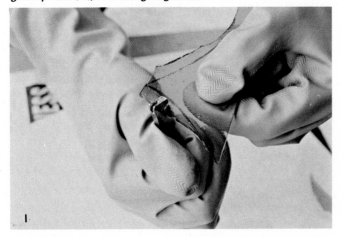

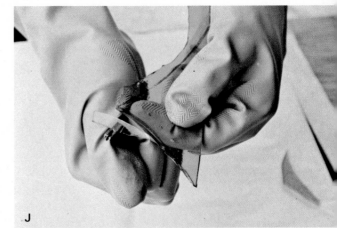

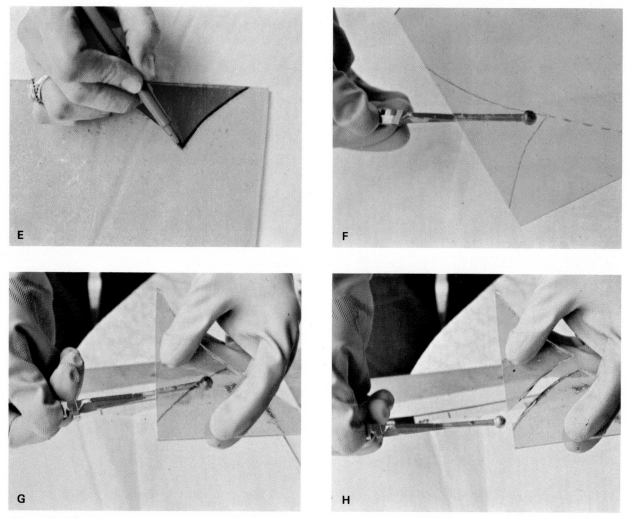

Figure 10. When working with light-colored glass, first transfer the pattern with a felt-tipped pen (E), then tap the ball end of the cutter directly under the score lines (F, G). If the score is even, the break will be even (H).

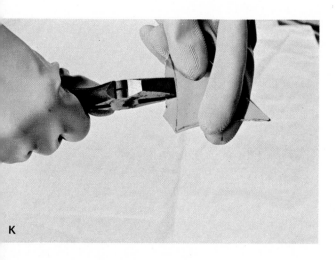

when glass is being cut because of the danger of flying chips. To avoid wasting precious colored glass, obtain some old window panes and practice using the glass cutter.

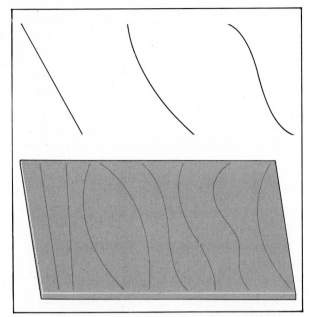

Figure 12. The natural breakage lines of glass are (from left) straight, curved, and wavy. A practice pattern is included for use on scrap pieces of window glass; score and break each line as instructed.

Cut the glass on a firm, even surface. Pad the area with newspaper before placing the glass down — less accidental breakage will occur if the cutting operation is done on a resilient surface. Keep the surface free of small chips of glass to prevent accidental breakage. The glass should be clean and dry. Always score on the smooth side of the glass. Straight, curved, or wavy lines are easy to cut simply because they are in keeping with the natural breakage lines of the glass. It is almost impossible to cut a circle in one cut — several cuts must be made.

Holding the Glass Cutter Properly

The glass cutter should be held as an extension of the index finger. This allows the wrist and the arm to act as the guiding factor. It is always better to stand when cutting glass — this allows for better leverage and lessens the temptation to use finger power only. Hold the cutter between the index and the middle finger, or with the index and the middle finger pressing down on top of the cutter. The teeth of the cutter should be toward you.

Hold the cutter perpendicular to the glass — if it is slanted the cut will be uneven.

Pull the cutter toward you while scoring straight lines. When scoring curved lines, it is easier to push the cutter. Move the cutter in a smooth, steady motion.

Start and stop within 1/16" from the edge of the glass. Running off the edge risks chipping the glass; once a line has been scored, do not go back over it. A glass cutter can be quickly ruined by going back over a line which does not seem deep enough.

Breaking the Glass

Once the glass has been scored, it must be broken immediately before it has a chance to "heal" or seal. Always break the glass away from the score line. The glass may be broken in any of the following ways:

1. By tapping with the ball end of the cutter directly under the score lines, causing the lines to "run." The tapping must be directly under the line or the effort is wasted.

2. For straight lines, place the edge of a flat ruler along the score line beneath the glass and apply downward pressure on both sides of the line. The glass will snap.

3. Narrow strips of the glass can be removed by using the teeth of the glass cutter or by using the glass pliers to break them off.

4. If there is sufficient leverage, the glass can be broken like a soda cracker, with a snap of the hands. Always remember to break the glass away from the score line.

If the score is even, the glass will run true when it is tapped; but if the score is uneven, it will run off when it comes to a flat spot and the line will not be as desired.

To avoid the inevitable nasty splinters and sharp edges, do not touch the edge of the broken glass until it has been filed smooth with the metal file. The file or glass pliers can be used at this point to smooth away any notches or bumps that remain on the glass.

Why a Cut Fails

Sometimes glass will not break. It is possible that the glass was not properly scored; if a good score was made, one can hear a high-pitched "hissing" sound. The glass cutter will not score the glass if:

1. Insufficient pressure was used. A pressure of about ten pounds is needed to score the glass. The weight must bear down vertically from the back of the hand.

2. The cutter was slanted so that the pressure was wasted — pressure was applied to the cutter instead of to the glass.

3. The cutter was dull: cutters will last through hundreds of uses if they are properly cared for and kept well lubricated.

4. The cutter skips because the wheel is damaged and needs to be replaced.

5. The cut was made on the rough side of the glass. (Most glass has a rough and smooth side; the cut must be made on the smooth side.)

6. The glass was not broken properly: either too much time lapsed between scoring and breaking or the glass was bent toward the scored side instead of away from it when the glass was being broken.

Difficult Cuts

The craftsman should avoid cutting difficult designs until he has become adept at glass cutting. Many different cuts can be made with only a little experience and practice. On a long difficult piece, lightly tap several times along the score line; do not allow the glass to break through at any one point before it has run through the entire length of the score line. If it does not easily fall apart, the design may be too complicated. All tapping of slight curves should start at the ends, meeting in the middle. All tapping of sharp curves should start at the apex and work toward the edges in both directions. A circle or concave curve cannot be cut away in one step, but requires several steps.

GLAZING

Assembling the glass with the lead and then soldering everything together is called glazing. Working on a sheet of plywood or some similar surface, position the glass pieces. Lay the pattern on the work area to help in positioning the glass properly. Select the desired lead. Preferably, U-channel lead should be used around the outer edge of the work and H-channel used in the internal part of the work.

The glass and the lead can now be assembled. Tack small nails into the plywood to hold the glass and the lead in position. Plan the joints so that they will come together wherever possible and so that their number will be minimal.

Press the lead firmly onto the glass and avoid leaving any space between the lead and the glass. The lead should be used in as long a piece as possible. The thinner leads, such as 1/8", 3/16", and

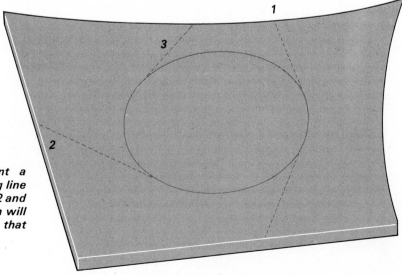

Figure 13. Circular shapes present a challenge in cutting. First score along line #1, then break away. Follow lines #2 and #3 in the same manner. A tiny notch will remain where the lines met; file that away.

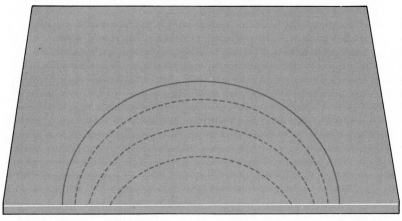

Figure 14. Another problem cut is a concave shape. First score along the line #1, then make a series of concentric scores inside the original score — at intervals of 1/8" on the glass. Tap out each waste section gently. Pliers can be used to remove stray bits.

1   1

1/4", can be cut with ordinary household scissors. The advantage of the utility or lead knife is that the lead can be cut right on the table without lifting it. With scissors, it must be lifted from the table. Trim the lead so that the joints are as close fitting as possible.

Apply flux to the area to be soldered and lightly touch the tip of the iron to the solder and the joint at the same time. Keep the tip of the iron in the solder until the melted solder forms a smooth pool and then remove the iron straight up. A little practice will develop the skill required to run a smooth joint. Take care to avoid melting the lead — apply the heat to the solder over the lead, not on the lead. (Most difficulty encountered in soldering stems from failure to keep the soldering tip clean and shiny. A dirty tip will not radiate heat and, thus, will not melt the solder.) When all the joints are soldered, remove the nails, turn over the piece, and solder the joints on the other side.

The soldering of wire hooks requires a little more heat than lead, so heat the wire for a moment before putting it in the solder. The hook always seems to be the most difficult part of soldering an ornament, perhaps because of its size. Even though the wire hook seems to be tightly soldered, some have a tendency to pull out of the solder under stress, drop, and break.

There are a few simple ways to insure that the hook is "locked" in place. Make the hook by twirling the wire around the tip of the needle-nosed pliers, forming a circle with the ends meeting. The circle is then soldered in place with a ridge of solder going through it — hence, it is locked in place.

COPPER FOILING

Although copper foiling is more time-consuming than working with lead came, it yields worth-

Figure 15. An important stage in assembling the project is wrapping the glass with lead (left). U-channel lead is generally used on outside edges, H-channel lead on inside edges. The ends of the lead must be trimmed (right).

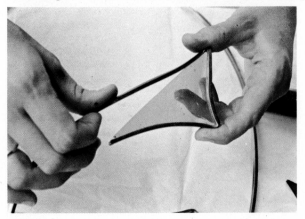
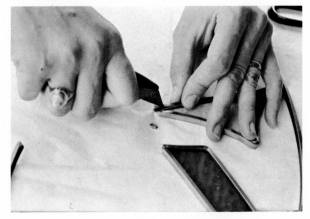

Figure 16. The first important step in glazing is to position the object securely on a board or other solid working surface. Apply flux to all areas to be soldered.

The tip of the soldering iron is then applied to the solder and the joint at the same time. Care and practice will produce a smooth joint.

After the wire hook for hanging has been attached, finishing touches can be put on the piece and the excess flux cleaned away from the joints.

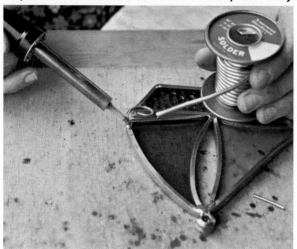

while results. Once most people learn to work with copper foil, they never return to the lead came.

When scoring the glass, a 1/16" allowance need not be made for the lead width. The glass can be scored directly on the lines of the pattern because the copper foil is only 1.6 millimeters thick.

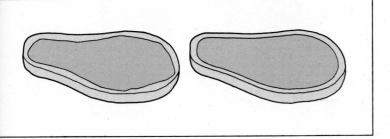

Figure 17. When using copper foil instead of lead, be sure to fold the foil neatly and evenly on each piece. Sloppy folding (left) will show on the finished piece; even folding looks much better (right).

When using copper foil as a substitute for the lead, wrap the edge of each piece of glass with foil. Be sure to remove the adhesive backing to expose the sticky surface. It will adhere easily if the glass is clean and free of oil and flux. It may be necessary to clean the glass before attempting to wrap the foil. It is important to be consistently neat and fold over exactly the same amount of foil on each piece. Any buckles around curves or in the corners can be smoothed down with the back of a spoon or a fingernail.

To position the glass on the board, tack small nails into the board, completely surrounding the glass. Apply flux to the copper and then solder a continuous joint between the pieces of glass, completely covering the copper and giving the appearance of solid lead. Keep a clean tip and use a smooth, steady motion — this goes faster than the lead because the copper takes the solder very rapidly. It is best if the seams form a slightly raised and rounded bead rather than being flat — this gives more strength and is neater.

The soldered seams can be left shiny, can be painted, or can be treated with chemicals to take on an aged patina. The last is the most popular and the most finished looking.

Before treating the work with chemicals, clean it well with alcohol to remove all flux. In an old can,

combine 1/2 ounce copper sulfate with 1/2 cup of water; heat the solution to boiling and stir to dissolve the crystals. While keeping the solution hot, dab it onto the solder with an old toothbrush. A darker finish can be achieved by the addition of tinner's fluid to the solution. Continue the treatment until all the metal has the desired effect.

The chemicals will not harm the glass, but will give it a patina of its own. When finished, wash the work under water and shine it. If any deposits remain, scrub them with a soft brush. Do not use abrasives.

There is one limitation to copper foil: it can be used only for interior work. There is no provision for cementing, which is necessary to make a stained-glass window waterproof.

Projects You Can Do

The three projects suggested here are small but will serve as a foundation for larger and more complicated designs. Fairly quick to do, each makes an excellent gift. Almost any design can be adapted to glass once one learns the mechanics of cutting the glass. Read through the projects first to determine what materials are necessary.

AN OWL

For this project, glass nuggets are used so that concentration will be on the soldering. The owl consists of one large nugget for the body and two smaller ones of a different color for the eyes.

1. Cut a length of U-channel lead for the top.

2. Frame the nuggets with the U-channel. Fit the joints as snugly as possible and then solder them.

3. Trim a piece of U-channel for the beak.

4. Twist a length of H-channel for the branch which the owl sits on.

5. Position the nuggets, top lead, and branch. Now, solder where they touch.

6. Place the beak piece on top and solder.

7. Turn the owl over and solder the back joints.

8. Attach a hook on the top.

9. Clean the owl with alcohol, shine it, and hang it up.

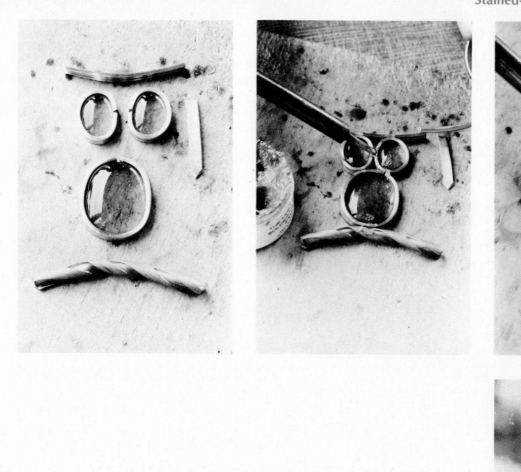

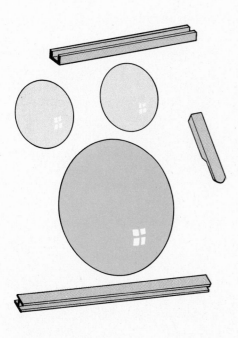

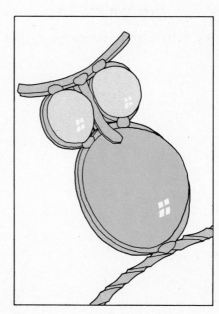

Figure 18. This pattern for the owl project shows the pieces needed and how they fit together. Follow the photographs if a review is needed on final assembly and solderings. The finished product is cleaned, shined, and hung up.

A SAILBOAT

Select the colors for the base and for the two sails on the boat. Position the pattern pieces and glass and prepare to cut.

1. Position the straight edge of pattern along the straight edge of the glass.

2. Score and break line (1-2 in the accompanying illustration).

3. Score and break line (3-4), then (5-6).

4. Score and break line (A-B).

5. Score and break line (B-C).

6. Score and break line (D-E).

7. Lay straight edge (X-Y) of pattern along straight edge of glass.

8. Score and break line (X-Z).

9. Score and break line (W-Y).

10. After cutting the glass, file the edges to remove any slivers and rough spots.

11. Using U-channel lead, frame the pieces of glass, bending the corners to make them pointed and fitting the joints snugly.

12. Position the pieces and solder them together.

13. Curl a piece of heavy wire and solder it to the front sail.

14. Curl a piece of wire for the top ring or, if desired, add a small glass flag.

15. Turn the boat over and solder the joints on the backside. Clean the piece.

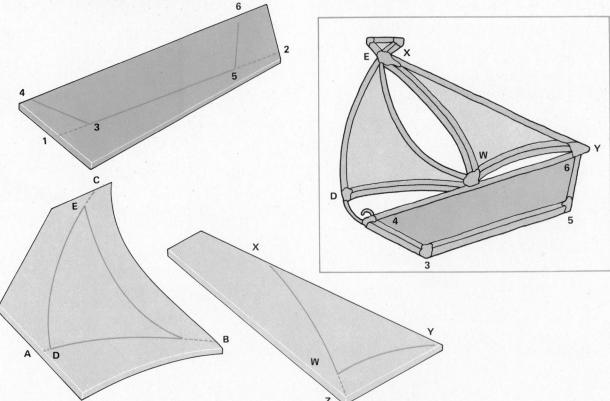

Figure 19. A sailboat can be assembled using this pattern. Follow the dotted lines on the pieces for scoring. In the photo of the finished boat, note the appearance of the lead where the three pieces are joined.

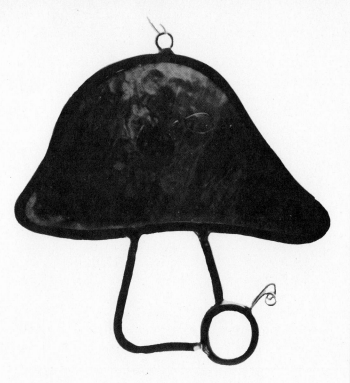

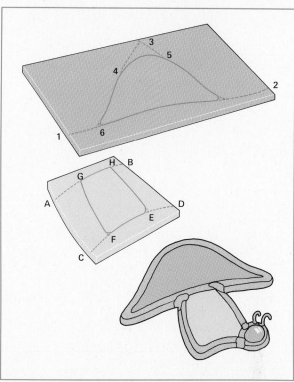

Figure 20. This pattern for a mushroom (left) shows scoring lines for the main pieces. The curve at the top of the mushroom will probably need to be filed, in order to obtain the smooth look shown in the photo.

FRIENDLY MUSHROOMS

This project will combine opal glass with cathedral glass to complement each other. A nugget is used for a ladybug.

1. Score and break line (1-2).

2. Score and break line (2-3).

3. Score and break line (3-6).

4. Score and break line (4-5).

5. Score and break line (A-B).

6. Score and break line (C-D).

7. Score and break line (G-F).

8. Score and break line (H-E).

9. Nibble away at the corners to round them off, and file the glass smooth.

10. Frame with U-channel and solder joints on both sides.

11. Frame the little nugget with U-channel, make an antenna with wire, and solder it in place; determine where it should go under the mushroom and solder. Determine the center of gravity and solder on a hook. Clean.

For Additional Reading

Bing, Samuel, **Artistic America, Tiffany Glass, and Art Nouveau,** MIT Press, 1971.

Hamilton, Walter J., **The Advanced Techniques of Making Leaded Glass Projects,** Laral Press, 1972.

Inesberg, Anita and Seymour, **How to Work in Stained Glass,** Chilton, 1971.

Lloyd, John Gilbert, **Stained Glass in America,** Foundation Books, 1963.

Reyntiens, Patrick, **The Techniques of Stained Glass,** Watson-Guptill, 1967.

Wood, Paul, **Stained Glass Crafting,** Sterling, 1971.

String and *Wire Art*

The artistic discipline of creating geometric designs with string and wire is a relatively new creative phenomenon.

Although man has been using string and wire for centuries, it was only recently that these items have been used to create the kinds of art objects to be discussed here. Primitive man used string for weaving, wrapping, and holding objects; wire and string have also been used since early times to create beautiful sounds on musical instruments.

Figure 2. The Brooklyn Bridge, designed by John Roebling in the 19th century, is famed as a feat of engineering but also deserves recognition as a work of art. (*Courtesy, Paul Popper Ltd.*)

All of the designs in this new art form have one thing in common: they are rooted in geometry. Some designs emphasize the geometric form itself, while others combine forms to create the impression of some object — for example, a butterfly, a flower, a bridge, or the sun. The designs are generally flat, two-dimensional shapes, constructed of colorful strings or threads stretched back and forth around nails.

Of course, it is also possible to work with string and wire in a three-dimensional way. Many modern sculptors have been experimenting with this new concept. The work of the Russian constructivist, Naum Gabo, is an excellent example. Gabo used string in his sculptural work to stress space, time, and "dynamic rhythm." He wanted to open up solid volumes to show the stress tensions inherent therein. Gabo denied that volume was an adequate expression of space and saw his work as a germinating point for architecture of the future.

Figure 1. Henry Moore's sculpture "Bird Basket" (opposite), 1939, uses string to emphasize the massive hollows of the basic hardwood structure. (Courtesy, Henry Moore.)

Another artist who experimented with string in his work is the British sculptor, Henry Moore. Moore's work is basically concerned with volumes and mass. He used stringed areas to help delineate the hollows and holes incorporated into the solid forms. Barbara Hepworth, another British sculptor, used string much in the same manner.

The principle behind stringed design work can also be seen in architectural structures. John Roebling's Brooklyn Bridge is a perfect example. In combination with the heavy stone masonry, the steel suspension cables are delicate but structurally strong. Besides being a practical object, the Brooklyn Bridge has often been called a work of art. The George Washington Bridge in New York and the Golden Gate Bridge in San Francisco are also excellent examples of cable work that inspire string designs. In fact, from spider webs to power lines, such geometric artistic designs can be seen everywhere.

The basis of string design work comes from geometric principles. For years, high school and college teachers have used stringed two- and three-

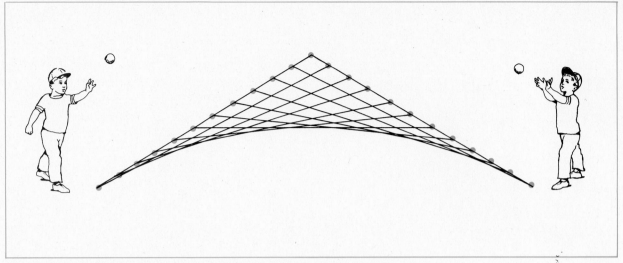

Figure 3. In this design, lines are set along points to form a parabolic curve.

Figure 4. The sculpture "Winged Figure," by artist Barbara Hepworth, was commissioned for the John Lewis department store in London. This work is a prime example of wire art in sculpture.

dimensional designs to illustrate certain mathematical ideas, such as the parabola, which involves the making of curves with straight lines. This principle is also used to illustrate the flight of an object, such as a baseball.

There are a variety of basic geometric forms used to create stringed designs: the circle, triangle, square, rectangle, and ellipse are a few common examples. Certainly part of the appeal of string and wire design work is the modern, futuristic look that can be achieved with clean geometric forms and colorful, crossing lines.

In recent years string design work has been called "symmography." As Lois Kreischer in her book *String Art: Symmography* explains: "The word symmography is derived from 'symmetry' and the suffix '-graphy.' Together they describe a linear representation in which proportion, balance, and harmony are used to create the proper relationship of rays of yarn to one another, thus producing an aesthetically pleasing picture."

Common Terms Used In String and Wire Art

Axis: any lengthwise central line, real or imaginary, around which parts of a body are symmetrically (proportionally) arranged.

Diagonal: the line that crosses a square or rectangle from opposite angles (corners).

Grid: a pattern of horizontal and vertical lines crossing each other at 90° angles.

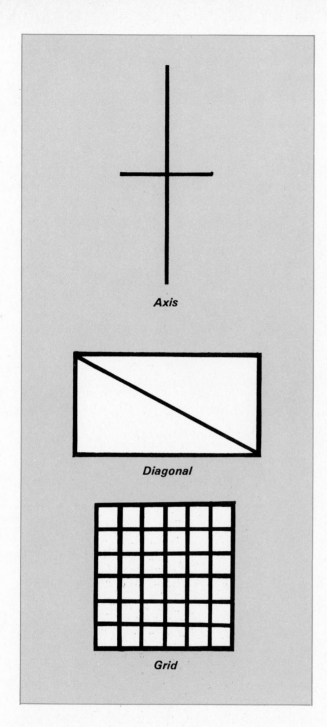

Axis

Diagonal

Grid

Mat Board: thick cardboard, which comes in colors; and used by artists to mat pictures for framing.

Mandala: a Hindu or Budhist symbol used for meditation; a design in which a circle encloses a square.

Parabolic Curve: a curve formed from only straight lines.

Symmography: a term used for string designing.

Basic Equipment And Supplies

The equipment necessary for creating string and wire designs is fairly inexpensive and easily accessible. Most items can be purchased at hardware stores, retail stores, knitting supply outlets, artist supply stores, and lumber yards.

STRINGS AND WIRES

Strong, thin strings are best to work with. It is possible, but not always practical, to know exactly how much string you are going to use for any given project. It is best to estimate how much string will be needed so that extra string is available in case something goes wrong. It is also best to purchase your strings, threads, and yarns at a store where a complete stock is always maintained. The kinds of fiber materials that may be used for almost any project are described below.

String

Any kind of colorful strong string is appropriate. One of the best is crochet string, which comes in an assortment of vivid colors and is strong and durable. It is generally better not to use especially hairy or slippery strings and cords, like jute and fine silk, because these materials are difficult to manage. However, the decision on what string to use ultimately depends on the desired effect. One may be striving for a very earthy look, or for a delicate and fragile motif. The type of room in which the finished design will be placed also has an effect, as does the size of nails or tacks being used. Crochet string works very well with the size tacks suggested below.

Thread

Mercerized cotton thread is also good for string art. It has the desirable characteristics of being thin and strong and is also available in many colors.

Yarn

Yarns can also be used effectively, especially orlon acrylic or four-ply knitting worsted. Because yarn thins out when it is pulled tight, the thickness of the yarns in the finished product will look different from the thickness in the skeins. Be careful of yarns that unravel easily, or that tear

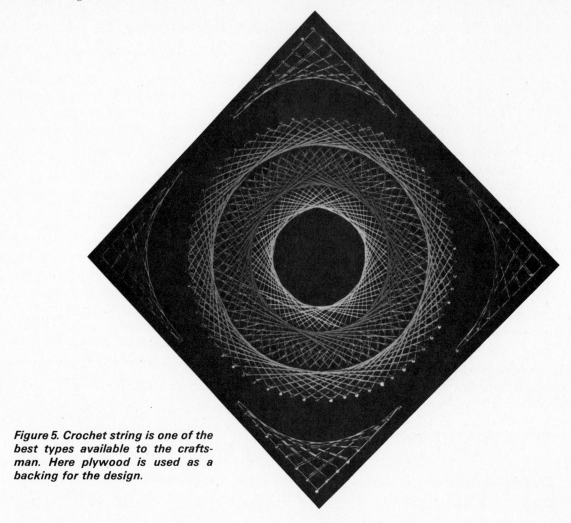

Figure 5. Crochet string is one of the best types available to the crafts- man. Here plywood is used as a backing for the design.

when pressure is applied to them. For special ef- fects, experiment with very fluffy yarns, like mo- hair and Icelandic mountain sheep's wool.

Wire

Wire is generally more expensive than string. The most commonly used wire for design is galvan- ized steel wire, copper, brass, and aluminum wires are also available. These latter allow for dif- ferent color effects, but are more expensive than steel. Wire comes in different gauges, a few of which are practical for general wire art: gauges 30 to 18 are recommended. Gauge 30 wire is 0.0140 inch in diameter and gauge 18 is 0.0475. A pound of 30-gauge wire yields 1913 feet of working wire. Wire can be purchased in small or medium-sized spools but that is the most expen- sive way to buy it. Purchasing it by the pound is much more economical.

NAILS AND TACKS

The kind, color, and size of nail or tack is, of course, a matter of personal preference. There is only one necessary characteristic: it must have a small head to prevent the string, thread, yarn or wire from slipping off. A nail also needs to be long enough to carry the required layers of material, which sometimes can be quite thick. The best size nail to use for the first project is a 1 inch or 7/8 inch nail with a small head. Later, as proficiency increases, experiment with all kinds of tacks, hooks, pins, and even thin dowels of wood.

WOODS

To create background for the design, the nails or tacks are pounded into a piece of wood. The least expensive and most readily obtainable is indoor plywood. It is generally best to use 1/2-inch plywood. Anything thicker is difficult to frame and heavy to hang; thinner pieces can be penetrated by nails and tend to warp. Wood with an excessive number of knots is also to be avoided. Paint or stain the wood as desired. The final product will be affected by the manner in which the wood is cut: edges should be smooth and even.

Once again, experiment with varieties and shapes of wood. These can lend interesting textures, colors, and characteristics to each project.

CARDBOARD AND MAT BOARD

Not all designs have to be worked on wood with nails. Interesting effects can also be achieved by stringing thread, yarn, string, and wire through cardboard or mat board. Almost any kind of sturdy, noncorrugated cardboard is usable, although it may be necessary to glue together two or three thicknesses of cardboard to create a sturdy surface. Mat board can be purchased at any artist supply or framing store and is available in a large range of colors. It is usually sturdy enough to use as is.

PAINTS AND STAINS

Depending on the desired finished effect, the wood can be either painted or stained. The wood may be painted either before or after putting in the nails, according to whether one wishes to keep the original color of the nails or to cover them with paint. Following are some suggested paints and stains.

Acrylic

Acrylic paints come in a wide variety of colors and have the advantages of drying fast and leaving a durable, attractive coat. Two coats are sometimes necessary, depending on the color.

Housepaint

Both water-based and oil-based housepaints are a practical possibility for covering wooden backgrounds. These often have the advantage of matching the accessories in one's home and of already being on hand.

Spray Paint.

Spray paints can be used on both wooden and cardboard surfaces.

Stain

There are a variety of stains from which to choose. Wire designs look especially good on stained wood.

Figure 6. This attractive, carefully planned geometric design, deceptively simple to make, uses crochet string on a background of stained plywood.

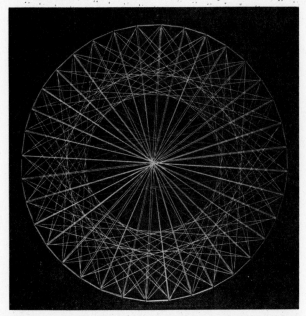

Figure 7. Cloth can be stretched over the wood used as a basic background for string art. Burlap was used in this example. The cloth is stretched tight and glued or tacked to the back of the wood.

FABRIC

Some craftsmen prefer a fabric background instead of paints or stain. There are a number of interesting possibilities: Colored burlap, velvet, velveteen, corduroy, and terrycloth make fine backgrounds. Solid colors are best because they allow the string design to be prominent. The material can be stretched over the wood and either glued or tacked to the back. Be careful that the edges do not wrinkle or bulge.

MISCELLANEOUS ITEMS

Other materials that are needed include hammer, scissors, masking tape, yarn needle, crochet hook, sandpaper, pencils, ruler or yardstick, eraser, compass, protractor, T-square, brushes, and paper designs. Also, some basic knowledge about parabolic curves and other shapes made from straight lines is required.

CREATING PARABOLIC CURVES

This technique can be practiced by first using paper and pencil and then transferring the ideas to cardboard and wood. There is some difference in technique between stringing a cardboard with holes punched in it and stringing a piece of wood with tacks in it. Both will be explained for the dia-

gram shown, which represents a 90° angle. On each axis, X and Y, there are five points — the zero is shared and five is an arbitrary number. There could be 100 or more points if desired. Start with cardboard. Lightly draw a right angle on the board. Place the points an equal distance from each other on both axes. Using the point of a compass, punch through the cardboard at each point, including zero. Now take a single strand of crochet string and thread a yarn needle that will fit through the holes. Tie a large knot at one end of the string. Starting the threaded needle from the back side of the cardboard, proceed as follows:

1. Up through 1 on X.

2. Down through 4 on Y.

3. Up through 3 on Y.

4. Down through 2 on X.

5. Up through 3 on X.

6. Down through 2 on Y.

7. Up through 1 on Y.

8. Down through 4 on X.

9. Up through 0.

10. Down through 4 on Y.

11. Up through 4 on X.

12. Down through 0 and, keeping the string tight, tie a knot in it at the rear of the cardboard behind 0.

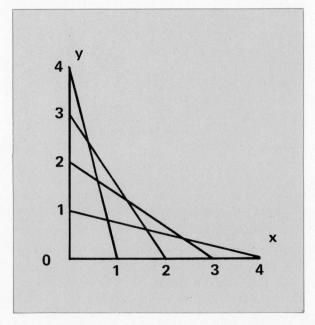

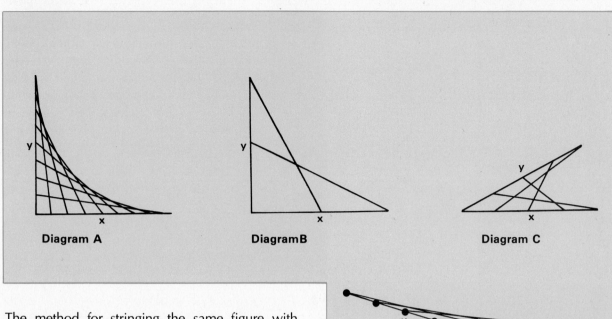

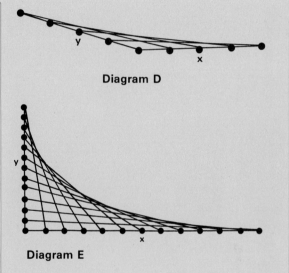

The method for stringing the same figure with tacks on wood is as follows:

1. Tie the string to tack 4 on X.

2. From 4X go to 1Y and, keeping the string tight, wrap it around 1Y once.

3. From 1Y go to 3X, wrap, then back to 2Y, then to 2X.

4. From 2X go to 3Y, and then to 1X.

5. Finally carry the string to 4Y and then go from 4Y to 0 and back to 4X. Tie the string off.

Make sure that the knot is strong. Clip the string close to the knot and put a small drop of any clear drying glue on to prevent unraveling. This is the basic technique for simple parabolic curves. Variations will come from the position of holes and nails and the length of the axis. Some examples of variations follow.

Variations on the Parabolic Curve

A smoother curve can be constructed by having more holes/nails per inch or foot on the axis. In one of the accompanying illustrations there are eight points on each axis — each point is 1/4 inch apart. In the other drawing there are two points on each axis, each 1 inch apart.

Another way to change the curve is to reduce or widen the angle, as illustrated. It is sometimes difficult to work with wide angles because the string has a tendency to lay unevenly. In such cases, a thin string or thread will work best.

Figure 8. Diagrams A and B show that use of more nails produces a smoother curve; C and D demonstrate that changing the 90° angle changes the curve; E stretches out the curve by lengthening one axis.

Also illustrated is still another way to vary the shape of a parabolic curve. Axis Y is twice the length of axis X. Each has the same number of points; however, the points on axis Y are twice as far apart as the points on axis X. This creates a less regular, but more dramatic curve — one that suggests flight and motion. The curve could be made even steeper by making the Y axis four times the length of the X axis. Of course, it is also possible to make the X axis longer than the Y axis. In either case, there always should be the same number of points on each axis. More variations on the curve can be achieved by widening or reducing the size of the angle between the axes and simultaneously lengthening one of the axes.

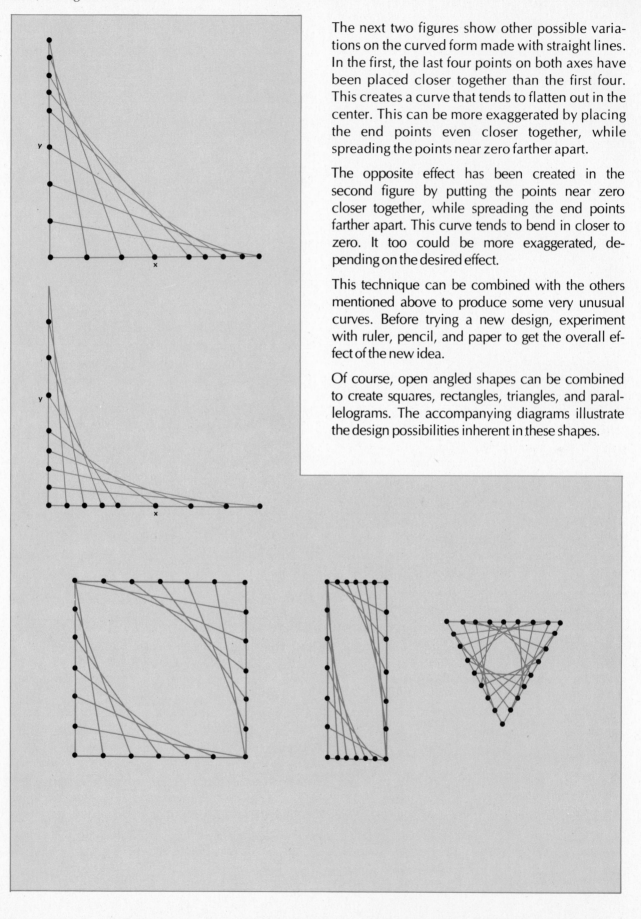

The next two figures show other possible variations on the curved form made with straight lines. In the first, the last four points on both axes have been placed closer together than the first four. This creates a curve that tends to flatten out in the center. This can be more exaggerated by placing the end points even closer together, while spreading the points near zero farther apart.

The opposite effect has been created in the second figure by putting the points near zero closer together, while spreading the end points farther apart. This curve tends to bend in closer to zero. It too could be more exaggerated, depending on the desired effect.

This technique can be combined with the others mentioned above to produce some very unusual curves. Before trying a new design, experiment with ruler, pencil, and paper to get the overall effect of the new idea.

Of course, open angled shapes can be combined to create squares, rectangles, triangles, and parallelograms. The accompanying diagrams illustrate the design possibilities inherent in these shapes.

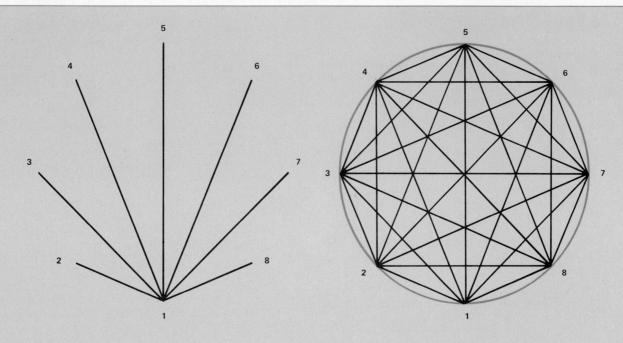

CIRCULAR FORMS

There are a number of techniques for creating unusual designs with circles. The first one to be demonstrated is especially effective on colorful cardboard with crochet string. Cut a square of cardboard and locate its center by lightly drawing diagonals from opposite corners. Where these lines cross is the center of both the square and the circle. Use a compass to draw a circle of the desired size. Place an even number of points on the circumference of the circle. Punch a hole at each point with a compass or another sharp-pointed instrument. Thread the needle with a colored string and tie a knot at the end of the string. Choose a hole and draw the needle through it from the rear of the board. Then proceed as follows, using the diagram as a guide:

1. Down 2, back up 1 from behind.

2. Down 3, back up 1 from behind.

3. Down 4, back up 1 from behind.

4. Down 5, back up 1 from behind.

5. Down 6, back up 1 from behind.

6. Down 7, back up 1 from behind.

7. Down 8, tie a knot behind 8.

Tie on a new piece of string if the first runs out, but make sure the knot is at the back of the cardboard. Carefully erase the light diagonal lines.

Follow the same procedure for each new starting point. Notice that previous strings will have already filled certain lines, so that with each new point there should be one less hole to string than at the previous point. The finished product gives the impression of rays radiating from each point. Experiment with this technique by not filling a certain number of holes. This also yields an interesting result.

The next technique is an excellent one to use with tacks on either stained or painted wood. Necessary supplies are a pencil, a piece of paper the size of the wood, a compass, masking tape, and a ruler. Tape the paper over the wooden shape. Using the compass, draw a circle at the center of the board. Subdivide the circumference of the circle into a prime number, that is, a number which is evenly divisible only by 1 and itself — e.g.: 1, 2, 3, 5, 7, 11, 13, 17, 19, 23. By using such a number of points, each colored layer in the design can be laid with one continuous string.

Take the circumference of the circle and divide it by the chosen prime number. Set the compass at

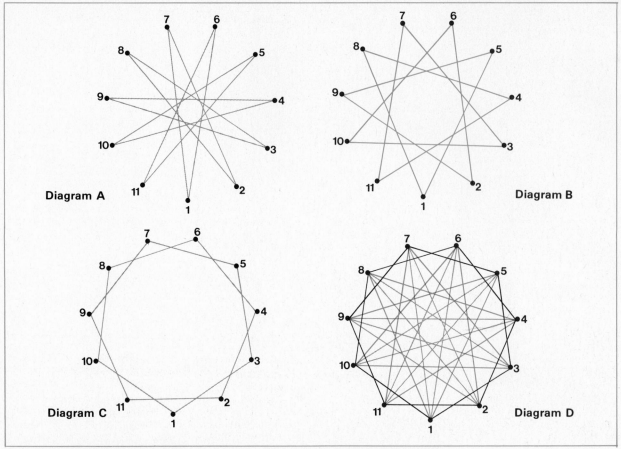

Figure 9. A design based on circles of different sizes is achieved by skipping tacks while stringing. Skip four tacks (A) to create the first circle, then three (B), then one (C); and finally string the border (D).

that amount and mark it off along the circle. Don't expect perfect results with the first effort — adjust and remark as necessary.

Having marked the prime number of points, hammer a nail into each point. Try to keep the nails at equal height above the wood. Once the nails are in place, remove the paper (carefully if keeping the pattern). The effect achieved with the stringing technique varies with the number of tacks skipped while stringing. The bottom layer of string should be the one that closes in the most; it can be any color desired. In the illustration the string was tied on nail 1 and then carried to 7, wrapped once and carried to 2. This pattern of skipping four tacks between connections was carried out until each tack had a string coming to it and going from it. When a large number of tacks is skipped, the finished circle will be small. Take care to keep the string taut from nail to nail. It is also a good idea to wrap the string once around each nail to help secure the finished design.

The next layer of the design can be a second color. This time the string starts at nail 1 and goes to nail 8, wraps once, and goes to nail 4, then to 11, 7, 3, and so on. In this layer the string skips three nails between each connection. Notice that the circle created here is larger than the one created by skipping four nails.

In the next figure, the string starts at nail 1 and goes to 10, wraps once, goes to 8, 6, 4, and so on until each nail is filled. In this case the string is skipping one nail and the resulting circle is very large. This is the third layer of the design.

To finish the design as illustrated, a final layer of string is attached from nail to nail, which creates an edge. There are many possibilities for this circular technique. The more nails on the circumference of the circle, the smoother the inner circles will look. Also, the number of colored layers used depends upon the number of nails.

Once all the strings are laid, the lines can be straightened so that the inner circles are even.

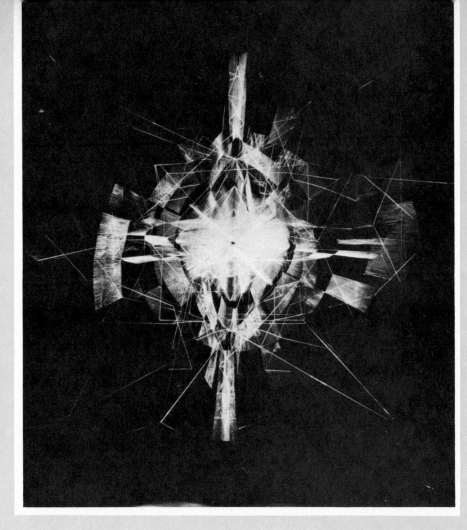

Figure 10. Richard Lippold used gold-filled wire in this dazzling sculpture (left), "Variation Within a Sphere, No. 10: the Sun." (Courtesy, The Metropolitan Museum of Art, Fletcher Fund, 1956.)

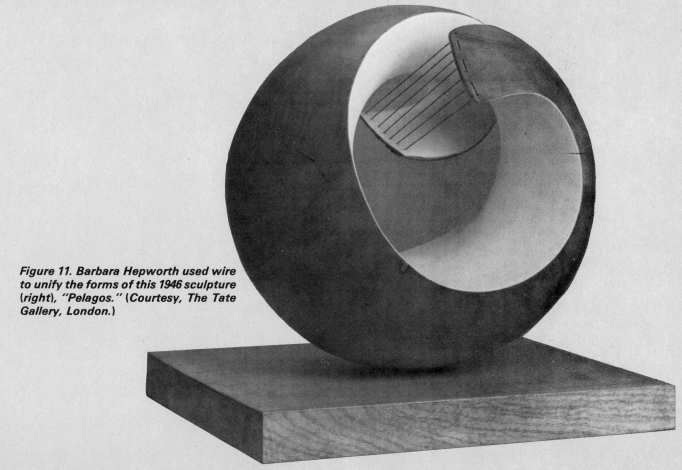

Figure 11. Barbara Hepworth used wire to unify the forms of this 1946 sculpture (right), "Pelagos." (Courtesy, The Tate Gallery, London.)

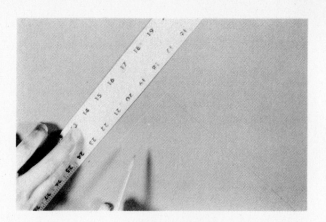

Figure 12. The circle project in this series of diagrams requires the use of ruler and compass. Threads originate from each point on the circle as shown.

Projects You Can Do

This section describes, step-by-step, several simple projects for interesting string and wire designs. The projects are done with materials that are readily available. After working through these projects, one will be prepared to expand on them in original ways.

PROJECT I

This project employs the techniques that were described under "Basic Procedures" for stringed circular shapes on cardboard. The materials needed are: (1) a square piece (from 1 to 3 feet per side) of fairly sturdy cardboard or mat board of any color (for practice use a piece of shirt cardboard with wrapping string); (2) two colors of crochet string to contrast with the color of the board; (3) a compass; (4) a ruler; and (5) a yarn needle.

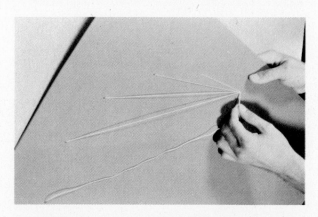

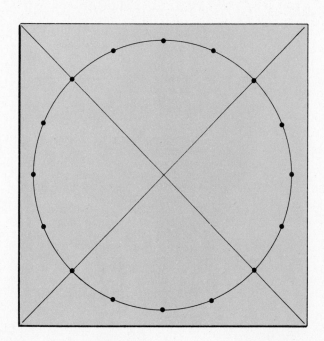

rear of the board. From that point bring the needle to the next hole and through. The needle then comes back to the original point of insertion before going to each of the other points on the circle. When the needle has been brought through the last empty hole, tie the string off at the back of the board.

Now move to a hole next to the one used as the starting point for the previous stringing. Change the color of the string and repeat the process. The first hole strung is the center point for seven holes — the companion color will be at each end of the set of seven.

The design created with this project is one of a circle in the process of being drawn. This is accomplished by leaving the other nine holes half empty. It is also possible to create a series of circles in various stages of development either on different colored boards or by adding different colored strings with each new hole.

Find the center of the square piece of board by lightly drawing two diagonals from opposite corners. With the point of the compass at the center (where the diagonals cross), draw a large circle. Do not go to the very edge of the square, but leave 1 or 2 inches between the circumference of the cirlce and the edge of the cardboard.

Now, with the compass or using the ruler, mark off 16 points on the circumference of the circle. These points should be equidistant from each other. Then, take the point of the compass and punch a hole in each point from the *front of the board to the back*. Lightly erase the diagonal and circle lines.

Next, pick a point at which to start stringing. This is an important step because every hole is not going to be fully strung. If the finished board is to be hung as a square, choose a point that is the nearest to the middle of one of the edges. If it is to be hung as a diamond shape, then use a hole that is nearest one of the corners. Thread the needle and tie a large knot at the end of the piece of string. Put the needle through the hole from the

Figure 13. Many pleasing variations can be obtained using the basic circle pattern. In this example, seven of the points are completed and the others are not — suggesting a fan shape.

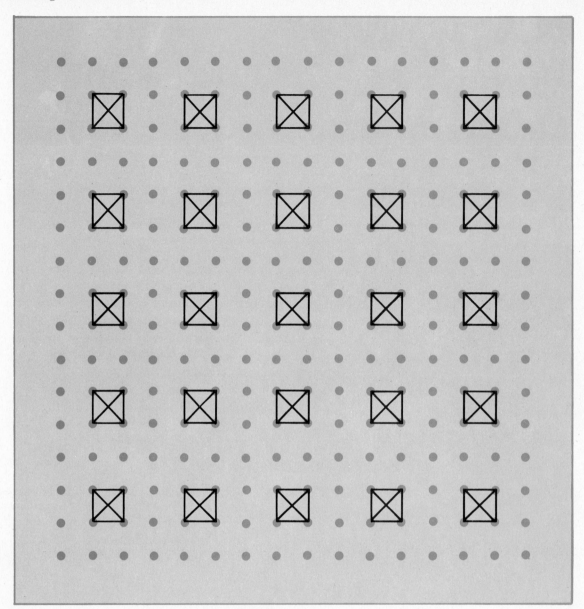

PROJECT II

This project is somewhat more complicated than the first. It is called the "Coptic Cross" because it is reminiscent of the shape of the crosses used in Ethiopia by the Coptic Church. Needed are: (1) a piece of 18″ x 18″ plywood (the corners can be curved or right angles); (2) 3/4-inch tacks with small heads; (3) a can of flat black spray paint; (4) four colors of crochet string; (5) a small spool of metallic thread (gold or silver); (6) a hammer; (7) scissors; and (8) a yardstick.

Work on the smooth side of the wood and avoid a side that has any knots or irregularities. With the yardstick, draw a line 1½ inches in from the four edges of the wood. There should be an equal margin on all sides, leaving a 15-inch square in the center of the board. Now take a pencil and mark off every inch on the drawn line. Connect the dots on lines opposite each other with a light pencil line — the result will look like a piece of graph paper. Once the grid is completed, hammer in a tack at every spot where two lines meet. This requires exactly 256 tacks. Do not hammer the tacks in completely, but be sure they are sturdy. Now look at the upper right hand corner of the grid. Count left four tacks and then down four. Then go back right four and up four to the original point. This will delineate a small square with four tacks within it. Hammer the inside tacks in farther than the surrounding ones. Now look at the grid. There should be 25 such squares each with a small square comprised of four tacks inside of each. Hammer down the four tacks inside each of these 25 small squares.

Once all the tacks have been hammered in, the board can be spray painted. To apply, read the directions on the can. It is usually best to spray a number of light coats. Let dry and then begin to string the tacks.

Stringing the Tacks

The first tacks to string are the 25 very small 4-tack squares that were hammered lower than the others. String these with the metallic thread. Start at one corner, go to the next, wrap around, and continue until a small square is strung. Then string the diagonals, producing a small square with a cross in it. This can be done with only two small knots. Use a drop of clear drying glue on these knots. When all the small squares are completed, turn the board so that it is in a diamond shape. It is now time to string the four large corner squares: the top and bottom squares should be the same color; the 2 side squares should be the same color also but different from the top and bottom.

To delineate the top and bottom squares, do the following. From the top nail count down seven nails in both directions. At the last nail on each side, turn a 90° angle and count over seven nails. This marks out a square with seven nails per side. The nails will be strung so that the curve goes from the top nail to the bottom one (see diagram). Follow the same procedure for stringing that was shown for stringing the first figure illustrated in the section "Creating Parabolic Curves" — the only difference is that there are now seven nails. After stringing one side of the square, string the other.

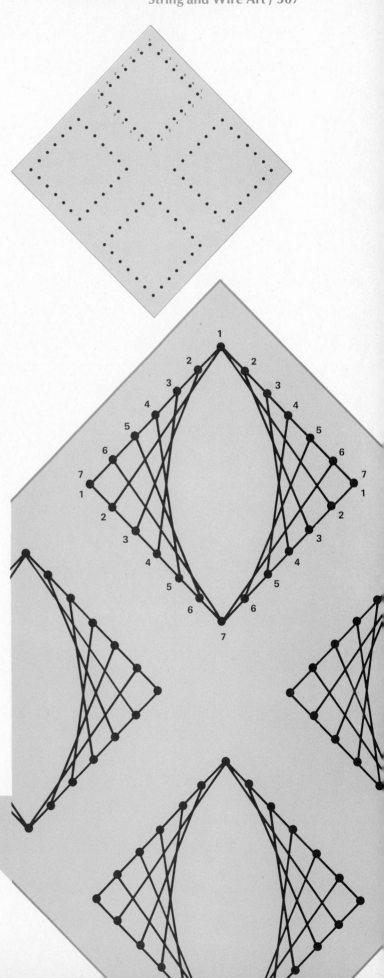

After the four corner squares are completed, string the large center square. To do this, find the nail at the center of each of the corner squares. These four nails are the corners of the large square. String the large square. When that is completed, string the small square in the center of the design. This is easy to do: the four corners of this square are the four inside corners of the top, bottom, and side squares that are already strung. The project is finished and can be framed or not.

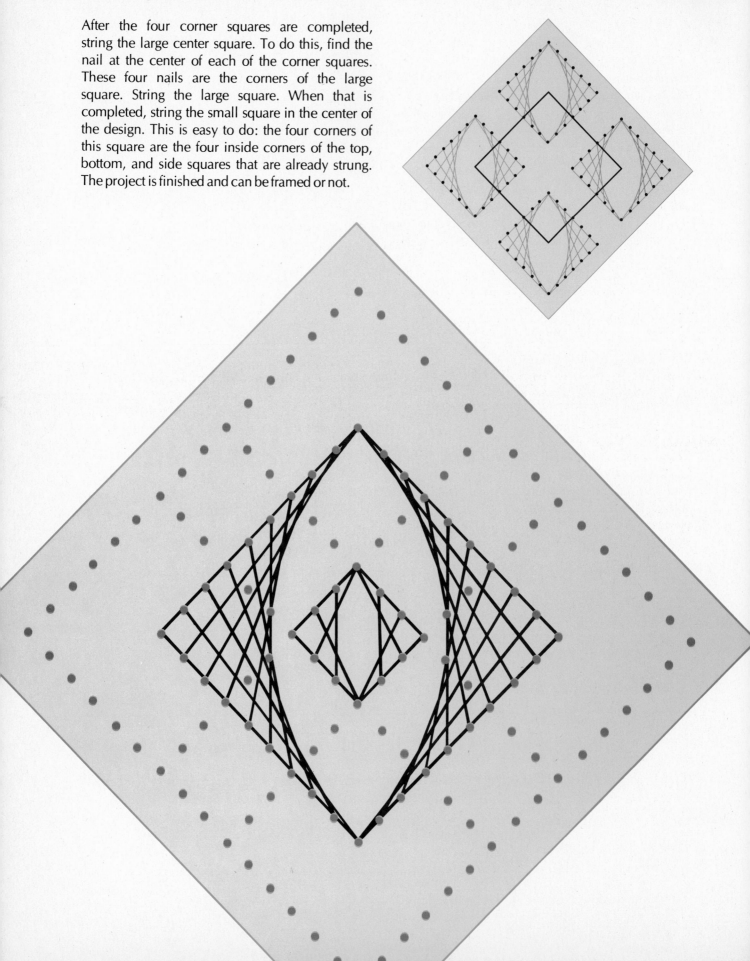

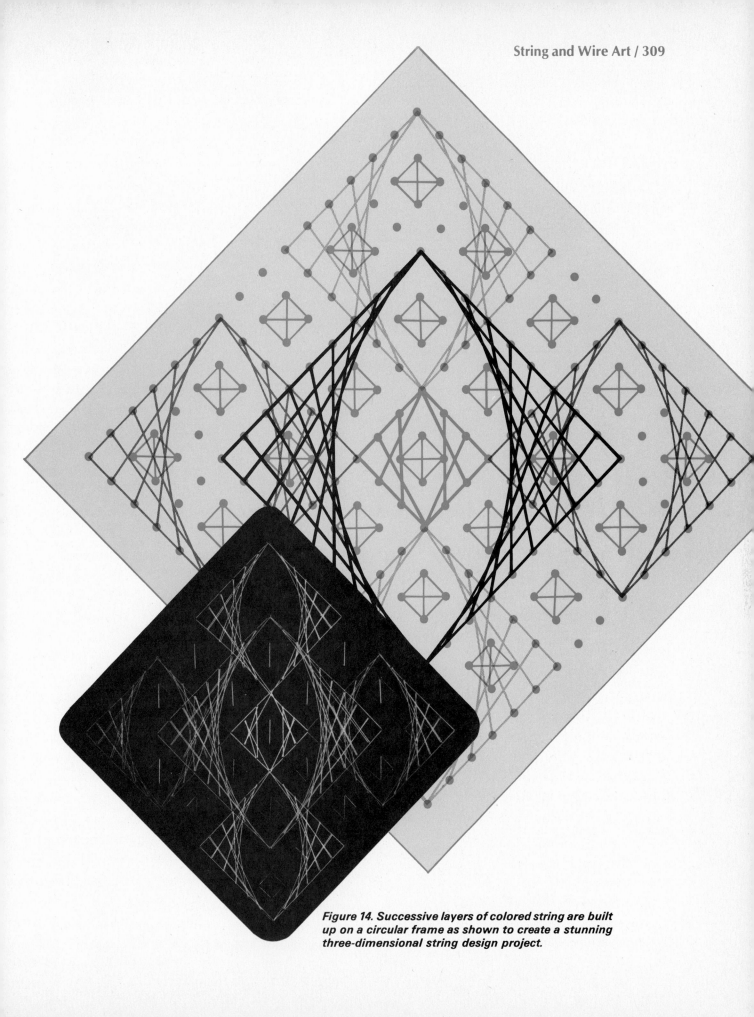

Figure 14. Successive layers of colored string are built up on a circular frame as shown to create a stunning three-dimensional string design project.

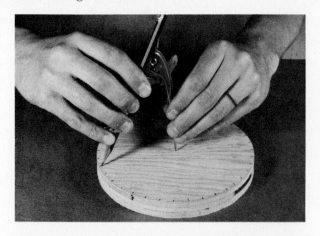

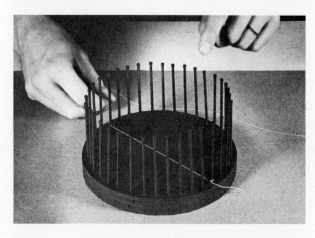

PROJECT III

This project provides a sense of the depth possibilities of string design. Needed are: (1) a circular piece of wood 6½ inches in diameter; (2) 37 nails, 3 inches in length; (3) between 13 to 18 colors of mercerized cotton thread (it is wise to get colors that are close in color (lightness and darkness) value and of an interesting chromatic range); (4) a can of spray paint (if using light-colored strings, it would be best to get dark paint, and vice versa); (5) clear drying glue or some acrylic medium; (6) a brush; and (7) a pencil, compass, and ruler.

Divide the circumference of the circular wooden shape into 37 parts. Mark off the spots with a pencil and then hammer in the nails so that they stand erect and perpendicular to the wooden base. Once all of the nails are in, spray paint the entire piece and let dry.

Arrange the threads in a preferred color order. Each color thread will be a layer on the design. For stringing the design, refer to the section on stringing a circular design with tacks. This procedure is similar. To determine how many nails must be skipped in each layer; use the formula $(X-1) \div 2$. To find the number of nails to skip over in the bottom layer, subtract 1 from 37 and divide by 2: $(37-1) \div 2 = 18$. For the next layer the formula is the same except that 3 is subtracted: $(37-3) \div 2 = 17$. For the third layer, subtract 5 from 37 and divide by 2: $(37-5) \div 2 = 16$; for the fourth, $(37-7) \div 2 = 15$; and so on. This simple formula can be used with any amount of nails on other circular designs.

Now begin stringing. Choose a nail and tie the first color to it. Starting with the next nail, count 18 nails and wrap the thread around the 18th. Continue until each nail has a thread going to and coming from it. Because this design is to have a depth dimension, the next layer should not be directly on top of the bottom one. Instead, move up a little on the nail and thread the second layer. Do this for all successive layers until the last, which should lie close to the nail head. Once all the layers are completed, take a yarn needle and

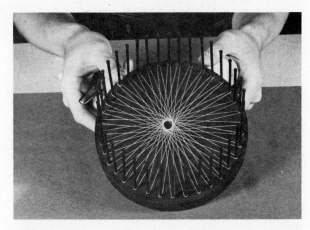

adjust them. Make sure that each layer is even and equidistant from each other.

Once all the thread is in place, take some clear drying glue or acrylic medium and lightly brush it on the threads covering the nails. This will prevent the threads from slipping and falling down.

For Additional Reading

Carelson, Jim, "Space Looms: Thread in Three Dimensions," **Creative Crafts,** June 1974, Vol. 4, No. 3

Jansen, Mark, **The Art of Geometric Thread Design,** Open Door Company, 1972.

Kreischer, Lois, **String Art: Symmography — Three Dimensional Design with Yarn Without Knotting or Knitting,** Crown, 1971.

Open Door Company, **The Art of Thread Design,** Open Door.

Saeger, Glen, **String Things You Can Create,** Little Craft Book Series, 1973.

Sharpton, Robert, "Symmography: String Pictures," **Creative Crafts,** Aug., 1972, Vol. 3 No. 4.

Wasserman, Burt, "String A Design," **Arts and Activities Yearbook,** 1967.

Rug Making

Thousands of years ago cave dwellers converted animal skins and woven grass into floor coverings. From that time to the present, rugs have been used for the same reasons: warmth, comfort, and beauty.

What is thought to be the earliest rug fragment dates back to 2000 B.C. Found in a tomb in Egypt, the pieces were all of natural color linen. While the Egyptian rug-making technique was very well developed at an early period, other cultures in various parts of the world were also experimenting with similiar ideas. Fragments from central Asia (Circa 500 B.C.) show wool being used not only in a pile (see definition below) but in colors as well.

Figure 1. This rug, "South American Sun," was made by the author using the rya method, with yellow and rust-brown yarns. An extra row was skipped to create a fringed effect.

By the sixteenth century, probably the richest, most luxurious rugs ever known were made in Turkey and Persia. These rugs are still famous for their elaborate designs and their rich colors, which were made from rare natural dyes. Since these dyes are not only expensive but difficult to find, aniline (synthetic) dyes, which not even age can mellow or blend, are being used today as substitutes. As a result, the quality of these carpets has suffered tremendously.

One of the most famous Persian rugs is the Arde-bil, now in the British South Kensington Museum. It has a jewel-like design of rich colors scattered over a deep blue background and measures 34 feet by 17 feet. It took 10 weavers working 3½ years to complete it, and its value is estimated to be $500,000.

In the mid-sixteenth century, Emperor Akbar of India imported Persian weavers to his country to start a rug-making industry. One rug in particular which demonstrates the Persian skill was woven in silk and is now at the Metropolitan Museum of Art in New York. This rug is said to have 2,500 knots per square inch. The same knotting technique, based on Oriental carpets, was introduced into France in the seventeenth century. It was used to weave the beautiful Savonnerie rug, which is known for its soft pastel colors and detailed floral patterns typical of the French Renaissance. It is said that during the reign of Louis XIV, two of these rugs were sold to the King of Siam for $90,000. The name Savonnerie, meaning soap, was given to the rugs because they were first made in an abandoned soap factory.

Examples of the pile technique have also been found in the Scandinavian countries dating back to the ancient Vikings. At that time, the thickly knotted materials were used mainly as linings in garments for protection against the cold. The Scandinavians called the knotting method *rya* and used it to make coverings for beds, sleighs, boats, horses, and doorways. Old rya fragments, usually done in monochromes of white, gray, and black and seldom with a pattern, are quite different from those of today. A rya pile, in comparison with the Oriental or Persian, was quite sparse, rarely having more than 30 knots per square inch.

Articles made by hooking loops of yarn into a woven fabric (now called punchwork) are

Figure 2. An excavation at Thebes in Egypt uncovered the ancient linen rug fragment (above). The art of rugmaking produced this patterned Savonnerie rug (below) in 17th-century France. (Both courtesy The Metropolitan Museum of Art; above, Museum Excavations, 1915-1916; below, Rogers Fund, 1952.)

Figure 3. The Scandinavians used the rya method of knotting to line clothing. Although the pile was sparse, it helped to protect against the cold. (Courtesy, Norsk Folkemuseum.)

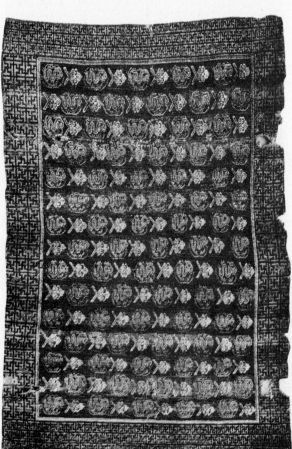

Figure 4. Chinese motifs and characters form the overall pattern of this 17th-century Ming Dynasty silk rug. (Courtesy, The Metropolitan Museum of Art, Rogers Fund, 1908.)

Figure 5. New techniques were used to design this 19th-century Chinese carpet. (Courtesy, The Metropolitan Museum of Art, the James F. Ballard Collection; Gift of James F. Ballard, 1922.)

Figure 6. The gros point technique was used to make the intricate floral designs of this large carpet (122'' x 81½ '') created by H.M. Queen Mary of Great Britain. (Courtesy, The National Gallery of Canada, Ottawa.)

thought to have been produced by the Copts (descendents of Egyptians), the Chinese, Moors, and Arabs early in the Christian Era. This method was used mainly for clothing. Hooked rugs were made later in the Scandinavian countries, England, Europe, and the United States. Colonial housewives in America often dyed strips of old cloth to create beautiful and durable hooked rugs.

These same basic techniques spread throughout the world, reflecting the character of many individual countries. This is the rich heritage upon which today's rug making is based.

Common Terms Used In Rug Making

Backing: the foundation canvas or fabric on which the yarn is worked.

Cut Pile: loops that have been cut to form a velvety or shaggy surface.

Latchhook Method: precut pieces of yarn knotted onto a canvas by using a hook.

Loop Pile: upright loops that are left uncut.

Margin: a border of at least two inches that is left unworked around a rug; usually turned under and sewn down after the rug has been completed.

Mesh: the number of holes per inch in canvas backings.

Pile: the upright yarn that projects from the backing.

Ply: the number of single strands that have been twisted together to form a length of yarn.

Punchwork Method: yarn threaded through a hook then pushed through a fabric backing, forming a loop on the other side of the fabric; worked from the wrong side, loops may or may not be cut.

Rug Yarn: usually wool or acrylic; has a rougher feel or texture than knitting yarn, making a rug more durable.

Rya Method: several long strands of different colored yarn threaded through a needle and then worked on a canvas backing in a stitch that locks the yarn in place; loops are cut unevenly to form a shaggy surface.

Basic Equipment And Supplies

Listed below are the few basic supplies used for rug making in general, as well as specific supplies for Latchhook, Punchwork, Rya, Quickpoint, and Crochet work. All can be bought at hobbycraft stores, yarn shops, or hardware stores. The cost of each project varies with the choice of materials — that is, the number of different colors, textures, and yarn necessary for a particular rug size.

GENERAL SUPPLIES

1. One large pair of scissors used for cutting backings and hanks of yarn and one small pair of scissors for clipping yard ends.

2. A yardstick and/or tape measure for drawing borders and for measuring and transferring designs.

3. Masking tape (one-inch wide), which is used for binding the edges of all rug backings, to prevent ravelling and to keep yarn from snagging on the canvas edges. The tape is folded over the raw edges as soon as the proper backing size is cut.

4. Large tapestry needle and carpet thread for sewing hems and binding.

5. Permanent felt tip markers in various colors for drawing designs and margins on the backing. It is essential that the markers be labelled permanent and waterproof. If not, they are likely to bleed on the yarn.

6. Skeinholder and ballmaker used for all yarn not in pull skeins. The skeinholder holds the yarn and turns as it feeds the ballmaker, which winds the yard into a flat ball that pulls out from the center. These are invaluable timesavers, although winding can be done by hand.

7. Rug binding, a wide (about 1½") firmly woven strip of cloth used to bind raw edges of rugs.

8. Anti-Skid Rug Backing Spray, which helps prevent rugs from sliding on slippery floors.

9. Fibers. The yarns normally used for the Latchhook, Punchwork, Rya, and Needlepoint techniques will be described under those headings below. In addition to those, there is a wide va-

Figure 7. An ordinary skein of yarn can be made into a pull skein by winding it from a skeinwinder (top) to a ballmaker (bottom). Both instruments are easily set up on a table.

SUPPLIES FOR LATCHHOOK METHOD

1. Backing. An open canvas with 3½, 4, or 5 meshes to the inch. A 5-mesh canvas makes a thicker rug than a 3½-mesh because there is more yarn per inch.

2. Yarn. Wool or acrylic rug yarn. Both may be purchased in 1-ounce precut packages. These strands are a standard 2½ inches long and make a 1-inch pile. One package will cover about 5½ square inches of 3½-mesh canvas or a little more than a 3½ square inches of 5-mesh canvas. If you wish to cut your own lengths, rug yarn is also available in skeins. (NOTE: The yarns described are those normally used and are suggested for the beginner. Rug makers already familiar with the Latchhook method are encouraged to experiment and create.)

Figure 8. Supplies needed for the latchhook method (below) include a yarn cutter and a supply of canvas backing material. The canvas should have 3½, 4, or 5 meshes to the inch.

riety of exciting and unusual fibers available today that can add interest and texture to your rugs. Some natural fibers, such as jute, twine, and rope, can be very effective. Narrow strips of fabric from old clothing or leftover sewing scraps can add varied texture. Plastic bags and garbage bags cut in strips can be used for rugs. Leather, swisstraw, and even thin wire can be used for artistic effects in making wallhangings by using rug techniques. One needs only to explore and experiment.

Rug-making supplies also may be purchased in kit form. These kits supply everything necessary to make a specific item *i.e.,* instructions, yarn, backing, and design. Kits are available in many designs, colors, and sizes so a beginner, wanting to learn a particular technique, may choose to start this way. Once the technique is learned, however, it is simple and far more satisfying to design an original rug. Many preprinted canvases also can be bought in craft shops and art/needlework sections in department stores. Although the design has already been prepared, the beginner can still make an original by doing any or all of the following: changing the colors, changing the type of yarn, mixing the textures of yarn, or changing the height of the pile.

Figure 9. The yarn cutter is a simple but ingenious tool that automatically cuts yarn into 2½" pieces. This is the length needed for a 1" pile.

3. Yarn cutter. This extremely simple tool automatically cuts yarn into 2½-inch lengths for a 1-inch pile. It is handy to have, particularly when using yarn not available in precut packages. The yarn cutter is worked by merely threading it, winding the knob clockwise while the cutter draws in the yarn, cuts it, and then drops it into a pile.

4. Graph paper (optional). For drawing or copying designs.

SUPPLIES FOR PUNCHWORK METHODS

1. Backing. Burlap or a sturdy, loosely woven fabric such as monk's cloth.

2. Rug yarn for the punch needle and speed punch needle; knitting worsted weight yarn for the automatic rug punch.

3. Tools. There are different types of tools, each one being slightly different. All of them come with complete instructions, which should be studied carefully. (Try a practice swatch before beginning a rug.) Each tool achieves the same effect, so use whichever is preferable to meet individual needs:

a. Punch needle. Small and lightweight, this needle is available either in one size or a style that has changeable needles to accommodate various thicknesses of yarn. This tool is not as fast as the following two and is well-suited for working at a slower pace.

b. Speed punch needle. This needle moves by itself, and is adjustable to five different lengths of loops from ⅜ inch to 1 inch. The spacing of loops is automatic.

c. Automatic rug punch or "eggbeater." This is similar to the speed punch in that it also moves or "walks." It is operated by another apparatus — in this case, a crank turned either clockwise or counterclockwise, depending on the desired direction. The yarn used must not be heavier than knitting worsted.

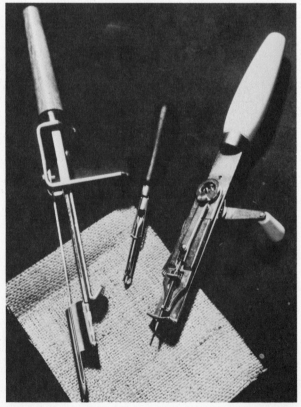

Figure 10. Tools for the punchwork method include a small punch needle, a speed punch needle, and an automatic rug punch. These are shown against a background of backing fabric.

4. Rug frame. A frame is needed to hold the backing taut while punching through it, especially with speed hooks. A frame may be small enough to hold in one's lap with one end propped against a table or it may stand alone. Small frames are most suitable for small pieces or sections of a rug to be joined later. The best types of frames are those on which the backing can be easily moved. One type has protruding nails that pierce and hold the backing. Another type has four long wooden strips (one for each side of the frame) with holes about every inch. A nail that can be easily removed is put through each hole, the backing, and a groove in the frame.

5. Liquid latex (rubber-based) backing and small brush. After the rug has been completed, the wrong side is brushed thoroughly with liquid latex which dries overnight to a permanent flexible backing. By using latex, the loops are secured and will not be pulled out accidently. Follow the directions on the can. The brush can be cleaned with soap and water.

Figure 11. Rug frames, available in a variety of sizes, must be used in the punchwork method to hold the backing taut. Try to get one which allows the backing to move easily.

Figure 12. Supplies needed for the rya method are very simple: rya canvas or rug canvas for backing, plus one 3'' yarn needle with a blunt end and a very large eye. Rya or rug yarn may be used.

SUPPLIES FOR RYA METHODS

1. Backing. Rya canvas or rug canvas. If using rug canvas, skip every other row.

2. Rya yarn. A medium-weight plyed wool yarn. With rya yarn three strands — usually of two or three different shades of a color — are used at one time. With rug yarn two or three strands may be used at one time depending on the weight of the yarn.

3. A large 3-inch metal yarn needle with a blunt end. Use one with a very large eye that can be easily threaded.

SUPPLIES FOR QUICKPOINT

1. Backing. Any sturdy large mesh canvas ranging from 3½ meshes per inch down to 10 meshes per inch. For beginners, 3½-, 4-, or 5-mesh is best.

2. Yarn. Bulky yarns should be used with 3½-, 4-, and 5-mesh canvas, and lighter weight yarns with 7- to 10-mesh canvas. Ask a salesperson where you are buying your supplies for advice if you are unsure about the proper yarn size. If yarn is too thick, it will be hard to pull through the canvas and will distort the design. If the yarn is too thin, it will not cover the canvas adequately.

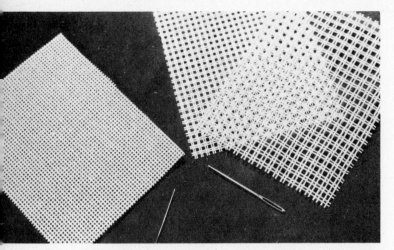

Figure 13. Two metal tapestry needles are used for quickpoint, and sturdy canvas with a large mesh is suggested for backing.

3. A large metal tapestry needle for 3½-, 4-, and 5-mesh (same as rya needle). Tapestry needle number 17 is suitable for 7- to 10-mesh.

4. Graph paper for drawing or copying designs.

SUPPLIES FOR LOOP CROCHET

1. Backing. None, since the backing and the loops are made at once.

2. Yarn. Rug yarn of either wool or acrylic; select a yarn which will suit the type of rug you propose to make. For example, if you are planning a rug which will receive hard wear, use a heavy, durable yarn that will not mat down.

3. A crochet hook. The most common sizes used in rug making are J, K, and Q. The size used is determined by the thickness of the yarn.

4. A large yarn needle for joining the pieces together.

Basic Procedures

Before buying any supplies, decide upon a design. Designing is perhaps the most rewarding and satisfying part of any craft and rugs are among the easiest projects to design. Absolutely no previous training and very little practice is necessary before beginning. The basic rule is to *keep it simple.* Children's coloring books, geometrics, and the alphabet are excellent places to look for ideas. A clue to any design is its function. Where will it be used? What colors or patterns will surround it?

LATCHHOOKING

This method is so simple that it can be learned in a matter of minutes. Speed and a rhythm are quickly acquired. Simple, bold designs are best, making it an excellent method for children as well as for adults.

Yarn may be bought in skeins or precut. If necessary, use the yarn cutter as described earlier. For a pile longer and deeper than 1 inch, cut the pieces twice the finished length plus 1 inch for the knot — *i.e.,* for a 1/2-inch pile cut the pieces 4 inches long. To cut them, wind the yarn around a piece of cardboard being careful *not* to overlap. Cut along one edge only. Example: For pieces 4 inches long, use a 2-inch by 8-inch strip of cardboard. Cut along one 8-inch side.

No frame is needed, so work with the canvas in the lap. Refer to the diagram while reading the following steps:

1. Hold the latchhook in the right hand. Fold one piece of precut yarn in half (making sure the ends are even). Holding the folded piece in the left hand, slip it over the hook beyond the latch.

2. Starting at the lower left corner, insert the hook through one mesh and out the mesh directly above so that the threads of the canvas are over

Figure 14. This beautiful example of latchhook technique was created by artist Traute Ishida. She entitled the flowing design "Three Leaves."

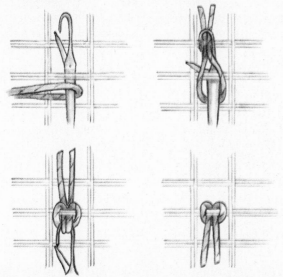

the hook and the latch is open. NOTE: To make the work go faster, fold the canvas back on the row being worked. This allows the hook to go straight through the canvas instead of going down into one hole and up through the next.

3. Start to pull the latchhook out of the canvas and, before it closes, *catch the yarn in the hook.*

4. Pull the hook back through the canvas, closing the latch over the yarn. This pulls the ends of the yarn through the loop, forming the knot. Pull the ends to tighten the knot. If the ends are not even, pull the shorter end. This will even and tighten the knot at the same time. Work across the rug, row by row. Complete each row before starting the next.

5. To finish, there are two ways to treat the edges of the canvas:

a. Simply cut the canvas to size, allowing a 2-inch margin along each side. Draw the margins with a permanent marker. When the design is completed, turn the edges under. Miter the corners and stitch on rug binding.

Figure 15. Precut yarn is folded over the shaft of the hook (above left); the latchhook is held in the right hand as it is inserted under and through the mesh until the open latch clears the canvas (above right). As the latchhook is pulled out of the canvas, the yarn should be caught in the hook by pulling it with the left hand up and to the right (below left). The hook is then pulled back through the canvas, closing the latch over the yarn and forming the knot (below right).

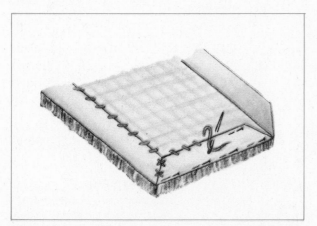

Figure 16. A true hem is made by folding over the margin of the finished rug, mitering the corners and securely stitching them down with carpet thread.

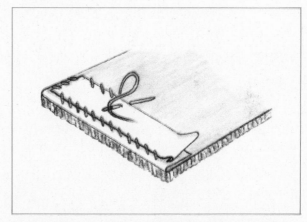

Figure 17. Rug binding is stitched on the turned-over 2-inch margins of the finished rug. This binding is a firmly woven cloth that both binds the raw edges and adds durability.

Figure 18. When finishing a circular rug, cut slits along the margin of the finished rug. When each cut section is turned under and stitched down, there will be a smooth, circular hem.

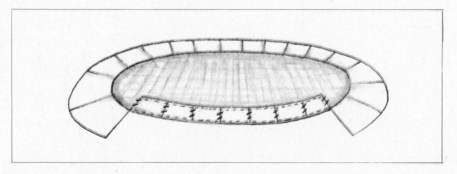

b. Cut the canvas to size allowing only a 1- or 1½-inch border. Instead of taping the raw edges, turn them under the latch through double canvas. This method gives the rug more protection along the edges. When finished, the rug may be left as is or rug binding may be added to the edges, if desired.

PUNCHWORK

This method is really centuries old. It was one of the most popular techniques used by the American colonists. Many beautiful examples are still in existence today and are especially valued now that rug making is gaining popularity in the craft world. Originally done with a hook, the older and slower rug-hooking methods gradually gave way to the newer and much faster punching methods. Fortunately, the finished appearance is not sacrificed to the faster methods. Except for the new and bright colors, these rugs are exactly the same as those made by our ancestors, even though they can be completed in less than one-fourth the time it took them.

Punchwork allows the greatest freedom in designing since the pile may be high or low, cut or uncut, or a mixture of any of these. It also lends itself to intricate detailing. All types of geometric and pictorial designs are possible. The pattern and the background can be hooked in straight rows, in various angles, or contoured to the design. It is also the fastest method (up to 500 loops can be made per minute).

A frame is necessary when punching a rug because it gives more control and prevents the work from stretching out of shape. Stretch and tack the backing (marked side up) in place, using the longer upholstery tacks or following the directions with the frame. The backing should be taut. If the design is larger than the frame, just remove and retack in a new area after completing each section. When there is an edge that will be con-

Figure 19. Hooked rugs were a typical craft form of 19th-century New England. (Courtesy, The Metropolitan Museum of Art, Rogers Fund, 1918.)

tinued in a new area, the best way to blend the dividing line is to make each line shorter or longer than the one next to it.

Following the manufacturer's directions, thread the yarn through the eye in the point of the needle. Practice making loops on a scrap piece of backing. Read and follow the directions that come with the punch tool since each of the three tools described in "Basic Supplies" varies slightly. Work on the marked side of the backing, which is the wrong side of the rug. When changing from

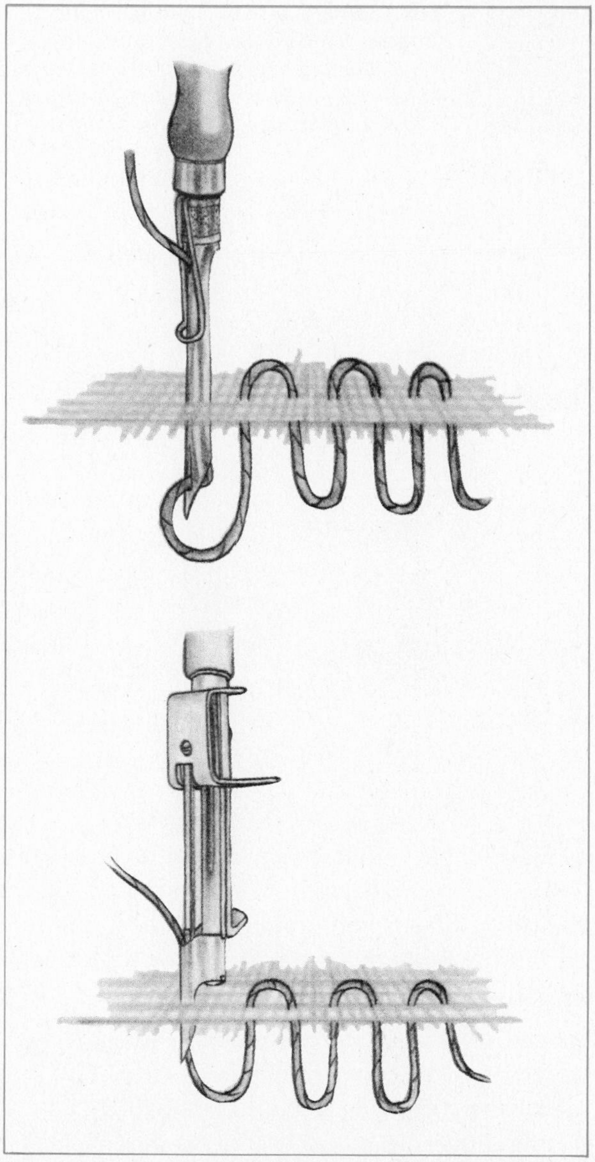

Figure 20. The manual punchhook (top) creates a loop stitch as the hook is pulled back through the canvas. The automatic punch hook (bottom) creates the same loop design but is operated with a crank that makes the process easier and faster.

one color to another, put the index finger on the stitch, pull out the punch tool, and cut the yarn, leaving about a 1-inch tail.

Bring these tails to the right side of the rug and clip them even with the loops. No ends should show on the wrong side. While working, be sure that the yarn is feeding freely through the needles or uneven loops will result. If a mistake is made, simply pull it out and repunch. Retack as often as necessary to take up the slack in the backing. If the backing can be seen from the right side, the rows are too far apart.

When making a design that has a background, start with the smaller areas of the design itself. Outline them with two rows of loops, then fill in at random. Next, outline the larger areas with two rows of loops and fill them in at random. For the background, outline the outside of the designs with two rows of the background color. Fill this in at random, also leaving room for two rows as a border. Add these two rows; putting an additional row of loops between the two border rows will prevent the backing from showing through when the rug is turned and hemmed. Hooking randomly creates a more uniform look on the right side than hooking in lines. As each area is completed, turn it right side up and look for bare spots. These can be easily filled in by adding a few rows where needed.

The rug can be made in pieces that are later joined together. Cut all of the margins evenly (about 1½ to 2 inches wide). Using a rug needle and strong carpet thread, sew the pieces together. Glue down the loose edges on the wrong side with liquid latex.

To finish, thoroughly brush a coating of liquid latex on the back of the rug. Brush a heavy coat of latex on the edges. Turn them back and press down firmly. No rug binding is necessary.

RYA

Rya rugs are known for their long, shaggy pile and their bright bold designs. Since this technique is best suited to very simple designs and large areas of color, it is excellent for beginners.

Making a luxurious rya rug is simple, fast, and very satisfying. There is only one stitch to learn, the locking stitch. The beauty of the rya is in its

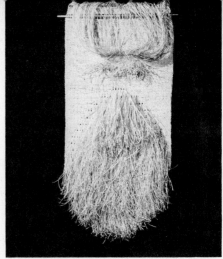

Figure 21. Two examples of rya weaving: "Centering Environment" (left) by Ted Hallman, Jr., and "White Peacock" (above) by Nell Znamierowski. (Courtesy, Museum of Contemporary Crafts, Photo by Ferdinand Boesch/Courtesy, The Art Institute of Chicago, Collection

Figure 22. Begin the locking stitch by inserting the needle through one mesh and out the mesh directly above. Bring the yarn around to the left, under the ends (A), and pull it firmly through the next mesh to the right (B). The second stitch goes through the same mesh (C) used to complete the locking stitch. As the yarn is pulled through the canvas, leave a 1½-inch loop (D); bring the yarn around to the left under the loop and into the mesh directly to the right, completing the second stitch (E).

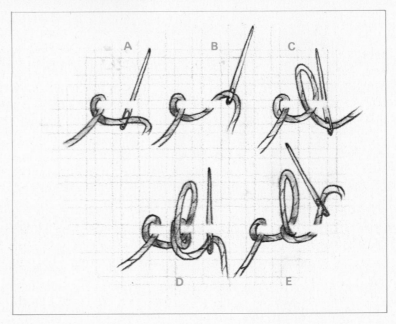

colors. Usually three to five shades of a color are used in one rug. Using several strands at once allows for a variation in shading that is not possible with other rug methods. Whereas rya yarn uses three strands in the needle at once, rug yarn may use two or three, depending on its thickness. Cut canvas to the proper size, allowing a 2-inch margin. Tape all raw edges and draw the design on the canvas. No frame is needed.

Cut through each of the skeins of yarn once to provide the correct working lengths. Start the first stitch at the top left corner, inserting the needle through one mesh and out the mesh directly

above. Pull the yarn through, leaving an end measuring about 1½ inches. Next, bring the yarn around to the *left* and under these ends. Pull the yarn firmly through the mesh directly to the right of the first stitch. This is the lock stitch.

For the second stitch, go through the same two meshes used to complete the lock stitch. Pull the yarn through, leaving a loop of about 1½ inches. Use the fingers to adjust each loop as it is made. Bring the yarn around to the left, under the hook, and into the mesh directly to the right, completing the second stitch. Repeat across the row.

When finishing a length of yarn or changing colors, finish with the backstitch and begin the new length of yarn in the same holes. Bring the yarn to the left and around the old and new ends and make a backstitch.

The loops of the rya look best when cut unevenly. To do this, cut the loops about 1/2 inch from the top. To avoid missing any loops, cut them open after completing each row. To finish, stitch the edges securely to the wrong side with carpet thread.

QUICKPOINT

This method is used for a flat smooth rug. It can, however, be very attractively combined with the latchhook method for a multidimensional rug.

Many different stitches can be used; some, however, will distort the canvas more than others. The basketweave or diagonal stitch (see *Needlepoint* article) is recommended because it distorts the least. It is also excellent for rugs because it covers the canvas well. It is the best stitch for any item that will receive hard wear, particularly rugs.

NOTE: To thread a tapestry needle with yarn, double it over the end of the needle, squeeze it tightly between the thumb and index finger, and slip it off the needle. Holding it tightly, push the yarn through the eye of the needle.

To start, open the skein; if not a pull skein, cut through all thicknesses at *one* end. Start a stitch by coming up through the canvas from back to front, leaving about a 1-inch tail on the wrong side of the canvas. Hold this tail against the canvas back so that succeeding stitches will cover it. The beginning tail of a new thread should be woven through an inch of previous work on the back side of the canvas to hold it in place. Never knot yarn because it causes lumps. If the yarn becomes twisted, simply let the needle dangle while the yarn untwists itself. Pick up the needle and continue working. Allowing the yarn to untwist produces a smoother and more even finish.

When nearing the end of a strand, weave it back through four or five stitches and clip it close to the work. Always pull stitches evenly. If a mistake is made and must be removed, pick out the stitches with the needle. Never snip with scissors because the canvas may be cut by accident.

Blocking is nearly always needed for any needlepoint piece, particularly if the stitches are pulled tightly. Mark the exact size of the rug on a softwood board that measures at least several inches larger than the piece. Use a ruler and a permanent waterproof marker to draw the exact finished size of the rug. Make sure the corners are square. Place the rug right side down over the guidelines. Tack along the edge of the canvas about every 3/4 of an inch. Using a sponge, thoroughly wet the entire rug. Allow it to dry completely. If a piece is still warped, block it a second time.

To finish the edges, trim the margin to 1 inch around the rug. Turn this margin to the back and stitch down using a large, blunt needle and carpet thread. A rug binding is then applied over the hem. Stitch one edge of the binding next to the folded edge of the canvas (where the stitching ends) and the other edge to the back of the rug, covering the raw edges. Anti-skid rug backing spray may then be used, if desired.

Figure 23. This pillow was made with a combination of techniques. Quickpoint was used on the background, but the owl was done by the latchhook method.

LOOP CROCHET

This is one of the quickest rug-making methods; it is done with a crochet hook and yarn. The method is quick because the backing and loops are made at the same time. The only stitches necessary are the chain and single crochet stitches (see *Crocheting* article). An infinite variety of rugs are possible: solids, stripes, blocks, and tweeds are but a few examples.

Figure 24. The chain and single crochet stitches were used to make the backing and the loops of these rug samples. This rug-making technique is quick and requires only a crochet hook and yarn.

Decide on the size and design of the rug. It may be made in one piece or in blocks that will be sewn together later. Before beginning, study the diagram of basic crochet stitches. Practice on a swatch first if the stitches are unfamiliar.

To make a chain stitch, tie a slip knot near the yarn end and leave a small tail. Insert the hook through the knot end and under the main length of yarn. Draw a loop through, making the first chain stitch. Continue for the desired length.

To do a single crochet stitch, insert the hook in the chain then pull the yarn over and draw it through. There are now two loops on the hook. Pull the yarn over again and draw it through both loops.

When actually ready to begin, very loosely chain the desired length. The first row should be single crochet beginning with the second stitch. Do a chain stitch to turn all rows. In the second row, insert hook into the first stitch, *grasp yarn around middle finger* (see illustration), draw loop through first stitch, pull yarn over, and draw through two remaining loops. Repeat rows 1 and 2 for the pattern. Loops may be cut if desired.

Figure 25. The loop crochet method is one of the easiest techniques in rug making because the front (above) and back (below) of the carpet are made at the same time.

Projects You Can Do

The following examples are suggested projects for beginners. It is hoped that they will be used as a guide. The design in each project is quite basic and can blend well into most homes. The sizes and colors can and should be changed to fit

HOUNDSTOOTH CHECK LATCHHOOK RUG AND PILLOWS

This ageless design looks bright and cheery in green and white or more formal in red and black. It is ideally suited to a man's study in beige and brown or to a child's room in pink and blue. It can be used under a coffee table, in an entrance hall, or in a bathroom.

Materials and Directions

For the rug, you will need 3/4 yard of 3½-mesh canvas 36 inches wide (21 x 28 inches finished size, 25 x 32 inches cut size to allow for 2-inch margins) and 9 ounces of white and 13 ounces of

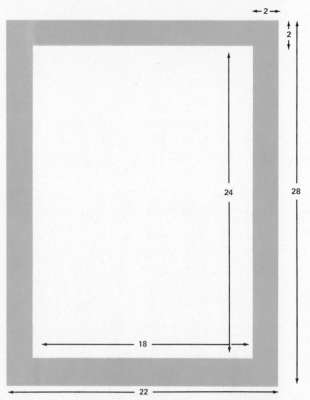

Figure 26. The border of the houndstooth check rug is 2". An additional 2-inch margin should be allowed for finishing the rug. (Diagram measurements are given in inches.)

Figure 27. The houndstooth check latchwork rug is made with 3½-mesh canvas 36" wide. The houndstooth pattern should be worked first; work horizontally row by row, following the graph (left).

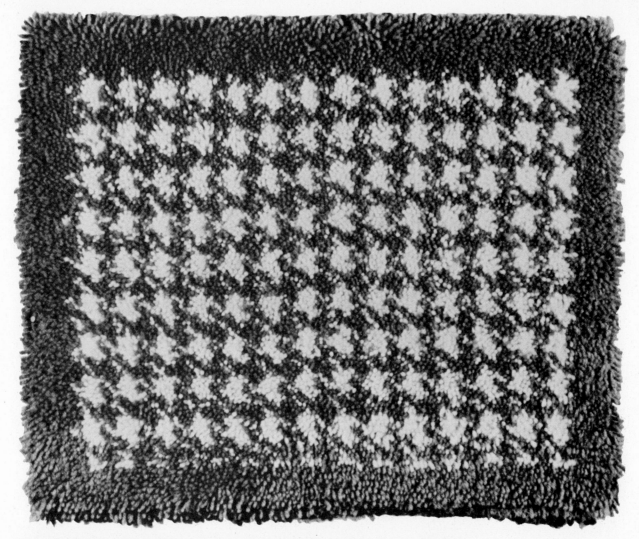

Figure 28. This houndstooth patterned rug was worked in horizontal rows, beginning at the bottom lefthand corner. The same latchhook method used in this rug can also be used to make a pillow.

green precut wool yarn. The pillow requires 1/2 yard of 3½-mesh canvas (14 x 14 inches finished size, 18 x 18 inches cut size to allow for 2-inch margins) and 4 ounces of red and 5 ounces of black precut wool yarn.

Cut and tape raw edges of desired size canvas. Draw margins, using a permanent marker. Start at the bottom left-hand corner. Work horizontally, row by row, following the graph. Repeat the motifs on the graph as many times as necessary to complete the rug. To finish, see "Basic Procedures."

Variations for Latchhook

1. Use the houndstooth check as a background for a design such as a bold initial or large flower.

2. Make a matching pillow reversing the colors in the rug.

3. Make a rug or pillow in Quickpoint using the houndstooth check.

"AGATE" PUNCHWORK RUG OR PILLOWS

This is a deceptively simple design, inspired by a popular motif used in colonial America.

Six colors in shades of creams, rusts, and browns may be used to make this rug. However, the design would be equally effective in shades of blues and greens, or reds and purples, or white, grays, and black. The beauty of this pattern is in its variety — no two squares are alike.

Materials and Directions

For the rug, you will need 1 yard of burlap in either 40- or 50-inch widths (finished size 24 x 36 inches, cut size 28 x 40 inches, allowing for 2-inch margins). The pillow requires 1/2 yard burlap, any width (12 x 12 inches finished size, 16 x 16 inches cut size, allowing for 2-inch margins). Also needed are 6 ounces of each of the following colors of rug yarn: cream, light gold, burnt orange, rust, medium brown, and very dark brown.

If using different colors, try to choose two light colors, two medium, and two dark colors. The amount of each color used is approximately the same. Cut the burlap, allowing 2-inch margins on each of the four sides. Tape the edges then draw the pattern on the burlap, using a permanent marker and a yardstick. Each square is 6 x 6 inches. Secure the burlap in a frame large enough to hold a set of four squares at a time. Work, following the described steps below, by filling four squares at once so colors need not be changed as often. Do as much as possible within one frame before moving the rug.

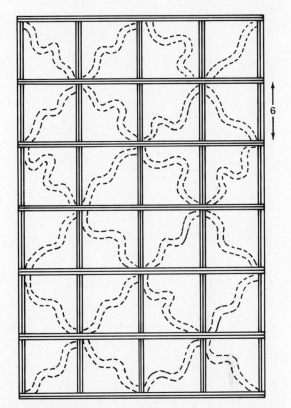

Figure 29. An intricate "agate" design can be worked quickly in punchwork. The burlap is blocked off (left), and then the unifying lines are marked across the rug (top). Four squares (below) should be worked at a time; start with the major lines and work outward.

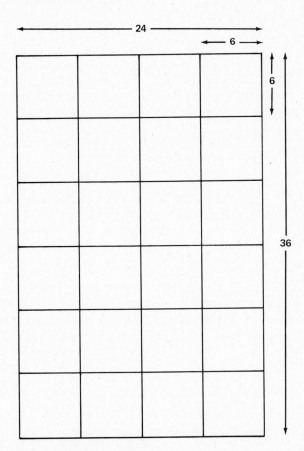

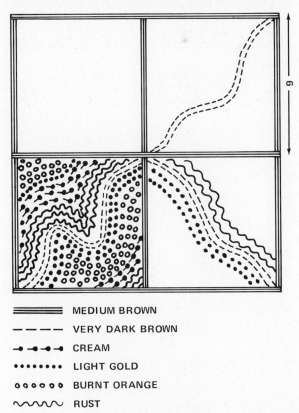

≡≡≡≡≡	MEDIUM BROWN
– – – – –	VERY DARK BROWN
⊷⊷⊷⊷	CREAM
••••••••	LIGHT GOLD
ooooooo	BURNT ORANGE
∿∿∿∿∿	RUST

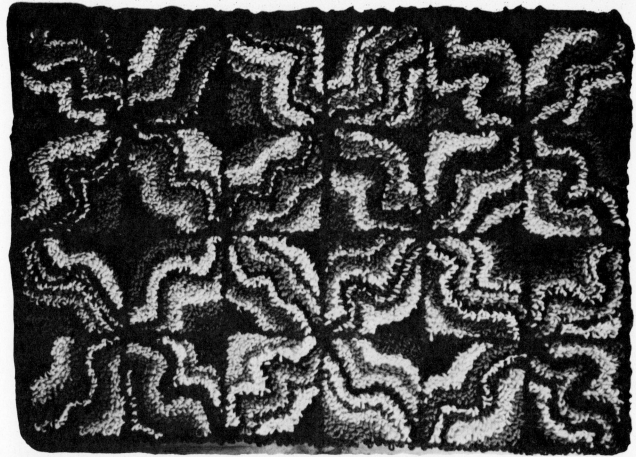

Figure 30. The punchwork technique was used to create this intricately patterned rug. Six colors of yarn were varied in sequence so that no two sections of the rug have exactly the same design.

1. Using color A, punch a line along the lines marked on the burlap. Then punch a line on each side of this first line, thereby making three lines. Color A is used only for outlining.

2. Next, work a group of four squares using color B, punching two wavy diagonal rows all going toward the center of the group of four and varying these so that no two squares are alike.

3. The last step is simply to fill in on either side of the diagonal line in every square. Try to use each color of the four remaining colors on both sides of each square to give a balanced look. Vary the color sequence for each square as well as the number of lines punched of each color. About 12 to 14 lines of punchwork on either side of the center line are needed to fill in each square. Use 1, 2, 3, or 4 lines of a color at one time. Frequently check the front side of the rug to see that the rows are close together and that the backing is covered. Loops are left uncut. Latex the back. (See "Basic Procedures" for details on latexing.)

Variations for Punchwork

1. The size of each square may be larger or smaller than those described above. The size of the squares should be in proportion to the size of the rug.

2. The wavy diagonal lines in each square may be changed so they all flow in one direction instead of toward the center of each group of four.

RYA "TILES" RUG

The rya, because of its long shaggy pile, is best used where it will not be subjected to hard and constant wear. It is most effective when used to highlight a room whether on the wall or on the floor. Its appearance is unlike any other type of rug; it is a joy to make and to own.

Materials and Directions

For this rug, you will need the following: (1) several large yarn or tapestry needles; (2) 3/4 yard of rya or rug canvas 30 inches wide or more (24 x 24 inches finished size, 28 x 28 inches cut size); and (3) 5 colors of yarn (49 ounces total) — 9 ounces of very dark green (A), 15 ounces of dark olive (B), 12 ounces of olive (C), 9 ounces of chartreuse (D), and 4 ounces of medium yellow (E).

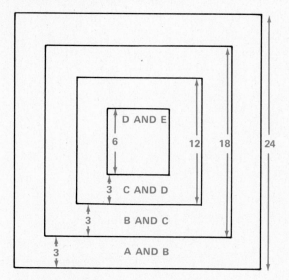

A DARK GREEN
B DARK OLIVE GREEN
C LIGHT OLIVE GREEN
D CHARTREUSE
E YELLOW

Figure 31. The rya pattern is a series of decreasing symmetrical squares, with the lightest color in the center square. Make sure the pattern is marked on the canvas to ensure accurate measurement.

Any color may be used as long as the shades of that color blend well with each other. Cut the backing, allowing a margin of 2 inches on each side. Tape all raw edges. Draw the design, following the diagram and using a permanent marker. Thread the needle with two strands at once, following the colors on the diagram. Begin at the top left corner. When nearing the middle, it is helpful to keep several needles threaded with different colors. See "Basic Procedures" for finishing.

Variations

This rug design may be used in a rectangular shape or it may be made into a pillow, using knitting worsted for softness. This same design in yellows, oranges, and reds adds warmth to a room; neutral beiges and browns lend sophistication; blues denote a calm and relaxed atmosphere.

Figure 32. Five shades of one color were used to create the contemporary design of this rya rug. The locking stitches make loops which should be unevenly cut to give the rug a long, shaggy pile.

PLAID QUICKPOINT RUG

In this plaid, which was adopted from the authentic Wallace Scotch Plaid, the basketweave stitch is used for the red and black squares. The chain stitch is used for the yellow and black lines, which are stitched over the squares later. This eliminates having to follow a graph and gives the rug added dimension. Each square is 4 x 4 inches. They can be enlarged if you choose; however, the size of the squares should be in proportion to the size of the rug.

Materials and Directions

The materials required include the following: (1) 1 yard canvas, 5-mesh per inch (20 x 28 inches finished size, 24 x 32 inches cut size, allowing for 2-inch margins); (2) 13 ounces of black, 8 ounces of red, and 2 ounces of yellow wool rug yarn; and (3) a large tapestry needle.

Proceed as follows:

1. Cut and tape the canvas. Using permanent markers and a ruler, draw the design by following the diagram.

2. Using a double thickness of yarn, begin stitching the squares. Follow the basketweave diagram (see Quickpoint procedures) for the solid red and black squares. Do these first. Follow the 2-color basketweave diagram for each red/black

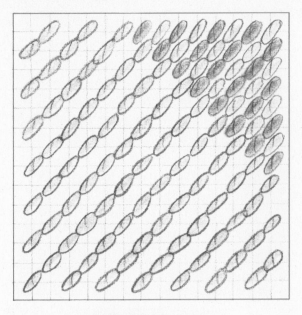

BASKETWEAVE STITCH

Figure 33. The basketweave is worked in diagonal rows by inserting the needle up and down through the mesh. Start the next stitch in the mesh to the left; then work down one row in a diagonal and up a row for the next.

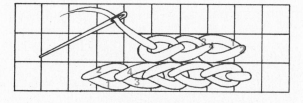

CHAIN STITCH

Figure 34. Bring the needle up and around to the left. Insert the needle down in the same mesh and bring it back up through the loop, then down through the next mesh to begin the second stitch.

square. When doing the 2-color basketweave, start with one color and skip every other row. Finish filling in with the other color. The basketweave is done diagonally across the canvas.

3. After completing the squares, chain stitch over them with yellow and black lines. Go through all thicknesses, including the canvas. Skip over three mesh with each chain stitch. Use a single thickness of yarn.

4. Block if necessary. (See instructions for blocking under "Basic Procedures.")

Variations

1. Change the colors from red and black with yellow to blue and green with black.

2. This same method can be used to copy any moderately simple plaid.

3. This design can also be worked in the punchwork method. However, the lines that were chain stitched in the quickpoint rug would have to be drawn on the canvas in the punchwork rug and worked at the same time.

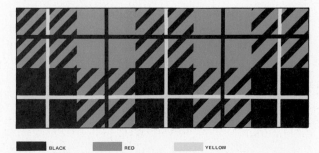

BLACK   RED   YELLOW

Figure 35. The Scottish plaid rug is a checkerboard pattern of repeated squares and overlapping lines. A detail of the pattern shown here keys the colors used to create this design.

Figure 36. This rug displays the authentic Wallace plaid. The quickpoint method used in making this carpet incorporated three colors of yarn and two stitches — Basketweave and chain stitch.

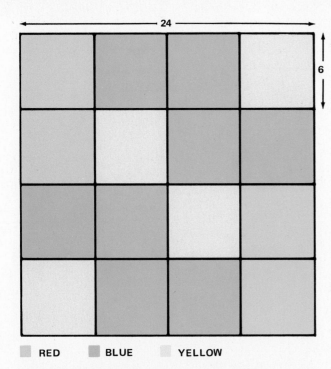

RED   BLUE   YELLOW

Figure 37. The primary colors indicated by the key make a bold design for the loop crochet rug. The squares should be 6" x 6". Stitch them securely together when they are finished.

Figure 38. Sixteen individual squares were made with the loop crochet method and then joined to create this rug (above). The bold design was achieved by using simple primary colors.

LOOP CROCHET RUG

This eye-catching rug, done in the primary colors, is a quick crochet rug. The method is a simple one: 6-inch squares that are stitched together. Use two strands as one, which makes it twice as fast.

Materials and Directions

You will need the following materials: (1) canvas (24 x 24 inches finished size); (2) 8 ounces yellow, 8 ounces red, and 16 ounces blue wool or acrylic rug yarn; and (3) a size K crochet hook.

Make 4 yellow squares, 4 red, and 8 blue, all 6 x 6 inches. Using two strands as one, chain 12 stitches *very loosely*. Following the directions for Loop Crochet in "Basic Procedures," repeat the first 2 rows approximately five times for a 6-inch square — there may be fewer or more rows depending on how tight or how loose the stitches are. Loops may or may not be cut. When finishing, use the same yarn and securely stitch the squares together, following the arrangements of color in the diagram.

Variations

1. Use either two or three strands each of a different color for a tweed.

2. Try different sizes and shapes of squares.

For Additional Reading

Hanley, Hope, **Needlepoint Rugs,** Scribner, 1971.

Laury, Jean Ray, and Aiken, Joyce, **Handmade Rugs From Practically Aynthing,** Countryside Press, 1971.

McCall's (eds.), **Rugmaking,** McCall Pattern Co., 1974.

Seagroatt, Margaret, **Rug Weaving for Beginners,** Watson-Guptill, 1972.

Wilcox, Donald J., **Techniques of Rya Knotting,** Van Nostrand Reinhold, 1971.

Znamierowski, Nell, **Step-by-Step Rugmaking,** Golden Press, 1972.

Plaster Crafts

Plaster is an inexpensive, readily available, and versatile material which may be carved, modeled, or cast in a wide variety of personally innovative as well as traditional ways.

Although there are several different kinds of plaster, most people refer to all plaster as "plaster of Paris." Plaster is associated with the capital of France because gypsum — the soft, white, mineral rock from which plaster is made — was mined commercially in the Montmartre section of Paris in the 1770s. The fine quality plaster made from this gypsum was widely used in making elaborate ceilings, moldings, and other interior architectural details, as well as for making reproductions of original stone or bronze sculptures. The popularity of these Parisian art products resulted in a permanent linkage of the words "plaster" and "Paris."

The use of plaster for sculpture and crafts did not originate in Paris, however. Plaster was known to the ancient Egyptians as early as 2500 B.C. and was used as a base for mural painting, original sculpture, casting, and molding. Despite the comparative softness and impermanence of plaster, many evidences of Egyptian plaster arts have survived in the tightly sealed tombs of the Egyptian nobility.

Although the elegance of marble and bronze sculpture comes quickly to mind when thinking of classical Greece, plaster was also in common use as a sculptural material as early as the time of Phidias (475-30 B.C.). The first-century Roman historian, Pliny, reported that such famous Greek sculptors as Lysistratus and Arcesilaus modelled both idealized and portrait sculptures using direct additive plaster techniques. Although only a few small statuettes have survived from ancient Greek times, it appears, from Pliny's writing, that the Greeks placed a surprisingly high value on plaster statuary and frequently erected large victory and commemorative statues in connection with their athletic games.

There is also evidence to support the theory that, prior to the Roman era, the Etruscans cast many of their terra cotta statuettes in plaster molds. Thus, ancient Rome abounded in plaster reproductions of antique Greek sculpture. While only the wealthy and powerful Romans could possess original Greek marbles and bronzes, those Romans of lesser means contented themselves with plaster reproductions.

During the Italian Renaissance, plaster again emerged as a sculptural medium. The noted sculptor Verrocchio (1435-88) made plaster casts of heads, hands, feet, and other anatomical features, retaining them as references for later works. Plaster "life masks" and "death masks" were cast directly on the faces of both living and dead individuals. Such masks have been an inexpensive means of accurate sculptural portraiture from the Renaissance to the present.

Many contemporary artists and craftsmen use plaster both as a means to an end and as a medium for their finished products. Scores of modern sculptors, in the development of their works and concepts, depend heavily on this unique white powder which turns to soft stone when water is added.

Figure 1. This finished sand casting (opposite) was made by an 11-year-old child. The sand remaining in the plaster gives the plaque a pleasant textured finish, and the design is highly personal.

Figure 2. This abstract plaster scultpure by French artist Jean Arp, called Human Concretion, *shows the possibilities of this art medium. (Collection, the Museum of Modern Art, New York, gift of the Advisory Committee.)*

Realizing, however, that the foregoing paragraphs scarcely scratch the surface of the history of plaster crafts, the reader should bear three things in mind. First, plaster has at least a 3500-year history as an art medium. Second, plaster usage throughout history has often been unfairly associated with inferior taste and lack of originality. Third, it is a versatile and inexpensive material which offers the artist/craftsman a wide range for creativity, after mastering only a few basic, manipulative techniques.

Figure 3. Plaster craft was known to the Egyptians more than 4,000 years ago. This death mask of Amenhotep III dates from the New Kingdom, about 1370 B.C. (Courtesy, Staatliche Museum, Berlin.)

Common Terms Used In Plaster Crafts

Armature: the inner support or skeleton of a modelled sculpture. Armatures may be of any material, but flexible wire is best for plaster.

Batch: a given quantity of a water and plaster mixture which is used for a specific task during the short period of time prior to its setting.

Casting Plaster: a plaster which is slightly harder and more dense than plaster of Paris; contains glue-size or other surface hardeners.

Dehydration: the heating of pulverized gypsum to a temperature of 350° F. Dehydration eliminates most water, leaving the resulting powder in a water-seeking or so-called "thirsty" state.

Gypsum: the single basic ingredient of plaster, gypsum is a soft, white mineral rock found in large deposits throughout the world.

Hydration: the setting process during which water is absorbed by the "thirsty" plaster particles.

Mold: the negative design, matrix, or impressed surface into which plaster is poured.

Molding Plaster: a soft plaster, commonly called plaster of Paris. It is pure dehydrated gypsum without surface hardening additives.

Patina: the final surface treatment of the plaster work. Patinas may be paint, stains, paste wax, shoe polish, spray lacquers, or any other coating applied for color, sheen, or surface sealing.

Plaster of Paris: a term used interchangeably with molding plaster.

Rasp: a coarse-toothed metal file used for shaping and smoothing set plaster.

Reinforcement: thin strips of gauze, burlap, or other open mesh fabric used in plaster to build up and strengthen the form.

Setting: the hardening of the liquid plaster mix. The batch sets when water is restored to the dehydrated gypsum powder. During the setting process, the gypsum particles realign themselves into long, thin crystals, forming a new rocky substance nearly identical to the original gypsum. Heat is spontaneously generated as some of the water recombines chemically with the dehydrated gypsum.

Slurry: a fluid mixture of plaster and water.

Stirring: the mixing of plaster and water either with a spoon or with the hands. During the stirring process, all air bubbles should be removed from the batch and the water evenly distributed throughout the mix.

Surform: a tool which has characteristics of both a carpenter's plane and a rasp; used for shaping and smoothing set plaster.

Basic Equipment And Supplies

Most of the basic equipment and supplies for plaster crafts may be purchased in the local hardware store, lumberyard, or building supply center. In all likelihood, most of the necessary tools and equipment are already in the kitchen, garage, or basement. As proficiency and enthusiasm for working in plaster increase, then it is time to invest in a few special tools and to set up a special work area. In the meantime, be inventive about tools and equipment, and avoid spending a lot of money. If the items listed below are ac-quired, one can undertake each of the three basic plaster-working techniques: casting, carving, and "additive" or built-up sculpture.

ARMATURE WIRE

Any wire which is flexible enough to bend with minimal assistance from a pair of pliers is acceptable for armature building. Soft aluminum wire (1/8" diameter) is ideal because it is fairly inexpensive, flexible, and does not rust from contact with the wet plaster. Soft copper wire is also good, but it is expensive. Coat hanger wire is usable, but difficult to bend and will rust. Unless a small piece of sculpture is planned, avoid "stove-pipe wire" because it is too flexible to support the weight of the wet plaster.

The purpose of the armature wire is not only to provide support for the plaster and reinforcement, but also to lend tensile strength to the otherwise brittle plaster sculpture. It is this inner skeleton of the piece which helps to prevent breakage. Many varieties of wire are available in the hardware store. Experiment with various gauges and varieties before buying in quantity.

Figure 4. Use soft aluminum or copper wire when building an armature, avoiding "stove pipe" or coat hanger wire, which will rust. Fasten ends securely by hand or with pliers.

BOWLS

Flexible plastic bowls are best for mixing plaster. Depending upon the size of the work, bowls as small as cereal bowls or bowls and basins with a capacity of several quarts may be used. Glass, ceramic, or metal bowls are usable, but difficult to clean if plaster dries on their sides. Flexible plastic allows for cracking and knocking out dried plaster. Plastic cups and margarine containers are handy throw-away mixing bowls for small jobs.

CASTING BASE

A firm base is necessary when reliefs are cast on soft clay slabs. It is possible, but not desirable, to work directly on a countertop or table. Look for a portable board, approximately 2' x 2' and 1" thick. An old pastry board or a scrap of heavy plastic countertop would be quite adequate.

CLAY

Natural clays, such as those used in ceramic sculpture and pottery, are best for casting plaster reliefs. These clays are commonly available in 50-pound moist lots, usually comprised of two 25-pound plastic bags, at a total cost of approximately $7.00. Natural clay will harden as its water content evaporates and, therefore, must be stored in a plastic bag or air-tight container when not in use. Clay may be purchased at art supply stores as well as at hobby, ceramic supply, or ceramic hobby centers.

Some plaster craftsmen prefer to use oil-based or synthetic modelling clay. It is more expensive but does not dry out between projects, is quite adequate for small casting jobs, and is available in the dime store. Both natural and oil-based clays are reusable and should be kept clean and free of plaster scraps.

FOUND OBJECTS

These are the infinitely varied and indescribable objects which are found in desk drawers, sewing baskets, toy chests, and on window sills over the kitchen sink. These are the things which are interesting for personal reasons and which are firm enough to be pressed into soft clay, yielding shallow impressions or molds into which liquid plaster may be poured.

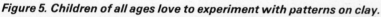

Figure 5. Children of all ages love to experiment with patterns on clay.

Figure 6. Creating design with clay and a stick.

Figure 7. An 11-year-old carefully rolls her clay.

KNIVES

Paring knives, spatulas, putty knives, or tableware are all acceptable. Wash and dry them between uses to avoid build-up of plaster.

PATINAS

Although plaster has its own pristine, white beauty and the surface of a piece does not necessarily have to be sealed, it is soft and chalky and will rub off on clothing or anything else. For color or surface sealing, experiment with spray enamels, oil or acrylic paint, paste wax, shoe polish, or other substances. Do not apply patinas until the plaster is bone dry.

PLASTER

For first attempts, go to the hardware store and purchase a five-pound box of plaster of Paris. If involvement with plaster develops into a major interest, buy the 100-pound sack of molding plaster at a building supply center. As with most things, the unit price of plaster sharply decreases as the bulk amount increases. Keep plaster in a dry place because it is always "thirsty" and will absorb water even from the air, becoming lumpy and of little or no value.

PLASTIC WRAP

Plastic bags, including garbage bags, cleaners' bags, and frozen-food bags, are useful for keeping clay moist, protecting working surfaces, and retaining moisture in cast plaster blocks between carving sessions.

REINFORCEMENT

The reinforcement strips, dipped in wet plaster, are wrapped around the armature wire to build up the sculptural forms. Surgical gauze is a good reinforcement fabric for small works. It is available in rolls of various widths at all drug and first-aid counters. Burlap, cut in strips of various widths and lengths, is used for reinforcement in larger sculptures. Use old burlap sacks or purchase it by the yard at a fabric store.

Rolls of gauze already impregnated with dry plaster of Paris are available commercially in art and hobby centers. Strips of this material, cut in desired lengths, are merely dipped in water and applied as needed to build up sculptural forms. The material is excellent and easily used by a beginner, but it is rather expensive. Because it is convenient and not messy, many craftsmen feel it is worth the expense.

Figure 8. These finished clay castings show the whimsy of a six-year-old (below), the mechanical interests of a nine-year-old (above right), the care and precision of an eleven-year-old (center right), and the happy creativity of the author (below). All were made from a variety of objects and plant materials.

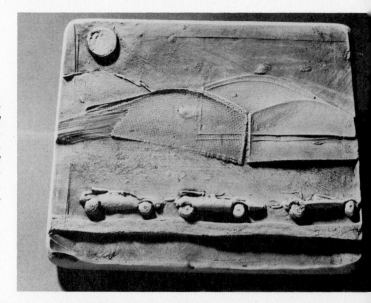

RINSE BUCKET

A large rinse bucket is absolutely essential. Use a mop bucket, a strong wastebasket, a dishpan, or a baby's bathtub. Rinse mixing bowls, tools, and hands before plaster sets on them. The plaster will settle to the bottom of the rinse water and may be thrown away after the water has been poured off. Never rinse plaster down the drain. It settles out and solidifies in sink traps and will eventually clog the plumbing.

An ordinary baker's rolling pin is useful for rolling clay into one-inch thick slabs used for casting plaster reliefs.

SAND

Any clean, coarse sand may be used for sand-casting with plaster. Very fine, "smooth" sand is less satisfactory because it does not hold its shape well in forming molds. Sand from a child's sandbox may be used or it may be purchased from a building supply company. Because only a bucketful is necessary, the cost is nominal. The sand may be reused.

SCRAPING TOOLS

In addition to the knives already mentioned, a variety of scraping and filing tools are useful for carving plaster blocks, texturing moist plaster surfaces, and smoothing dried sculptural forms. The advanced craftsman will want to acquire special plaster sculpture rasps at an art supply center, but these are not essential for the beginner. Be inventive. Use old hack-saw blades or three-inch sections of a broken wood-saw blade. A useful scraping tool can be made by bending the top of a tin can in half. This provides a semi-circular scraping tool with a smooth side that is in contact with the hand. When improvising scrapers from cut or broken metal, file down all nonfunctional sharp edges or cover them with adhesive tape.

SPOONS

A strong plastic mixing spoon is recommended. Others may be used, but these work best for stirring plaster, scraping the bowl, and spreading the slurry into a mold.

WOODEN STRIPS

Wooden strips — 3/4 inch thick, 3 inches wide, and in lengths varying from 12 to 30 inches — are used for building the box-like enclosures in which the plaster reliefs are cast. Use either plain boards or strips of plywood. Sand the rough edges and apply a coat of shellac or varnish to avoid water absorption and warping. The strips used to form the opposite sides of the box should be exactly equal in length. These strips are reusable as they are tied together or wedged in place with lumps of wet clay, rather than joined by nailing.

Basic Procedures

The basic procedures for working in plaster are governed by a few simple facts concerning the essential characteristics of the material. The craftsman should know how to mix the plaster, understand the setting process, and learn how to manipulate the material in its various stages of hardness. The rules are easy to learn; the medium is inexpensive and safe; and a satisfying end-product may be produced in a relatively short time.

HOW THE MATERIAL WORKS

Plaster is powdered, dehydrated gypsum. In its dehydrated state, plaster will absorb water up to approximately 20% of its weight. Normally, plaster and water are mixed in a 2:3 ratio — i.e., three parts of plaster to two parts of water (for example, three pounds of plaster would be added to two pounds of water). In a 2:3 ratio, 80% of the water used to mix the slurry merely provides a temporary surrounding or suspension fluid for the gypsum particles. Suspended in the fluid, these gypsum particles can again form into interlacing, needle-like crystals, thus reconstituting the original grainless, rocky substance. This 80% "free" water eventually evaporates, while 20% of the water is permanently combined with the gypsum. When more water is used, the interlacing crystals form farther apart, yielding a less dense and softer plaster. When less water is used, the crystals form closer together, yielding a denser, harder plaster. More water slows up the setting process, while less water accelerates the setting process.

THE MIXING AND STIRRING PROCESS

There is no point in trying to guess or prescribe the exact amount of plaster to be mixed for a given project. The craftsman, himself, must estimate the volume of plaster needed for his own project and select a mixing bowl which will hold about twice that amount. This allows room for stirring without spilling over the sides.

Weighing the Water and Plastic

Fill the mixing bowl to approximately 1/3 of its capacity with water. Weigh the water on the kitchen or bathroom scale, allowing for the weight of the bowl. Then, weigh out 1½ times that amount of plaster (e.g., one pound of water to 1½ pounds of plaster). Keep hands, container, and plaster dry until ready to begin the stirring process. Eventually one becomes so familiar with the look and feel of plaster that the weighing step can be skipped. Until then, use the scales.

Adding the Plaster

Sprinkle the plaster by hand into the water. Air bubbles will rise as the plaster sinks, and by the time all of the plaster has been added, one or more little islands or peaks of plaster will rise above the surface of the water. Keep hands dry while sprinkling the plaster.

Stirring

When all of the plaster has been added, begin to stir it thoroughly until all air has been released and the water evenly distributed. A strong plastic spoon is a good stirring tool. However, the hand is a better and more sensitive one because it can feel inconsistencies in texture. Scrape the bowl and pinch out lumps. Stirring is the first step in the setting process.

THE SETTING PROCESS

This process involves the absorption of water by the dehydrated gypsum particles, the formation of crystals, and the eventual hardening of the substance. Whether casting on clay or sand, casting a block for carving, or building a sculpture on an armature, the plaster will become increasingly rigid as each minute elapses. For all practical purposes, complete hardness is achieved in 20 to

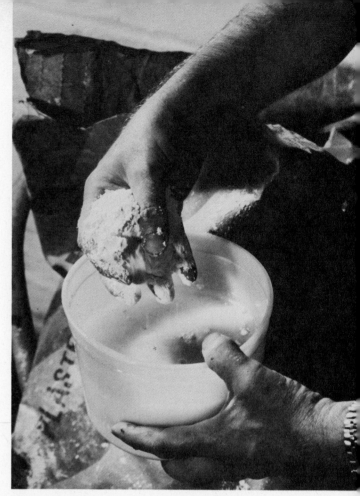

Figure 9. Sprinkle dry plaster into water.

25 minutes when the mix is a 2:3 ratio. As plaster sets, it loses its shiny, watery surface and generates a considerable amount of spontaneous heat. The larger the plaster mass, the more observable the heat will be. A one-quart milk carton full of plaster will be hot to the touch in a few minutes. Although plaster is considered fully set and ready to handle in 20 or 25 minutes, it continues to gain compressive strength as it dries out. Fully dry plaster has nearly twice the strength of wet plaster.

When casting a plaster block or plaque, do not disturb the wet plaster until it is fully set. On the other hand, when building up or modelling reinforced plaster sculpture, feel free to move, scrape, and smooth the plaster with tools or fingers as long as the setting process permits. The reinforcement will prevent breakage.

CASTING ON CLAY

Decorative wall plaques may be made by impressing designs or found objects into rectangular slabs of moist clay and pouring plaster into the

Figure 10. Peaks form as the bowl fills.

Figure 11. Stir carefully with a plastic spoon or, better, mix thoroughly with hands.

resulting mold. Follow the procedures outlined below.

Rolling the Slab

On newspaper, cardboard, or heavy cloth, roll out a thick slab of moist clay. For plaques of less than 12 inches long, a clay slab of one inch in thickness is ideal. Increase the thickness of the slab as the size of the plaque is increased. Strive for uniform thickness so that the plaster may be poured on a nearly level surface.

Impressing the Design

Create a design or a representational (realistic) picture by pressing objects into the clay. Press straight downward to avoid angular undercuts in the mold and pull the objects out of the clay carefully to avoid damage to the resulting impressions. Draw lines and details boldly with a pencil or sharp stick.

Building the Wooden Enclosure

Place the impressed slab on a firm surface. With the three-inch wooden strips, build a dam-like enclosure around the slab, wedging the strips in place with wads of soft clay. If the strips are placed in direct contact with the clay slab, the plaque will have the same dimensions as the slab. If the enclosure is constructed with about a 1/2 inch space on all sides between itself and the clay, a ready-made frame will be cast with the plaque. During the setting process, the plaster will adhere to the wooden strips. However, the bond is easily broken by a light tap with a hammer.

Pouring and Spreading

Do not mix the slurry until the slab is impressed and the wooden strips have been positioned firmly to form the casting enclosure. When the mix has been thoroughly stirred, but before it has shown any signs of setting, apply a thin layer (about 1/4 inch) over the clay. An initial thin layer will permit small air bubbles caught in the details of the mold to escape. If an air bubble seems trapped, pat the liquid plaster gently with the finger tips, being careful not to damage the mold.

Figure 12. A selection of materials for clay casting a decorative plaque.

Figure 13. Moist clay is rolled to form a thick slab of uniform thickness.

Figure 14. Objects are pressed straight down into the clay, then carefully removed.

Figure 15. *The slab is enclosed with wood strips.*

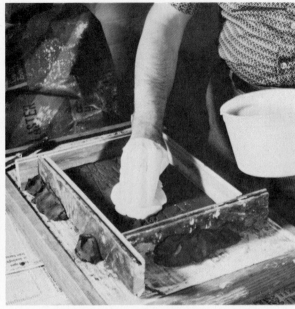

Figure 16. *A thin layer of mix is then applied.*

Figure 17. *A thicker layer of slurry follows.*

Figure 18. *A hanging wire is embedded in the mix.*

Figure 19. *In about 30 minutes, the clay peels off.*

Next, pour or spoon on the remainder of the slurry until the thickness of the plaster layer is at least 1/2 inch. Larger plaques require a greater thickness of plaster, but avoid making the piece too thick because the plaque may be too heavy for hanging. While the plaster is still soft, it is possible to embed some wire in the plaque near the top center, leaving a loop of wire exposed as a hanging fixture. Or, if the piece is very large, embed a layer of burlap in the plaster about halfway in the thickness for purposes of reinforcement.

Removing the Clay

Wait at least 30 minutes before trying to remove the clay from the plaque. Then, remove the wooden strips and loosen the whole clay and plaster mass from the casting base. Rest the piece carefully on a table, clay side up, and gently loosen and lift the clay from the plaster. The clay mold may lift off in one piece or it may tear. In either case, the mold is usable only once. Separate any plaster scraps from the clay and return the clay to a plastic bag to keep it soft for future casting. Traces of clay may be stuck to the plaque. These are removed by gently washing when the plaster is fully set.

SAND CASTING

Sand casting is similar in principle to casting on clay, but it is easier, quicker, and, perhaps, more fun. Pack two or three inches of clean, moist sand in the bottom of a plastic pan or a cardboard box. (A shoe box is quite suitable for this purpose.) Impress a design, pour the slurry, and embed some hanging wire. When the plaster is fully set, loosen by gently bending the plastic pan or by peeling away the wet cardboard. Brush off loose sand with a soft brush, but leave the sandy surface which is embedded in the plaster.

Sand casting will not reproduce minute details as clay casting will. Accept this limitation and have fun making quick, bold designs.

CASTING A BLOCK

Plaster sculpture may be carved from a cast block using the same general principles involved in carving wood, stone, or even soap. It handles easier than wood or stone and is not much harder

Figure 20. Moist sand is readied for sand casting.

Figure 23. Pencil drawing creates additional design.

Figure 21. The sand is impressed with a coffee can.

Figure 22. Wooden forms make design impressions.

Figure 24. Plaster is then smoothed over the mold.

Figure 25. The remaining plaster is poured.

Figure 26. The sand is removed from the cast with a brush, leaving sandy surface embedded in plaster.

than soap. The plaster should be cast in a container from which it can be removed easily. Cardboard milk cartons are particularly useful for casting a block because they come in many sizes, hold liquid without losing their shape, and are easily peeled away from the hardened block.

Select the appropriate size milk container, cutting off the top for ease in filling. Stir the slurry until it begins to thicken slightly. Otherwise, the plaster particles will settle to the bottom of the container, forming a harder, more dense plaster at the bottom with a puddle of water on top. Pour the slurry into the container. It is wise to have a small extra container handy to hold any extra plaster which may have been mixed.

If you wish to add color to the plaster, stir in any water-soluble paint or dye while mixing the slurry. Do not use acrylic, latex, or any oil-based paint. If desired, add texture to the slurry while mixing by adding sand, coffee grounds, or vermiculite. The addition of a tablespoonful of any of these, plus a teaspoon of brown tempera (poster paint) per cup of plaster will result in a block which will resemble rough-grained stone when carved. Experiment with colors and textures while casting a block for carving.

CARVING FROM THE BLOCK

Carving or "subtractive" sculpture may seem a bit formidable for the beginner. When part of a block is chipped or scraped away, it cannot be restored. Many carvers like to make pencil sketches of the finished form and mark guidelines on the block. Others prefer to dig right in, allowing forms to suggest themselves as the carving takes place.

Begin carving as soon as the block is removed from the mold. Damp plaster is more easily carved and less brittle than dry plaster. Any small knife with a short, sharp blade will suffice for plaster carving. Dig, chip, or scrape away the forms. Large areas of unwanted plaster may be removed with a coping saw, but do not attempt to chip away large chunks with a knife or chisel — this might split the block. Turn the block constantly, examining all angles for compositional interest. If more than one carving session is necessary, wrap the piece in plastic to preserve moistness. Otherwise, the block will become too hard and brittle for easy carving.

Figure 27. Drawing the design on a cast plaster block provides the artist with guidelines in creating a plaster sculpture.

Figure 28. An ordinary kitchen paring knife is used to trim away the unnecessary plaster carefully.

Figure 29. Different tools, such as the surform, can give the piece an attractive variety of surface textures.

Figure 30. A deep depression is cut into the moist plaster block as the carved design begins to take shape.

Carved pieces may be left roughly textured, smoothed to a satiny surface, or planed to have contrasting areas of roughness and smoothness.

BUILDING AN ARMATURE

Building an armature is essentially a matter of cutting, bending, and firmly twisting wire to form a sculptural composition and provide the inner support for a piece. The armature remains permanently embedded in the sculpture. The wire must be firm enough to support the wet plaster, yet flexible enough to bend into the desired shapes. Each piece of wire used must be firmly twisted and joined at all points of contact. A combination of thick and thin wires is sometimes desirable, with the thicker wire determining the large structural lines and the thinner wire providing secondary lines and details. Remember that the quality of the final sculptural forms will depend in large measure upon a well-designed armature. Examine the sculptural lines from every angle to assure a strong composition.

BUILDING ON THE ARMATURE

When building up sculptural forms on an armature, add the plaster-soaked reinforcement strips with thought and care. Start with gauze or burlap strips of 1-inch widths and no longer than 6 inches. Dip strips in wet plaster, dragging them over the rim of the bowl to remove dripping plaster. Wrap carefully around wire forms, building up the thickness of the wire gradually and uniformly. If the wire starts to sag slightly under the weight of the plaster, stop for a few minutes until the plaster sets and gives reciprocal strength to the wire. Mix only small batches of plaster at a time. If the sculpture is less than 12 inches high, work with batches of one pint or less. When the first layers of plaster and reinforcement begin to harden (or if they have become entirely dry between work sessions), successive layers will set quite rapidly and the piece will no longer be in danger of collapse.

When the piece has almost reached its full thickness, discontinue using reinforcement strips and apply pure plaster with a small knife or fingers. The top layers of plaster must be mixed with more water if the under layers have dried out to the point where they will absorb water from the new plaster. In such cases, the new layer of plaster sets almost as soon as it is applied, indicating that more water is necessary. Top layers may be modelled with the fingers or a small knife to achieve desired surface forms and textures.

SURFACING THE PLASTER FORMS

Plaster may be filed with a rasp, scraped with a knife, or sanded to complete smoothness. On the other hand, very attractive surfaces may be achieved by applying wet plaster with fingers or brushes, or even by dripping wet plaster over the piece.

When building up patinas, experiment with various methods of surfacing. Smooth sculpture may be enhanced by applying an even coating of color and sheen. Rough pieces may be enhanced by rubbing patinas into the crevices and buffing them off raised areas. Surface the sculpture in a way that is personally pleasing.

Figure 31. Tools needed for building wire armature.

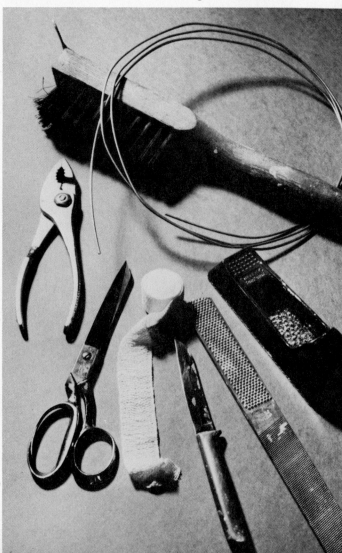

Figure 32. Wire is bent and twisted into the shape the artist desires.

Figure 33. Gauze or burlap strips dipped in wet plaster are wrapped around the wire form.

Figure 34. The surface is scraped with a rasp or knife to achieve the desired finish.

Figure 35. An interesting surface texture is obtained by dripping plaster from a knife.

Projects You Can Do

Now that you have acquainted yourself with this brief history of plaster, its tools and equipment, and the basic procedures of the craft, it is time to think about undertaking a project. The following projects should be thought of as suggestions, not as rules and regulations that must be observed. Copy them if desired, but do not underestimate your imagination or ability for original invention. If the directions and illustrations suggest other ideas and variations of the projects, trust intuition. The worst that can happen is temporary failure, but remember that plaster is inexpensive and creative thoughts are rare. One can always try again.

SEATED GIRL: REINFORCED PLASTER ON ARMATURE

This project is approximately 10 inches high. A seated figure is used because it provides several points of contact with the horizontal surface on which it is built. The beginner will encounter few problems of stability and balance with a seated figure as opposed to a standing figure. A small bird is added for a whimsical effect.

The materials used are as follows: approximately 12 feet of 18-gauge wire; 2 rolls of 1-inch surgical gauze; and about 5 pounds of plaster. (The actual amount of plaster in the sculpture is less than 5 pounds, but a certain amount of plaster is always wasted — even when mixing only small batches.) Working time for the project should consist of two sessions of approximately 90 minutes each. The surface plaster is applied with a paring knife and fingers and should be deliberately left roughly textured for interest.

When doing this project, feel free to vary details. The seated figure could be a boy instead of a girl. The secondary subject matter need not be a bird. Consider various other points of individuality which could be added: try distorting the figure, exaggerating fatness or thinness, increasing or decreasing the size of the head, or making amusing facial features.

Figure 36. This reinforced sculpture (opposite) of a seated girl begins (top row) with a wire armature, takes on shape and fullness as strips and plaster are added, and becomes a delightful finished figure (lower right).

CLAY CASTING: BOTANICAL FORMS

This project is approximately 10 x 12 inches and roughly 3/4 inch in depth. Collect three or four kinds of small branches, firm-stemmed weeds, or distinctive seed pods. One need not be limited to the botanical forms shown in the illustration. Choose specimens which are easily available and which are personally interesting.

Roll out a slab of clay, soft enough to take an impression but firm enough not to stick to the botan-

Figure 37. This decorative plaster wall plaque is a clay casting, the finished product of the process illustrated on pages 344-345.

ical specimens. Make the slab larger than 10 x 12 inches and trim to size. Read the instructions on impressing and casting on clay under "Basic Procedures." Proceed as directed. When the plaster plaque has been removed, use a rasp or surform to clean up and smooth off rough edges.

For a variation on the project, substitute either items from a child's toy chest or cooking gadgets from the kitchen drawer. Smooth metal or plastic items used to make impressions will stick less if dusted with talcum powder.

SAND CASTING: A SUNBURST

This project is an irregular shape, about 12 inches in the largest dimension. Fill a rectangular plastic pan with clean sand to a depth of about 3 inches. Add enough water so that the sand is firm enough to make an impression — about the degree of moistness necessary for making sand castles.

Find a small pan or tin can which is approxi-mately 5 inches in diameter, and impress a circle to a depth of about 1/2 inch. This will comprise the main form for the sunburst. Impress eyes and other features, augmenting impressed shapes with lines drawn with a pencil or sharp stick. Add rays around the face with a thin triangular object. Extend the rays by drawing wavy lines outward to achieve a pleasant free design. Cast as described in the section on "Basic Procedures."

Figure 38. The detailed steps in the author's creation of this sand casting of a cheerful sunburst are shown on pages 346-347.

ABSTRACT SCULPTURE: CARVED PLASTERS

Cast a plaster block in a 1/2 gallon milk container. Try to visualize in which areas of the block to carve deep holes and what the general outlines and curves will be when viewed from each of the four sides. Draw a design on the sides and start to remove that part of the block which is not needed. Use a rasp or a surform to round off corners, and a paring knife to chip and scrape away little bits of plaster in concave areas. In this piece, a tablespoon of brown tempera and 1/2 cup of sand can be added to the slurry for the effect of simulated stone. Blue watercolor can be brushed into the concave areas to increase the impression of cool shadows. To poise the piece at the proper angle, bore a hole 1/4 inch in diameter into the plaster and into the wooden base. Then insert a 1/4 inch dowel to a depth of approximately two inches and set with white glue.

For Additional Reading

Chaney, Charles, and Skee, Stanley, **Plaster Mold and Model Making,** Van Nostrand Reinhold, 1973.

Cowley, David, **Working With Clay and Plaster,** Watson-Guptill, 1973.

Meilach, Dona Z., **Creating With Plaster,** Reilly and Lee, 1966.

Miller, Richard McDermott, **Figure Sculpture in Wax and Plaster,** Watson-Guptill, 1971.

Figure 39. This attractive abstract sculpture was carved from a plaster block by the author.

Plastic Crafts

Because of its stability and versatility, plastic has become a new and revolutionary art medium.

The first true plastic form was discovered in 1909 by a chemist, Leo H. Baekeland. His material, called Bakelite, could be molded into a shape and become a solid composition when heated and compressed. Since 1909, much progress has been made in the study and manufacturing of plastic. However, not until after World War II was there a great increase in the production and use of plastics as substitutes for products made from natural resources. In many cases the plastic substitutes were better suited for a particular purpose than the original natural materials.

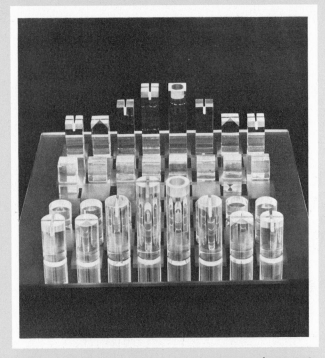

Figure 1. This stunning contemporary chess set, called "Urban Gambit," was designed by Robert A. Propper and made with plastic resins. (Courtesy, Robert A. Propper.)

Today, the science of plastics has merged with the fine arts to create an endless variety of art forms. Transparency, reflection, distortion, refraction, diminution, and magnification are all characteristics of plastics which allow the contemporary artist many expressive possibilities. Indeed, many established artists consider plastics a suitable medium for capturing their expressions. One such artist is David Weinrib of New York, who has said, "One of the primary advantages in the use of plastics for sculpture is that one can work directly with colored material. Plastic, in its immediate response to heat and pressure, opens for me the possibilities of greater and greater moldability and a fluidity which I want to bring to my forms as they move through space." Carolyn Kriegman has designed sculptural body ornaments in plastics to obtain light, color, and transparent qualities. Ted Hallman, who has experimented with synthetics in combination with his weaving, has used plastics for their transparent and luminous color qualities. Even for the arts and crafts enthusiast, plastics provide a new dimension of creativity in the home. The curious craftsman will surely enjoy the simple, basic techniques of plastic craft and will be fascinated with the results.

Figure 2. Jackson Woolley, a California artist, used acrylic sheets to form his sculpture "Oriel." This dramatic work of art is 30¾" high. (Courtesy, Museum of Contemporary Crafts.).

Common Terms Used In Plastic Crafts

Acetone: a solvent for cleaning uncured polyester resin.

Acrylic: a synthetic resin, formed into rods, sheets, or tubes under heat (acrylic rods are 1/16" to 12" in diameter; acrylic tubes, 1/4" to 18" in diameter; and acrylic sheets, 3/64" to 4" thick).

Casting: the method of pouring liquid resin (thermosetting) into a mold to form an object.

Casting Resin: a thermosetting plastic, either of flexible or rigid polyester resin.

Catalyst: in plastics, a substance mixed with polyester resin to cause a chemical reaction within the plastic for the process of curing.

Cementing: a process of bonding two pieces of plastic by adhesives or solvents.

Cure: the hardening process which occurs when a catalyst has been added to liquid polyester resin to make it a solid.

Edge Lighting: because acrylic has the ability to transmit light from one end to another, when an unpolished edge of an acrylic sheet is placed on a light box, light is filtered through the sheet.

Embedding: a process of laminating materials or casting objects in resin.

Epoxy: a thermosetting plastic, used as an adhesive.

Fillers: inert materials added to resin to make it stronger or paste-like.

Gel: a stage during the curing process of resin when it becomes gelatin-like.

Lamination: a process of impregnating absorbent materials within resin to build up layers.

Light Box: a structure containing a light which is transferred through an acrylic art form.

Shelf Life: the amount of time a plastic can be stored before it becomes unusable.

Thermoplastic: a plastic that becomes soft when heated and hard when cooled.

Thermosetting plastic: a plastic which, after a chemical reaction, assumes a solid state.

Translucent: a partially transparent quality; light can pass through but objects cannot be clearly distinguished when viewed through a translucent substance.

Transparent: the ability of a substance to transmit light so that objects are clearly visible when viewed through the substance.

V-Support: a rectangular board, with a V-shape cut at one end; it is clamped to a work table with the V-cut end extending from the table's surface.

Welt: the change which occurs in an acrylic surface when it is heated over a strip heater.

Basic Equipment And Supplies

Plastic craft supplies can be purchased at hardware stores, craft and hobby shops, and plastic manufacturers and distributors. Many items are also found in the home. Of the following materials, not all are necessary for particular projects but are included here for easy reference: (1) acetone; (2) acrylic plastic; (3) an aluminum cooking sheet for fusing polyester mosaics and pellets; (4) asbestos, a fireproof material on which acrylic can be heated in the oven; (5) a small pointed tool

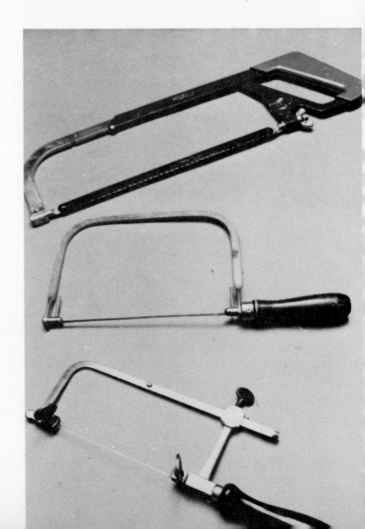

for making holes; (6) a candle for polishing polystyrene mosaics and pellets with the flame; (7) catalyst; (8) cellophane for use as a separator when embedding polyester resin and fabric; (9) a clamp to secure plastic when cutting, drilling, or filing; (10) epoxy; (11) an eyedropper for measuring catalyst; (12) fabric for use in the resin-embedding method; (13) files for smoothing plastic; (14) a fine-grain abrasive powder to be used with water for polishing acrylic; (15) a flat edge, such as a piece of wood or spatula, for smoothing resin when embedding material; (16) a grease pencil for marking acrylic surfaces; (17) a hand drill for drilling holes; (18) handsaws, such as hack, back, straight, coping, and jeweler's saws, to cut plastic; (19) a pliable plastic container for mixing resin and catalyst; (20) a mold, purchased ready-made, for casting resin forms; (21) polyester coloring, in liquid, powder, or paste form, for adding to polyester resin; (22) polyester resin, a thermosetting plastic for casting and laminating; (23) polystyrene mosaic, a thermoplastic that fuses under heat; (24) polystyrene pellets, another thermoplastic that fuses under heat; (25) a respirator with a chemical filter to be worn when working with polyester resin for long periods of time or when using large amounts of resin; (26) a ruler for measuring and to serve as a good straight edge when marking layouts; (27) sandpaper, medium to fine grit, for smoothing polystyrene plastic; (28) a spatula to remove fused polystyrene mosaics and pellets from cooking sheet; (29) #00 steel wool for the polishing of acrylic; (30) a stirring stick for mixing polyester resin and catalyst; (31) a strip heater for bending acrylic; (32) tile clippers for cutting polystyrene mosaic tiles (substitutes are nippers and nail clippers); (33) tweezers for forming polystyrene mosaics; (34) a vise; (35) a V-support; (36) wet or dry sandpaper to use with water for smoothing a plastic surface; and (37) wire for connecting fused sheets of polystyrene mosaic tiles and pellets.

Plastics are a new and exciting medium for the craftsman. Their physical properties permit endless creative possibilities for functional and aesthetic art forms. Moreover, the craftsman should find the learning of plastic art form techniques a stimulating and enjoyable experience.

Within the family of plastics, there are two basic types that will be dealt with here: thermoplastic and thermosetting plastic. A thermoplastic substance becomes soft when heated and hard when cooled. It is shaped when heated after which the new shape is retained by cooling. However, although the process of heating, shaping, and cooling may be done repeatedly, the plastic will eventually become lifeless. Thermosetting plastic is a liquid that becomes a solid when it goes through a chemical change. Once it is a solid, it is a permanent form.

WORKING WITH THERMOPLASTICS

A thermoplastic substance is hard and rigid. Two basic types, fusible and acrylic, will be discussed here.

Figure 3. A variety of hand saws can be used to cut plastic; three are shown (opposite), and many more are available. A good selection of files (left) is needed to smooth the edges and the surface of the plastic.

Fusible Thermoplastic

Fusible thermoplastic, better known as polystyrene, is very common in industry. It is easy to work with and ideal for the beginning craftsman. Because it has an indefinite shelf life, it will not change with time. Tools for working with this type of plastic are utensils commonly found in the home. Although there are two types of fusible thermoplastics, polystyrene mosaics and polystyrene pellets, only the former will be discussed here.

Polystyrene mosaics are 3/4″ tiles which can be purchased at craft stores. They are available in a wide range of opaque, transparent, and translucent colors. Fused tiles (fused together when heated in an oven) can be made into jewelry, flowers, mobiles, and many other attractive designs. The process of fusing polymosaic tiles is easy.

1. Create a design with 16 tiles but use only three colors. Arrange the design in a square.

2. Preheat oven to 350° F.

3. Place the created arrangement of mosaic tiles on a clean, scratchless, aluminum cooking sheet and put it in the oven. Make sure the oven temperature does not exceed 400° F or the tiles will decompose.

4. The tiles can stay in the oven between 45 to 60 minutes. The exact amount of time determines the texture that the mosaic design will have. For a rough surface, the plastic should stay in the oven for a shorter period of time so there is only partial melting of the mosaics. A smoother surface is achieved by a longer duration of heat; the tiles will melt down and make the surface more even.

5. Be attentive to the tiles in the oven: check them for any air caught between the tiles; this will cause a gap. If this happens, use a spatula to gently push the tiles together.

6. When the surface texture is at the desirable consistency, remove the tray from the oven. Let the design cool before removing from the tray.

This completes the basic procedure of fusing mosaic tiles. The craftsman can now experiment with the finished design by shaping, cutting, sanding and polishing, and puncturing.

Figure 4. Polymosaic tiles are fused together in a basic pattern of 16 tiles arranged as a square. After the tiles are fused together (below), the square can be cut or shaped into various objects.

Figure 5. To shape polymosaic tiles, place the large square over a metal object of the shape desired. The tiles should be warm when placed over the metal.

Shaping

When the design has been removed from the oven and while it is cooling, the craftsman can shape it into a creative form. Using a protective covering for the hands, lift the design from the cooking sheet with a spatula and shape into the desired form. Then, place it in cool water. The plastic can also be shaped by putting it over or into a form — such as a metal or glass cup, bowl, or bottle — and then allowed to cool.

It is also quite simple to shape a single tile into a bead form. Heat a tile until it becomes soft and moldable, then place a metal rod, such as a knitting needle, diagonally across the center of the tile. Using tweezers, fold one corner of the tile over the needle and adhere it to the opposite side. Roll the metal rod back and forth, making the bead symmetrical.

Figure 6. To make a bead from a tile, heat the tile until flexible, grasp with a tweezers, and fold over a thin metal rod (such as a knitting needle). Then roll the rod around to make the bead symmetrical.

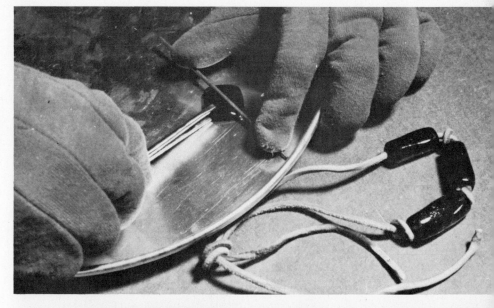

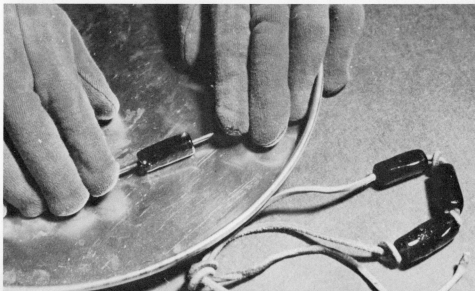

Figure 7. Tile clippers can be used to cut a single plastic tile into small pieces of various sizes and shapes. With practice, the craftsman can cut pieces at the angle desired.

Figure 8. To polish a sheet of polymosaic tiles, move the sheet rapidly over a flame. A deft touch and a careful eye are needed to avoid scorching the tiles during this procedure.

Cutting

A single tile can be cut with tile clippers, nippers, or nail clippers. A fused tile design can also be cut with a handsaw.

Sanding and Polishing

Polymosaics can be hand-sanded with regular sandpaper. Start with a medium-grit paper and work to a fine-grit paper. Areas that have been sanded, however, will become dull. To restore the brilliance, move the plastic rapidly and carefully over a candle flame — charring will occur if the plastic is held too close to the flame.

Puncturing

It is possible to connect separate fused design forms to create linked panels for such items as a room divider, window hanging, or — on a smaller scale — jewelry. To make the holes, heat a metal awl or other sharp metal instrument (stick a cork on one end if the implement does not have a handle) over a flame and push it through the plastic. During this flexible stage, wire can be permanently embedded in the plastic. After inserting the wire, let the plastic cool. A wire can also be permanently embedded in cool plastic by heating the wire first and then inserting it into the plastic.

Figure 9. To make a small hole in a tile or a mosaic, heat a metal awl over a flame and push it through the plastic. It may be necessary to push and twist the awl to open a larger hole.

Figure 10. To embed a wire in cool plastic, heat the wire and push it into the plastic with pliers. A glove should be worn — a necessary safety precaution with hot metals.

Acrylic Thermoplastic

An acrylic thermoplastic can be shaped while hot and will retain its shape when cooled. When reheated, however, the plastic will assume its original shape. Acrylic can be purchased in tube, rod, block, or sheet forms — the last being the most commonly used — and is available in various patterns and textures as well as mirrored, opaque, and transparent colors. It has an indefinite shelf life but will corrode if exposed to acetone, benzene, ketones, lacquer, turpentine, and other similar solutions. It may be sawed, drilled, carved, and sanded by metal and woodworking tools. Shaping and cementing are also possible. There are two methods used in working with acrylic design forms — (1) working with acrylic in its natural state and (2) by heat-forming — only the latter will be discussed here.

Acrylic is moldable when heated between 250° F and 340° F. When soft and flexible, its shape can be altered and retained after it is allowed to cool. If reheated, however, the new form will be lost, as the plastic will assume its original shape. As mentioned earlier, the heating, shaping, and cooling process can be repeated several times on one piece of plastic before it loses its workability. Acrylic can be heated and shaped in two ways: (1) to heat a large area, a kitchen oven is used; (2) to bend a straight line, a strip heater is needed.

Figure 11. A variety of tools can be used on an acrylic sheet, including a jewelry saw (below, left), a hand drill (below, right), a file (opposite, top), a wet-sanding device (opposite, lower left), and a carving needle (opposite, lower right).

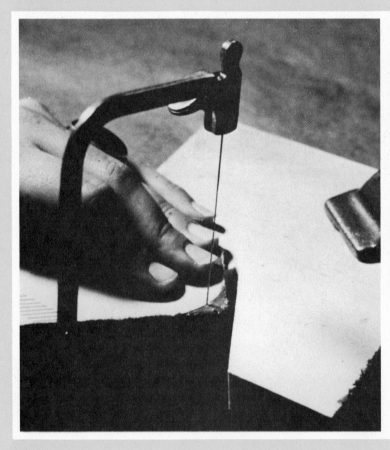

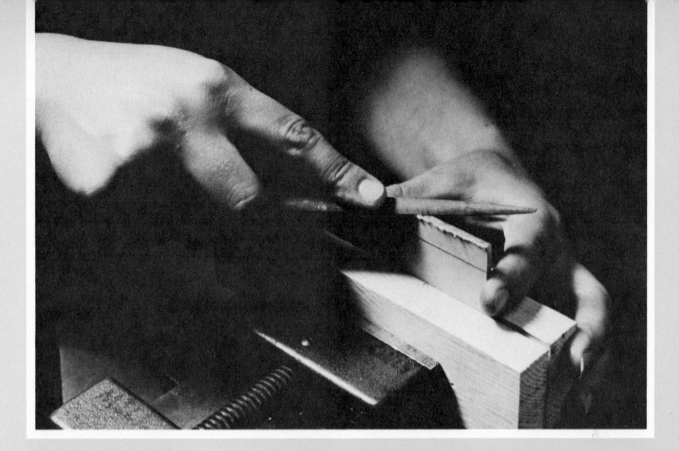

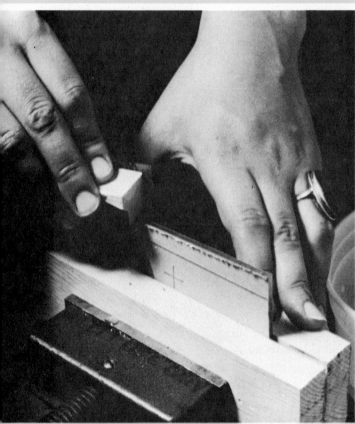

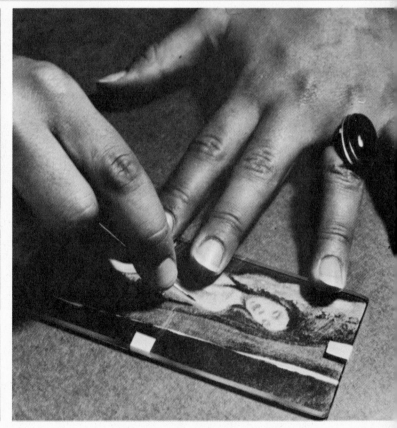

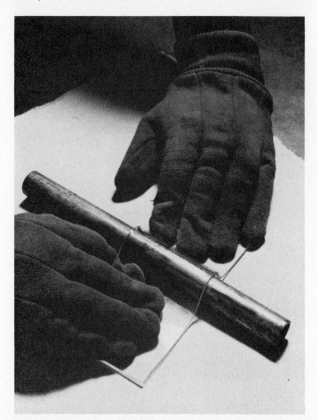

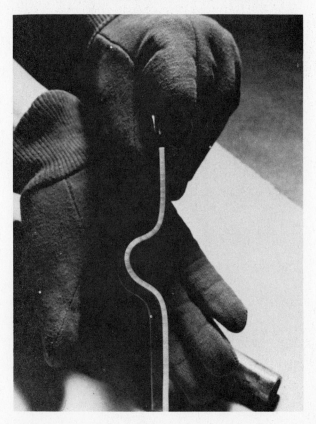

Figure 12. Wear protective gloves to mold a sheet of acrylic. The sheet is heated in an oven, then placed over a form of the desired shape and size (above). After the acrylic cools, the new shape is fixed.

Shaping in an Oven

When heating acrylic plastic in an oven, always use asbestos. Do not leave the flexible acrylic unattended. When the plastic is soft, remove it from the oven with protective gloves and shape the acrylic by hand (still using protective gloves) or place it over a form. The new shape must be kept in place until the plastic has cooled completely. Spring clamps can be used to secure the shape while cooling, but remove them before the plastic is completely cooled to prevent a marred surface.

Shaping With a Strip Heater

Acrylic can be bent with accuracy by using a strip heater, which can be purchased or easily constructed. Materials needed for constructing a strip heater are: (1) 1/2″ plywood, 6″ x 42″; (2) two 1/4″ plywood strips, 2-5/8″ x 36″; (3) two heavy-duty aluminum foil sheets, 6″ x 36″; (4) two asbestos

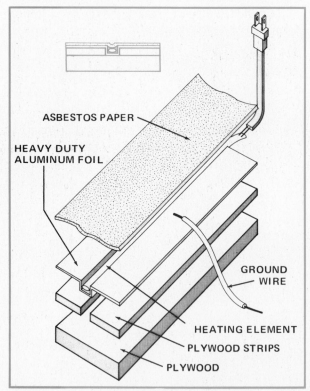

ASBESTOS PAPER

HEAVY DUTY ALUMINUM FOIL

GROUND WIRE

HEATING ELEMENT

PLYWOOD STRIPS

PLYWOOD

papers, 6-1/4″ x 36″; (5) staples; (6) ground wire and screw; (7) hammer and nails; and (8) a Briskeat RH-36 heating element, 1/2″ x 36″, wired with a two-prong plug and used in a 110-volt outlet (this item can be purchased from hardware stores or from the Briscoe Manufacturing Co., Columbus, Ohio 43216.)

Nail one of the two 1/4" plywood strips to each side of the 1/2" plywood base, leaving a 3/4" channel down the center. Place the two sheets of aluminum foil over the top surface, folding it to fit the 3/4" channel, and attach the ground wire to the aluminum foil with a screw. Make sure the ground wire is long enough so that it can be connected to a common ground — e.g., the screw in the cover plate of an electrical outlet. Place the two pieces of asbestos over the aluminum foil, folding them to fit the 3/4" channel. (Dampen the channel area to keep the asbestos and aluminum foil from cracking and tearing.) Staple the asbestos and aluminum foil in place along the outside edges of the two 1/4" plywood strips.

To prevent the edges of the asbestos and foil from fraying, tape them to the sides of the 1/2" plywood base. Place the heating element in the channel and hammer a nail 1-1/2" from the center of each

end of the plywood base. Attach the end strings of the heating element to the nails (the nails and heating element should all be in line with each other). Connect the ground wire to the common ground and plug into a 110-volt outlet when ready to use.

To bend acrylic, remove the protective paper from a sheet of the plastic. Place the acrylic on top of the strip heater and position the area to be bent directly over the heating element. Do not let the element touch the acrylic. Do not leave the plastic unattended while heating because scorching can easily occur. The plastic is ready for bending when the heated area begins to soften and become flexible. Bend the acrylic to the desired angle, with the heated side on the outside of the bend. Hold the acrylic in the desired angle until it has cooled enough to maintain its shape.

Figure 13. Important steps in making a strip heater are shown here (from top): nailing 1/4 " plywood strips on a base board; adding asbestos and aluminum; and installing a heating element.

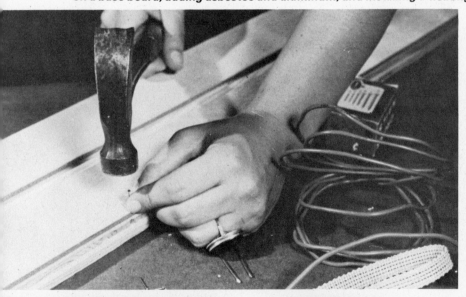

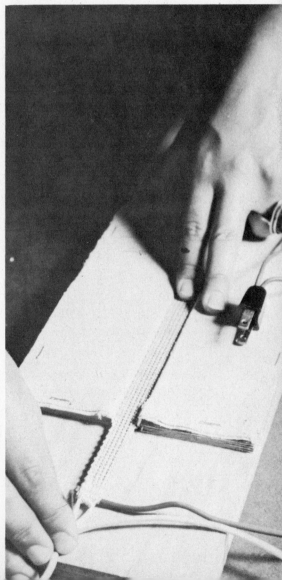

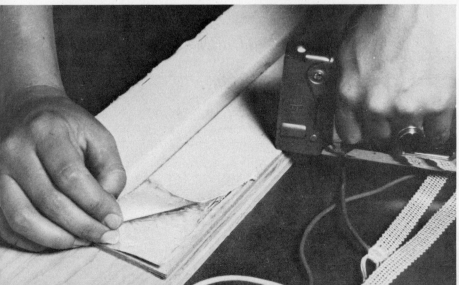

Figure 14. A careful layout of materials is just one of the precautions essential when working with polyester resins. The work surface should be covered with waxed paper or some other disposable paper.

WORKING WITH THERMOSETTING PLASTICS

Because thermosetting plastic comes in a liquid form, it must undergo a chemical change in order for it to become a solid. This chemical change occurs when a catalyst is added to the plastic. Once the plastic has been changed from liquid to solid, the change is permanent.

Polyester resin is a thick liquid plastic used for casting and laminating. When a catalyst is added to it, a chemical change causes the resin to heat up and harden. Before it hardens, however, the resin first goes through a gelling stage. The process which occurs between the liquid, gelling stage, and the solid state is called curing. The length of time the curing takes depends on the amount of catalyst used — *i.e.*, the less catalyst used, the longer the curing period; conversely, the more catalyst used, the shorter the curing period. The curing process, therefore, may take minutes, hours, or days. The amount of catalyst used is determined by the amount of resin used and whether the craftsman is casting or laminating (casting is the pouring of the resin into a mold; laminating is the building up of resin in layers). The resin can be opaque, transparent, or colored by mixing it with special pigments.

Certain preparations must be made and precautions taken before working with polyester resins. The work area should have good ventilation because the resin and catalyst give off fumes. If exposed to these chemicals for a long period of time or if working with large amounts of resin, wear a respirator with a chemical filter. Also wear protective gloves. When dry sanding, cutting, or filing the resin, wear a cloth filter mask or goggles if necessary. Store catalyst and resin in a cool, dark place and keep them away from exposed flames. Do not smoke near the chemicals. To remove resin or resin dust from the body, wash with cold water. If too much catalyst is added to the resin, it causes cracking and smoking. If this should happen, run cold water over the form.

Cover the work area with wax paper or other disposable paper. Have all equipment and supplies ready. Acetone is used to clean resin from hands, brushes, and clothes when it is still in a liquid or gelling state.

Types of Polyester Resin

There are two basic types of polyester resins: one designed for casting and the other for laminating. When casting, use either a flexible or a rigid resin. The flexible type is preferred when embedding materials into the resin.

Coloring

Special polyester resin colors are available in liquid, powder, and paste form. Before using the catalyst, a very small amount of color is added to the resin and mixed thoroughly to prevent streaking.

Catalyst

The catalyst, which is usually in a liquid form, is usually sold with the resin. It is measured out with an eyedropper. Lamination resins require more catalyst than casting resins in order to cure. (Use the proportions given in the directions because too much heat will cause the thick resin to crack.) Mix the catalyst and resin thoroughly with a stick.

Molds

Many types of molds can be used for casting resin. Molds are available at craft centers but they can also be made at home out of plaster, wax, aluminum foil, or flexible rubber. The beginning craftsman may find it easier to work with ready-made molds and experiment later with hand-made molds.

Casting

Casting is simply the process of pouring the catalyzed casting resin into a mold. The resin remains in the mold until it has cured properly. It is removed when hard. If the exposed surface of the resin is tacky (sticky) while in the mold, brush a thin layer of highly catalyzed resin (six parts resin to one part catalyst) over the top. Wait until this mixture hardens and then remove the form from the mold.

Impregnation

Impregnation is the embedding of materials in polyester resin. To prevent the resin from

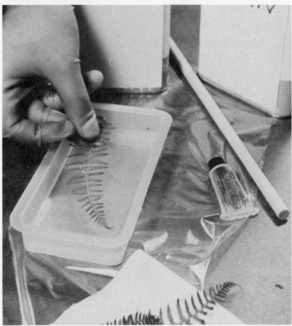

Figure 15. Casting is the process of pouring the liquid resin into the mold (top). Putting a fern or other material into the mold before it cures is called impregnation (bottom).

Figure 16. A handsome paperweight like this one can be made by casting and impregnating liquid resin. To prevent cracking, use a flexible polyester resin.

cracking while it cures, a flexible polyester resin should be used. Different types of materials can be impregnated, such as paper, burlap, canvas, cloth, dried flowers, leaves, seeds, and legumes.

Fillers

Fillers are used to strengthen the resin and make it putty-like. Materials used as fillers include wood chips, sawdust, crushed stone, metallic flakes, sand, and talc. The putty-like consistency achieved by adding fillers allows for a buildup of resins over a wire armature or over such other forms as candles or molds. Before putting the filler into the resin, Cab-O-Sil (a type of filler) can be added. This thickens the resin and prevents the filler from settling to the bottom when it is added. When using Cab-O-Sil, wear a mask. After the catalyst is added, use a putty knife to apply the resin.

Once the polyester resin has cured, it can be cut with wood or metalworking saws with sharp blades. Hand or electric drills with bits for drilling into metal may be used for drilling into cured polyester resin. When drilling, use a mild soap-and-water mixture to reduce the friction. Also, clamp down the form to be drilled.

Sanding and Polishing

When sanding, use wet or dry sandpaper, working from a coarse grit (#150), to medium grit (#220), and then a fine grit (#400). If sanding a flat edge, use a sanding block to prevent dipping. After sanding, the worked areas will be dull and marred. To polish these areas, brush over them with a highly catalyzed polyester and let cure.

Projects You Can Do

Plastics offer many opportunities to the avid craftsman. The following projects demonstrate the basic skills a craftsman must know in order to create original art forms. If the craftsman's workshop already contains basic metal and woodworking tools, this craft can be relatively inexpensive.

ACRYLIC BOOK STAND

An acrylic book stand is an attractive yet functional form that can be used to hold a cookbook and keep it clean while following a recipe. Materials needed for this project are: (1) a 1/4" thick acrylic sheet, 12" x 25"; (2) a strip heater; (3) grease pencil; (4) ruler; (5) files; and (6) wet or dry sandpaper; and (7) a 14" strip of wood.

Before starting the project, check the edges of the sheet of acrylic. If they are rough and file and sand them. After this has been done, remove the protective paper and, working lengthwise, measure 7" in from one edge. Draw a vertical line with a grease pencil and ruler from the top to the bottom of the acrylic sheet. Now turn the sheet over and measure 7" in from the first 7" line. Make another vertical line. From this line, measure 2" and draw a third vertical line. Turn the acrylic over and center the first vertical line over the channel of the strip heater. When the line is centered, gently rub it off with a soft cloth and heat the plastic to the flexible stage. Place a strip of wood along the area to be bent. Bend the heated acrylic, with the heated side on the outside of the bend, to a 90° angle. Hold in position until cooled.

Figure 17. To build up resins over a form—such as a candle—fillers are added to the liquid resin to give it a putty-like consistency. Various fillers are available.

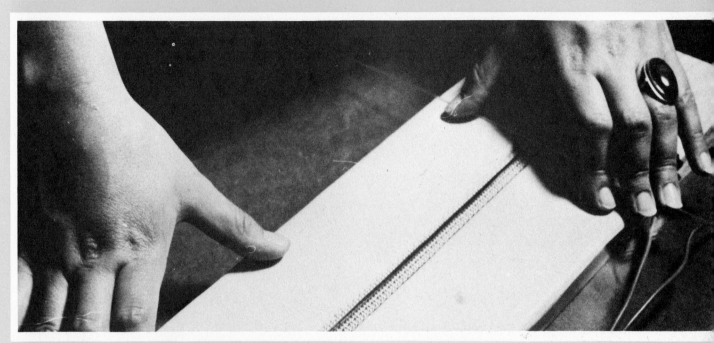

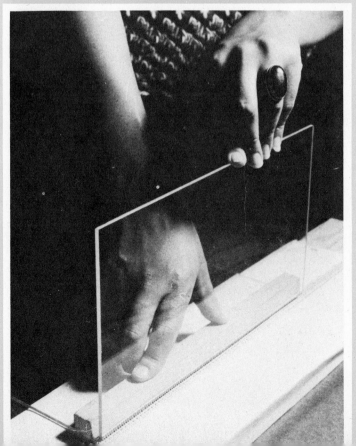

Figure 18. Directions for making an acrylic book stand include the following steps (from top): marking the surface with a grease pencil, positioning the mark over the heating channel, and bending the acrylic.

Follow this same procedure for the second and third vertical lines. Always remember that the greased line is on the surface facing the craftsman and that the heated side is on the outer side of the bend. After the third bend has cooled, clean the surface with a soft, damp cloth.

EMBEDDING CLOTH IN RESINS

The craftsman can embed any type of cloth in resin. The material should have a beauty of its own, making it worthwhile to display. Be sure, however, to follow all precautions mentioned previously.

Materials needed for this project are: (1) cloth; (2) flexible polyester resin; (3) catalyst; (4) eyedropper; (5) cellophane; (6) flat-edged piece of wood or spatula; and (7) pliable plastic bowl.

Figure 19. An acrylic book stand, most often used for holding cookbooks, is shown in completed form. Remember to sand the edges of the acrylic before beginning the bending process.

Figure 20. The steps required to embed cloth in resin include pouring the resin onto cellophane (top left), placing the cloth (top right), adding resin over the cloth (lower left), and spreading evenly (lower right).

Lay a sheet of cellophane, a little larger in size than the cloth, on a level, smooth working surface. Pour the flexible polyester resin into the plastic mixing bowl. Add the correct amount of catalyst with an eyedropper, according to the directions on the can, and mix thoroughly. Pour the resin into the center of the cellophane and let it spread evenly. Place the cloth on top of the poured resin. Then, pour another layer of resin in the center of the cloth and let it spread evenly again.

Place another piece of cellophane at one edge of the resin and, as smoothly as possible, lay the cellophane across the top of the cloth in the resin.

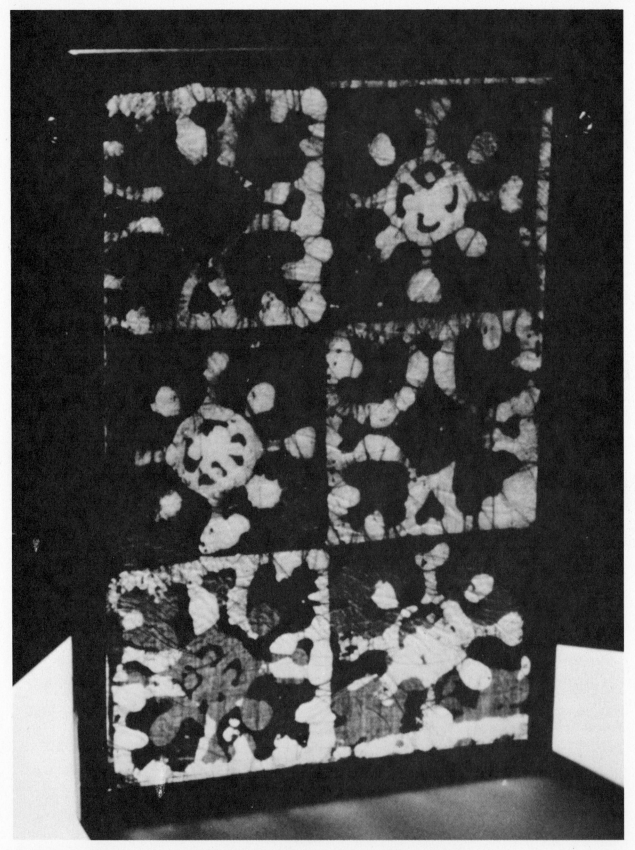

Figure 21. The finished object, cloth embedded in resin, can be framed for a colorful and attractive display. Or, if desired, hooks can be fastened to the back of the acrylic with epoxy, eliminating the need for a frame.

Figure 22. An important step in making plastic jewelry is bending the acrylic around a form of the required size (above). The finished jewelry (below) suggests avant garde design.

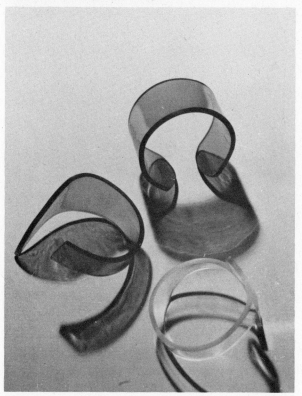

With a smooth, flat edge, gently work out air bubbles and even out the resin so it is the same thickness throughout the cloth. Let the resin cure. Remove the cellophane after the resin has solidified. The edges may be left as they are or they may be cut, sanded, and polished. If this display of fabric is to be hung, hooks can be adhered with epoxy or the fabric can be framed. Remember, use acetone to clean utensils and resin spills before the resin has time to cure.

CLEAR PLASTIC BRACELET

Contemporary plastic jewelry can be made with ease. Materials needed are: (1) a 1/16" thick sheet of acrylic, 7" x 1½"; (2) files; (3) wet or dry sandpaper; (4) oven; (5) asbestos; (6) protective gloves; and (7) circular or oval form.

Smooth out the edges of the acrylic sheet by filing and sanding. Round off the corners with a file and then sand. Edges may also be rounded if desired. Place the acrylic sheet on asbestos and put in into a preheated 275° F oven. Heat. When plastic is flexible (determined by the ease of lifting up a corner of it), remove from oven with protective gloves and wrap it around a circular or oval form. Hold until cooled (dipping in warm water helps the acrylic cool quicker). Clean with soft, damp cloth.

For Additional Reading

Newman, Day Hartley and Scott, Lee, **Plastic for the Craftsman,** Crown, 1972.

Newman, Thelma R., **Plastics as an Art Form,** Chilton, 1966.

Newman, Thelma R., **Plastic as Design Form,** Chilton, 1972.

Nordness, Lee, **Objects, U.S.A.,** Viking, 1970.

Painting, John, **Sculpture in Fiberglass,** Watson-Guptill, 1972.

Zechlin, Katharina, **Setting in Clear Plastic,** Taplinger, 1971.

Decoupage

The art of decorating with applied paper cutouts is easy to do, yet it allows the craftsman to design and produce imaginative and beautiful objects.

The origin of decoupage is historically unknown. However, there is evidence that in Siberia, as long as 3000 years ago, primitive people used cut decorations as appliqués on hangings. The Chinese cut paper for decorations 1500 years ago. Hiram Manning, a present-day decoupeur, owns a pair of Chinese pictures which date back centuries. These are composed of cuttings from silk robes which were glued on silver and placed under glass.

Decoupage, as it is known today, became popular in the eighteenth century in France and Italy. At that time, artists painted scenes and designs on furniture for nobles and wealthy people. Decoupage developed as a means of duplicating an artist's work at a fraction of the cost. In Italy, decoupage was called "l'arte del povero," or the poor man's art. Italian artists used the technique of pasting cut out prints on a surface and covering them with a transparent coating which produced a hand-painted look imitative of an artist's original creation.

Until the eighteenth century, the only reproductions available had been block prints. These were printed primarily for religious and educational purposes. Once engraving was perfected, however, a wealth of material became available.

As decoupage developed, engravers and printers began to make available good prints of original art works. The prints were colored and applied by skilled craftsmen to furniture and other small, decorative items. The decoupaged objects were so beautiful that they soon became appreciated for their own sake. Craftsmen were commissioned to use decoupage as a method of decoration, instead of hand painting.

The three main styles or periods of decoupage are eighteenth century, Victorian, and modern. Eighteenth-century decoupage was classic in feeling — hand-colored original designs and reproductions of fine art works were the basic design sources. Two artists closely associated with eighteenth-century decoupage are Jean Pillement and Francois Boucher. Pillement's work, for the most part, exhibited a Chinese influence and was very difficult to cut. Boucher's art was characterized by cherubs and garlands of flowers.

Because of greatly improved printing techniques, Victorian decoupage consisted of precolored prints, as well as embossed prints and the elaborate use of gold paper trim. Indeed, the trend of the Victorian era was toward overdecoration.

With all this activity, cutting soon became a distinct art. Probably the most famous cutters of the Victorian era were Miss Amelia Blackburn and a Mrs. Delany. Examples of their exquisite work may still be seen in the British Museum and the Victoria and Albert Museum, both in London. Queen Victoria herself was a collector of decoupage. Her collection was quite famous and differed from earlier collections because it consisted largely of a decoupage variation called "vue d'optique," in which the designs give an illusion of depth.

Robert Sayer, a famous collector of prints of the Victorian era, collected the works of Pillement, Boucher, and many other artists. He published them in a book entitled *The Ladies Amusement Book.* Sayer's collection was very popular in the Victorian era and many of his prints are still being used today.

As the name implies, modern decoupage makes use of all the modern products derived from today's printing processes. These include such items as greeting cards, calendars, and magazines as well as printed art work. Variations from the basic cutting technique, such as dechirage, collage, montage, and repousse, are also frequently used in modern decoupage.

In dechirage, the piece to be pasted on the surface is carefully torn instead of being cut. Collage is the artistic composition of designs, pictures, or any artistic material which have been pasted on a surface. Montage makes use of assorted designs and objects combined on a flat surface; repousse makes use of "raised" or embossed cutout designs on a flat surface.

Figure 1. An elegant example of l'arte del povero, *this Venetian secretary* (opposite) *is decorated with applied engravings, lacquer, and gold. (Courtesy, The Metropolitan Museum of Art, Fletcher Fund, 1925.)*

Figure 2. This Victorian decoupage panel, "Wood Vetch," is one of the series called "Mrs. Delany's Flora." Mrs. Delany was a British decoupage artist. (Courtesy, The British Museum, London.)

Originally, all prints used in decoupage were black and white and had to be colored by hand. However, modern color printing techniques have made possible beautiful color reproduction. In view of the current interest in the art of decoupage, it is fortunate that chemists have developed fast-drying lacquer-like finishes with which to cover the cutouts. Decoupage — taken step by step — is neither difficult to learn nor hard to do. One's first project can be a beautiful and lasting object of art.

Common Terms Used In Decoupage

Antiquing: a technique using color, most often brown, to "age" an object.

Base Coat: opaque colored paint or wood stain used to cover the raw wood.

Bleeding Print: a print in which the colors run or blur when sealer is applied.

Brayer: a rubber roller for flattening and adhering the cutout to the surface.

Bridge: an uncut connecting strip used to support the delicate parts of a cut out print before it is applied.

Curing: a process of hardening for preservation.

Cutout: a design cut out of a print and used as decoration on the decoupaged object.

Decoupage: the art of decorating surfaces with applied paper designs.

Finish: a clear, lacquer-like liquid used to cover the cutout.

Flowing On: the method of applying finish to the surface over the glued cutout.

Plasti-tak: plastic, sticky material used to hold the cutout to the surface while creating the design.

Sealing: covering with a liquid coating to prevent bleeding or running of color.

Submerging: the process of applying repeated coats of finish to the decorated surface for proper buildup over the design.

Wet Sanding: special sandpaper and water used to smooth and level the decorated and coated surfaces of a project.

Figure 3. Supplies for decoupage include scissors, brushes, sandpaper, steel wool, glue, sealer, finish, wax, and brush cleaner. Most are easily available locally or by mail.

Basic Equipment And Supplies

Before starting any decoupage project it is advisable to assemble all the necessary equipment and supplies. All are craft items and are easily purchased at a local craft shop or from a mail-order craft supplier. Many of the items, such as sandpaper, brushes, glue, turpentine, and steel wool, may be obtained at a hardware or paint store. Pens, India ink, tweezers, colored pencils, and scissors may be found in various retail stores. The special paints and finishes required are best purchased from a craft shop or mail-order craft supplier as ordinary paint stores do not usually stock them.

The selection of the box or plaque to be decoupaged and the print or prints to be used as the decoration should be decided upon first. The other supplies will be governed by this selection. For example, the selection of the plaque and the print will determine what base paint to use; whether antiquing will be desirable; whether to use ornamental trim, lustre wax, or hardware; and the style and type of hardware.

For a first project it is advisable to use a commercially manufactured box or plaque since these are made of new, unfinished wood. Later projects can include beautiful and unusual old wooden boxes containers or plaques, and even furniture, any of which may be purchased at auctions and antique shows.

Design prints for a first project are also best selected from the prints available in craft shops. The possibilities for design are, of course, limitless. It is fun, for future use, to assemble a portfolio of prints, designs, and decorations. Calendars, greeting cards, post cards, illustrations from books or magazines, even wedding announcements are just a few suggestions for sources of material for a portfolio.

Following is a list of basic equipment and supplies, with explanations regarding their use.

WOOD PLAQUE OR BOX

A plaque is a flat, shaped piece of wood. The size of a particular plaque should be determined by the area of wall to be covered, the decor of the room in which the plaque will be placed, and the selection of the cutout which will be decoupaged onto the plaque surface.

Wooden boxes are probably the most popular objects for modern decoupage. Selection of a box should be determined by the way it will be used and how it is to be decorated. Boxes come in various styles, depending on whether or not they require hinges and on the type of closure.

Both first-project boxes and plaques should be of new wood, free of knots, properly kiln dried and pre-sanded to a reasonable smoothness. They should be small in size.

Figure 4. Wood plaques and boxes are popular items for beginning decoupage projects. Boxes and plaques should be small, and made of good quality new wood.

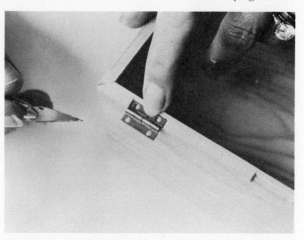

Figure 5. Hinges are a basic supply item in decoupage; notches for adding them are made with a "V"-tool. Choose the type and size of hinges at the time the box is chosen.

WOOD PUTTY

This comes as a powder and is mixed with enough water to form a stiff paste. The paste is applied to the holes and other imperfections on the plaque or box and allowed to dry. It is then sanded smooth. Do not mix more wood putty than will be used at one time. The mixture hardens quickly and cannot be reused.

HARDWARE

Hardware is the metal trim, closure devices, or clasps used on boxes; hangers for plaques; and decorative rings on the top of plaques which may be used for hanging or just as decorations.

If hinges are required with a particular type of box, they may be either concealed inside the box or applied as added decoration to the outside. Concealed hinges are usually rectangular in shape while outside hinges usually have decorative shapes. For best artistic results selection of hardware should be made at the time the box is selected.

PRINT

The "print" is the decorative paper print design or drawing which is applied to the surface being decoupaged. As previously recommended, a commercially produced, new, colored print should be used for a first project.

The thickness of a print is of great importance because it determines the number of coats of finish necessary to "submerge" the print after it has been cut out and glued to the surface. Embossed cards, post cards, and other thick paper prints should generally be avoided for first projects.

Black and white or uncolored prints may be used but also are not recommended as a first project because such prints must be hand-colored. Furthermore, some types of paper should not be used for decoupage, such as newspaper, wallpaper, and other papers where the quality of the paper and the printing ink are inferior.

ORNAMENTAL PAPER TRIM

This is an optional item on boxes and plaques. The most commonly seen trim is a gold-embossed paper, used as borders, on corners, or as the dominant design. Ornamental paper trim comes in various widths, shapes, patterns, and colors. Trim should also be selected when the design is planned.

SCISSORS

Scissors are the basic decoupage tool and should be of top quality. Be sure that they fit the hand comfortably and that a sharp, fine cut can be achieved with little effort.

Decoupage scissors are similar to cuticle scissors, having a curved blade. The curved shape and short length of blade insures a proper cut. Straight scissors — small scissors with straight blades — are also used in decoupage for preliminary cuts and for straight cuts.

HOBBY KNIFE

This is a sharp-pointed knife which can be used as a substitute for decoupage scissors. It is most effectively used to cut out the small, inaccessible inner areas of a print.

Figure 6. This selection of prints demonstrates the wide variety of subject matter available to the decoupage artist. Beginners will find it easier to use a commercially prepared print.

PLASTI-TAK

Plasti-tak is a sticky, plastic material used to hold the cutout print on the wooden object or pattern paper while creating the design. Plasti-tak will not mar the wood surface or leave sticky residues on either the wood or the paper. It can be reused and should be kept in one wad.

TWEEZERS

Tweezers are an optional, but frequently useful tool. They are used to lift delicately cut prints onto the pasted surface of an object to be decoupaged. Long-nosed tweezers are best.

SANDPAPER

Three weights of sandpaper are necessary for any project: #220, #400, and #600. The #400 and #600 must be "wet" sandpapers. One package of the three combined weights is sufficient for one project.

SANDING BLOCK

A hand-sized block of wood with a felt pad attached to the underside should be used when sanding whenever possible. A surface sanded in this manner is more level than would be possible if the sanding were done by hand alone.

BASE PAINT

Base paint is used to cover the raw wood before the print is glued on. Colored oil- or water-based paint or wood stain may be used. A two-ounce jar should be a sufficient amount for one project.

Water-based paints are used with lacquer-type synthetic, quick-drying finishes. Oil-based paints are used with varnish finish. Water-based paints and wood stains are suggested for a first project because they are quick drying, need little or no sanding and are compatible with quick-drying finishes.

BRUSHES

The average decoupage project requires three brushes: a one-inch brush for the base paint (nylon bristles for water-base, natural bristle for oil-base); a one-inch nylon brush with tapered tip for finish coats (except varnish, which requires natural bristles); and one small artist's brush for various small tasks.

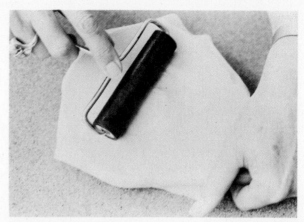

Figure 7. Use a brayer to secure the design to the surface. To protect the print, first place a clean cloth over the design, then roll the brayer back and forth briskly.

INDIA INK

This is a waterproof ink used for limning the fine lines of a design which are too difficult to cut. It can be applied with a pen or a very fine brush — the pen is easier to use. If a mistake is made the ink can be removed with a damp sponge before it is dry.

PEN

A pen is used to apply an ink signature or additional fine lines on the design. A "fine" nib is recommended.

GLUE

A white, clear-drying glue should be used for adhering print and trim to the painted or stained surface of the object to be decoupaged. One two-ounce bottle of glue is sufficient for several projects.

BRAYER

A brayer, a rubber roller attached to a handle, is used to adhere the design to the painted or stained surface by rolling it back and forth over the glued print. The brayer not only sticks the design down, it also helps to eliminate air pockets and any excess glue under the design.

A brayer should never be rolled in direct contact with the print. To do so might mar the colored surface of the design. Therefore, a clean lint-free dampened cloth is placed over the surface of the design before the brayer is used.

Figure 8. The decoupage on this box, designed by Fran Otnes, incorporates elements from many magazine illustrations and paintings. (By permission from Lithopinion #27, the graphic arts and public affairs journal of Local One, Amalgamated Lithographers of America and lithographic employers, New York. © 1973 by Local One, A.L.A. Photo by Wayne Ponton.)

SEALER

Sealer is a shellac-type coating which is used, in spray form, to seal the raw wood and prevent color variations from showing through the base paints. It is also used to seal the colors of the prints and to seal color when a project is antiqued. One can of sealer spray should be sufficient for a single project. It is advisable to purchase a sealer of the same brand as the finish and the brush cleaner to ensure that they are compatible.

FINISH

Finish is the clear, liquid coating used to "submerge" the cutout design glued to the painted surface of the wooden object being decoupaged. One quart is an adequate amount for a single project. There are two types of finish: one is a synthetic, lacquer-type finish; the other is a varnish. Because the former is quick-drying and is quicker and easier to apply than varnish, it is recommended for first projects. Finish is applied with a brush which should not be used for any other purpose. Finish should be stirred with a wooden stick so that it is always thoroughly mixed. It should never be shaken to mix.

Varnish is a natural finish. It is thinned with turpentine and one coat takes about eight to twelve hours to dry. It should be stirred, not shaken, and applied with a brush used only for this purpose.

BRUSH CLEANER

This is a special liquid used for cleaning the brushes used to apply synthetic, lacquer-type finishes. A one-pint can of brush cleaner should be sufficient for one project. For easier use, it should be stored in a small glass jar, but large enough to accommodate the brush being cleaned. The lid of the jar should be metal and tight-fitting. Brush cleaner can be used repeatedly and replaced only when it becomes too thick with excess finish.

TURPENTINE

Turpentine is used to clean varnish brushes, to thin varnish, and to mix with oil color for antiquing.

ANTIQUE COLOR

Antique color is applied after the print or prints

Figure 9. Imaginative use of decoupage on egg cups, by Fran Otnes. (By permission from Lithopinion #32, *the graphic arts and public affairs journal of Local One, Amalgamated Lithographers of America and lithographic employers, New York. © 1973 by Local One, A.L.A. Photo by Wayne Ponton.)*

have been glued on and several coats of finish have been applied. The purpose of the antique color is to yield an aged, antique look or to subdue color.

STEEL WOOL

Steel wool, #0000 weight, is used dry as a buffing agent to give sanded surfaces of a decorated object a soft patina or shine. When using the steel wool on a surface, rub with a brisk, *straight* motion so that the surface becomes warm to the touch. A hand-rubbed, soft shine is the desired effect. One small package of steel wool should be sufficient for one project.

FINISHING POWDER AND OIL

Finishing powder mixed with finishing oil is an additional and optional buffing process. It is used to add to the patina of the finish.

LUSTRE WAX

Lustre wax is a solid, decorative wax available in gold, silver, copper, and other metallic colors as well as in paint colors. It can be used instead of ornamental trim as a decoration on the edges of plaques and boxes or to adorn inside surfaces.

CLEAR WAX

Clear wax is applied to add shine and to protect the decorated surface. One two-ounce jar is sufficient to wax several projects.

COLORED PENCILS

Artists' colored pencils may be used to delineate fine lines on color prints which are too fine to cut. They may also be used to color black and white prints and to repair damage where premature or too-deep sanding has whitened or spoiled the colored surface of a print. Colored pencils are an optional item.

LINING MATERIAL

Lining material is used to line and decorate the backs of plaques and the inner parts of boxes. There is a wide choice of linings, such as velveteen, cotton, silk, or brocade. Felt is an excellent lining for the backs of plaques.

Linings for boxes should be selected to coordinate with the exterior decoration on the box, both in color and in style. These should be installed only after the outer surfaces of a box are completely finished.

Basic Procedures

After assembling all necessary supplies, the decoupeur is ready to begin. Close attention must first be given to planning the design for the project. This will display the decoupeur's creative ability.

THE DESIGN

There are several things to remember when planning a design. Be sure that the color of the base paint will complement and enhance the design. Make sure that the design dominates its area. A large expanse of plain painted wood is dull and uninteresting.

In planning a design, it is helpful to draw the exact outlines of the shape of the box or plaque to be decoupaged on a piece of plain paper. Then, with tweezers, place the cutout print on the paper. Arrange the design to fit each area. If necessary, cut the design apart, shift the cut pieces, and add or combine prints. When the design has been decided upon, the cutouts may then be held in place with plasti-tak.

In planning and laying out a design, the print or prints may extend over the slot between the edges of the base and lid of a box. The print will be slit along the opening after it has been glued and the glue has dried. Ornamental trim may be used in a similar manner.

CUTTING

The manual skills of cutting prints and designs should be practiced before starting a project. Select prints from magazines or similar sources as practice material. Attention should be paid to the shape of the subject matter being cut out. For example, blades of grass should be sharp, clouds or edges of garments should be soft and flowing. A simple way to judge a well-cut print is to reverse it and view it from the back. If the design is still pleasing, it has met the test.

Figure 10. A delicate design featuring birds was used for this decoupaged box. Decoupage is generally associated with traditional styles of interior decoration, although some artists have used the technique in innovative ways.

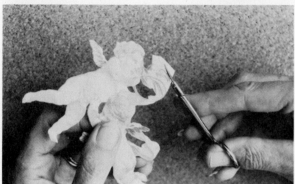

Figure 11. Cutting must be done with care and precision. Inside areas should be done first (top), leaving the outside area for last (bottom). A knife can be used for the outside cutting.

Cutting is important and must be planned. Analyze the print to determine where to make the first cut. Ordinarily, inside cuts and contained areas where cuts do not go out to the edge should be cut first. Both the decoupage scissors and hobby knife are good for such cuts. When scissors are used for inner cuts, the scissors should be held underneath the print. This exposes the cutting action. Use straight scissors to trim away any excess paper around the outside of the print. The outline of the print is always cut last, with either decoupage scissors or knife. (The procedure for cutting the outline is described later under *Essential Instructions*.)

If the outer parts of the print are intricate or delicate, "bridges" of paper should be left, to be cut last. If a print is to be torn, the outer edge should not be trimmed away. When tearing, tear the edge of the print to create an uneven edge, leaving enough plain paper around the print to enhance the design. Always tear the edge away from the print with a downward motion so that the bevelled edge projects from the top or printed side.

ESSENTIAL INSTRUCTIONS

Decoupage is not a craft to be rushed. Read the following instructions carefully to become familiar with the entire procedure. An understanding of these instructions will minimize mistakes and produce a first project of which one can be proud.

Making Surface Repairs

Examine the surface of the wooden box or plaque to be decoupaged for dents, knots or cracks. These cannot be hidden with base paints or stains. If imperfections are found, fill and repair them with wood putty. Apply the wood putty mixture with a finger or hobby knife. Work it into the imperfection on the box or plaque. Immediately smooth the place with the flat edge of a hobby knife blade. Wipe away any excess putty. Allow the wood putty to dry and sand it smooth with #220 sandpaper. If the box or plaque is to be stained with a water-based wood stain and not painted, substitute the wood stain for plain water when mixing the wood putty. The wood putty repair will then match the color of the wooden surfaces of the box or plaque once they have been stained.

Concealed Hinges

If concealed hinges are to be used, proper notches must be cut in the box base and the lid. On the edges of the base and lid (using the hinge for a pattern), mark the notch outlines with the hobby knife. Cut the notch to the marks with the knife. Make the cuts just deep enough to accommodate the thickness of the hinge. Notches in base and lid should be the same depth and at matching points.

Figure 12. Dents or cracks in the wood should be carefully filled in with wood putty. Apply the putty with a hobby knife, as shown, or with the fingertip. Smooth the surface immediately.

Figure 13. After the wood has been smoothed and sanded, apply sealer from a spray can. Hold the spray can about 12" from the wood, and apply a light even coat over the outside of the object.

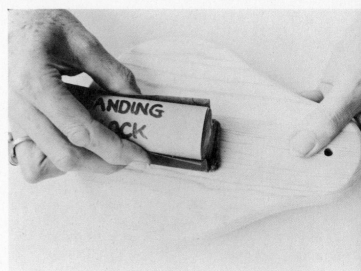

Figure 14. Use a sanding block, rather than just a sheet of sandpaper, for the sanding process. Paper is wrapped around the block and held there by pressure from the hand.

Sealing

Seal the wood object by spraying with sealer. To do this, hold the object about 12 inches from the spray can and spray three light, even coats over all outer surfaces of the object. Allow 30 minutes for each coat to dry. After the last coat of sealer has dried, sand all the sealed surfaces. Use #220 sandpaper on a sanding block.

When using a sanding block, a sheet of sandpaper four inches square is wrapped around the felt surface of the sanding block (sanding surface down). It is held on the block by finger pressure. Apply light, even pressure. The sanding block should be used both when sanding raw wood and when the surface is being leveled after the design has been submerged by the finish coats. Sand with the grain of the wood. Repeat the sanding and sealing processes twice.

If the base paint is to be a wood stain instead of a colored paint, omit the sealing process and sand surfaces smooth. Wipe sanded surfaces clean.

Applying the Base Paint

Thoroughly mix the base paint. Water-based paint is best applied with a one-inch brush in several thin coats. It can be thinned as necessary with water and mixed by shaking the jar. Apply a thin, even coat of base paint to all surfaces which are exposed or which will be coated with finish. If a partition box is being used, remove the partitions and paint them separately.

Apply paint along the length of the grain. Wipe out any drips and runs while the paint is still wet. Suspend the painted object on a can so that the paint can dry. The number of coats of base paint necessary to cover the raw wood varies. Light-colored paints require at least two coats. Dark-colored raw wood will always need a minimum of three coats when being covered with a light-colored paint. Proper coverage with colored base paints requires a complete opacity, with no wood surface showing. Two or three coats of paint is usually sufficient to achieve this.

Water-based paint dries quickly, usually in 15 to 30 minutes. Each additional coat of paint should be applied only when the prior coat is fully dry. Water-based paint should not be sanded between coats but may be sanded after the final coat has dried 12 hours. Light hand sanding with dry #400 sandpaper should be done to eliminate runs and drips, but minor roughness need not be sanded. Clean the brush immediately after each coat so that the paint will not dry on the brush.

For decoupage work, oil-based paints should be flat enamels. They may be used as base paints only when varnish coats are used to submerge the print. Flat enamel should be used because varnish adheres to it better than to glossy enamels.

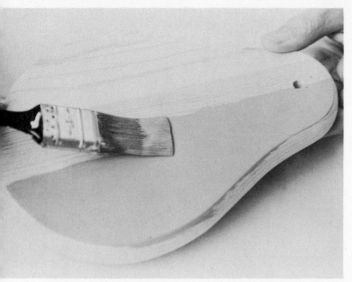

Figure 15. Apply paint with the grain of the wood, as shown. The number of coats needed will depend on a number of factors, such as the color of the paint and the darkness of the wood.

Each coat of an oil-based paint takes 6 to 12 hours to dry. Thin, light coats applied with a one-inch brush are recommended. Each coat should be lightly sanded with #400 sandpaper. Oil-based paint is thinned with turpentine and should be stirred to mix. Because oil-based paint and compatible varnish coats are slow drying, with repeated sanding necessary, they are not suggested for a first project.

Applying Wood Stain

Wood stains follow the same basic procedures for mixing and for use and cleaning of brushes as colored paints. These are used when a wood-grain background is desired. A water-based stain is recommended. The wood should not be sealed when a wood stain is used as the stain will not penetrate sealed wood.

Wood stain, which is mixed by just shaking the jar, should be applied in a thin coat with a one-inch brush and can be thinned as necessary with water. A two-ounce jar of stain is usually a sufficient quantity to do one project. Because water-based stain dries quickly (10 to 15 minutes), the stained wood should be wiped clean with paper towel immediately after the stain is applied. Repeat stain coats — wiping after every coat — until the desired shade of darkening is achieved. Allow base paint or stain to dry 12 hours before next step.

Preparing the Print

"Peeling" a print means reducing the thickness of the paper. This is done by first soaking the print in a solution of vinegar and water. Then, starting at an edge of the soaked print, split the layers of paper by peeling away the back (uncolored) part. When the print has been reduced to the desired thickness, it should be allowed to dry before cutting.

Place uncut print on sheets of newspaper and spray only the printed side with a light, even coat of sealer. If the print does not "bleed" when the sealer is applied, it is ready to be cut or torn. If the print bleeds, discard it.

If ornamental trim is to be used, the trim should be sprayed with three light coats of sealer. Let dry between coats. (Gold-embossed trim may be changed to silver by using a paper towel to rub paint-brush cleaner on the gold paper. This removes the gold finish.)

Figure 16. Wooden blocks by Fran Otnes. (By permission from Lithopinion #32, the graphic arts and public affairs journal of Local One, Amalgamated Lithographers of America and lithographic employers, New York. © 1973 by Local One, A.L.A. Photo by Wayne Ponton.)

Figure 17. A surreal effect was achieved on these two sides of a box by Fran Otnes. (By permission from Lithopinion #32, *the graphic arts and public affairs journal of Local One, Amalgamated Lithographers of America and lithographic employers, New York. © 1973 by Local One, A.L.A. Photo by Wayne Ponton.)*

After determining what part of the design is to be used and what part is to be cut away, cut or tear the print. The proper cut of any print used in decoupage is a bevel cut. A bevel cut means cutting the paper so that the cut edge is rounded toward the underside. To achieve a bevel cut, hold the decoupage scissors with the blades resting against the index finger. The curve of the scissor blades must be toward the back of the hand. Hold the cutting hand so that its palm is turned up enough to have the scissors cut at a slant, with the bottom blade closer to the cutting line. Hold the print loosely in the opposite hand. The paper should be turned as cutting progresses. Learn to move the paper constantly so as to cut an uneven, interesting edge. The cutting hand does not move.

If a hobby knife is used, the cutting part of the blade should be held at a 45-degree angle with the surface of the print. With smooth, even pressure guide the blade of the knife along the lines of the print which are to be cut. It is helpful to do knife cutting on a smooth, hard surface, such as masonite or plywood. When properly used, the knife makes a clean, sharp cut. Practice with scrap paper to perfect a proper cutting technique.

Next, spray two light coats of sealer on the colored side of the cut or torn print. Sprayed sealer coats on prints take about 10 minutes to dry.

Applying the Design

Using a finish brush, apply one coat of finish to the painted or stained wood. This coat of finish will be the base on which the design is glued. One brush-on coat is sufficient; it should be allowed to dry several hours.

Lay out the design on a paper outline of the box or plaque or on the box or plaque itself. When satisfied with the design, use plasti-tak to hold it in place until it can be glued. If trim is to be used, the necessary amount should be measured out at this time, but not cut.

After the finish has dried, glue on the cut out or torn print and any ornamental trim. To do so, moisten the back of the print with a damp sponge. Then, using the fingers, spread an even coating of glue on the surface where the print will go. Using tweezers if necessary, carefully place the print in position on the glued area. Press down with the

Figure 18. The design should be planned, laid out, and arranged carefully before it is applied permanently. Let the pieces dry on a model of the wood or on the wood object itself.

fingers to adhere all parts. Excess glue on the face of the print can be wiped away later.

Cover the glued print with a damp cloth and roll with the brayer to stick the print down flat. When using the brayer, start at the center of the design area and gently press and roll the entire design. Lift the cloth to determine that the design has been properly glued down and that air bubbles and excess glue under the print have been eliminated. Replace the cloth and reroll with the brayer if necessary. Stubborn air bubbles can be pricked with a pin to allow air to escape. Edges which have not stuck may be brushed with extra glue and restuck.

For ornamental trims, apply glue with a brush; glue in place and cut, miter, and remove extra pieces of trim as necessary. Brush the trim with a coat of glue to act as a sealer.

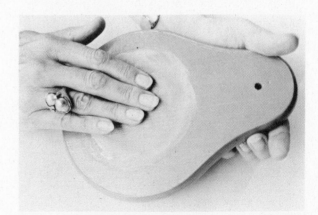

Figure 19. Spread a coat of glue on the prepared wood, using the fingers as shown. Then place the print in the proper position and smooth down with the fingers. Wipe away excess glue.

After the design is thoroughly glued but before any excess glue is dry, the painted part of the wood and the print face should be wiped clean with a damp sponge.

Now is the time to apply a signature to the project, if desired, using India ink and a pen. Any design feature which was too fine to cut, such as raindrops, butterfly antennae, or reins of horses, also can now be drawn in ink. Allow the project to dry 24 hours and reseal both the glued print and ink additions with spray sealer.

Applying Finish

Mix the finish thoroughly. Using the flow-on method, apply the proper number of finish coats to the area being decoupaged. (The flowing-on of a coat is done by first loading the brush with finish. Then, while holding the brush at a 45-degree angle, allow the finish to flow onto the surface. Do not go back and "brush smooth.") If the piece is to be antiqued, only six finish coats should be applied at this stage. If the project is a plaque with no ornamental trim and it is not being antiqued, 15 coats should be applied. If it is a box and it is not being antiqued, 20 coats should be applied. Between coats, suspend the project on a can above the work surface.

If a plaque or box has a fairly large area, each successive coat should be flowed-on at an angle 90 degrees to the direction in which the prior coat was applied. Edges of boxes and plaques not decorated by prints should not have finish flowed-on. Rather, they should be coated using a brushing action, so that the excess finish will not drip.

After each coat is applied, remove any bubbles or lint. It is not necessary to sand after each coat. After all necessary coats have been applied, let the piece cure for 24 hours.

Antiquing

If the project is to be antiqued, six coats of finish must first be applied over the print. Then spray or paint the antique color on all surfaces to be antiqued and allow to dry for only two or three minutes. Next, using paper towels, wipe to the desired degree of darkness. Allow antiquing to dry 24 hours. Seal carefully with spray sealer, using sufficient coats to cover completely. Allow sealer to dry several hours, then apply an additional 10 coats of finish. The first several coats of finish over the antiquing should be applied in the same direction as the antique streaking. Allow the project 24 hours to cure.

Sanding

Sand with #400 wet sandpaper. Using water with detergent added, wet the sandpaper and the wood surface. Carefully sand the outline made by the raised edges of the cut out print. If the cutout is not damaged by this hand-sanding, a sanding block can then be used. Sand until level. Wipe dry periodically to determine when the surface is smooth, level, and dull. When a proper surface has been achieved, wipe clean with clear water and dry.

After the first stage of sanding has been completed, apply an additional 10 coats of finish. Allow the piece to dry and cure for two to three weeks. Then, repeat the wet sanding with #400 wet sandpaper, using the sanding block on flat areas and hand-sanding on edges. Sand in the direction of the print or with the grain of the wood. Sand all surfaces until smooth and dull, leaving no low or shiny spots.

Next, repeat the wet sanding process using #600 wet sandpaper. Continue until the surface has a soft patina or shine. Wipe surface dry.

Figure 20. For antiquing, first apply six coats of finish to the object. Then brush or spray the antique color on the surfaces to be covered. Rub the color into the surface with a paper towel.

Figure 21. Trim a piece of cardboard to fit the space to be lined; then cut the lining larger than the pattern on all sides (top). The lining should fit the box snugly (bottom).

Polishing and Waxing

Polish with #0000 steel wool, rubbing briskly in the same direction as for sanding. The friction of hard rubbing makes the surface warm. This is normal. Rub until the correct soft shine is achieved. This takes time.

If more shine is desired, use finishing powder and oil. Apply with felt. Rub in the same direction as the steel wool. When the desired shine is achieved, remove excess powder and oil with a clean cloth.

Use a clear wax for decorated surfaces. Apply an even coat with a damp cloth and allow it to dry. Buff with a flannel cloth to shine.

Lining the Plaque or Box

Apply lining to back of plaque or insides of box. To cover the back of a plaque, first make a paper pattern of the plaque. Transfer the pattern to the lining material. Felt or contact paper may be glued directly in place, but velvet or other lining materials should be glued to cardboard first. Apply glue to back of plaque and position lining. Use brayer to adhere smoothly. Be sure lining on back of plaque is not visible from the front.

Box linings should be mounted on cardboard before being installed. Cut the cardboard pieces to fit sides, bottom, and lid; cut the lining material one-half inch larger on all sides than the cardboard patterns. Miter the corners by diagonally cutting off the overlap at the corners. Fold fabric back over the cardboard and glue one-half inch of material (preferably at the top edge) to the back of the cardboard patterns. Put lining pieces in place to test fit before gluing. Adjust as necessary by trimming cardboard at the bottom edge. Glue side linings in place first, bottom last.

Using Lustre Wax

If additional decoration or trim is needed, lustre wax may be used. It can be applied straight from the jar with the finger, or it can be diluted with turpentine and applied with a brush. If a mistake is made or the effect is not the one desired, the lustre wax may be removed by wiping with a paper towel dampened in turpentine. Allow to dry five minutes and buff with paper towel.

Attaching Hardware

The final step is attaching hardware. Position it on the object and mark the holes for screws with an awl. Then make holes with the awl at the places marked. Insert screws and turn in until heads are flush with the hardware surface.

Hinges are attached to the base of the box first, screws installed only half way. Then mark screw holes on lid with awl. Attach lid to base with hinge by installing screw in lid half way. Then tighten all screws. Install any other hardware items in the same manner.

Figure 22. After the box is lined, apply the hinges and hardware. Mark the screw holes with an awl, then use the awl to make the holes. Insert screws so that the heads are flush with the surface.

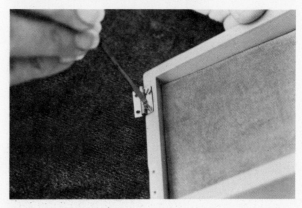

Projects You Can Do

Interest in a craft is stimulated by a particular project. The projects here are meant to give ideas for projects one might want to undertake. The mushroom plaque and antique trunk box projects detailed here are excellent projects for beginners. They incorporate all the basic techniques needed to learn the craft of decoupage without sacrifice of utility or beauty.

MUSHROOM PLAQUE

The necessary supplies for making a mushroom plaque are: (1) a wooden bread-board plaque; (2) a mushroom print; (3) dusk blue water-based paint; (4) one package of wet sandpaper, including #220, #400, and #600; (5) spray sealer; (6) a sanding block; (7) base paint brush; (8) scissors; (9) finish brush; (10) glue; (11) brayer; (12) one pint of synthetic lacquer finish; (13) one pint of brush cleaner; (14) #0000 steel wool; (15) clear wax; (16) lining material; and (17) hardware (a bracket for hanging).

Procedures

1. Examine wood for cracks or imperfections. Fill

Figure 23. The decoupage craftsman can create a variety of interesting gifts. These two purses (left) are good examples. The egg-shapes mounted on stands were also decoupaged (right).

with wood putty if necessary. Allow wood putty to dry.

2. Sand wood with grain, using #220 sandpaper on sanding block. Hand sand the end grain on the edge of plaque.

3. Spray-seal wood with sealer. At proper intervals, spray and seal two additional coats.

4. Apply base paint to wood by brush. Allow paint to dry 30 minutes. Add additional coats sufficient to cover. Allow base paint 12 hours to dry.

5. Stir lacquer finish. Brush one coat of lacquer finish on painted wood. Allow lacquer finish coat one hour to dry.

6. Cut out print. Spray-seal print with three coats of sealer.

7. Glue print to wood. Sign with ink. Dry 12 hours.

8. Spray-seal print and signature with sealer.

9. Apply 15 coats of lacquer finish over painted and decorated surface by brush, at one hour intervals. Use flow-on method over top surface but brush finish on edges of the wood. Rotate the direction of each coat 90 degrees. After last coat, allow to dry 24 hours.

10. Wet-sand by hand, using #400 sandpaper, until level and dull. Clean with water. Let dry.

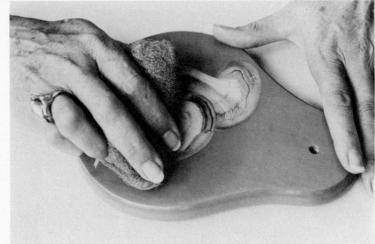

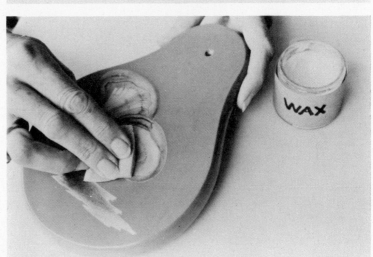

Figure 24. To finish the mushroom plaque project, coat the design with lacquer and wet-sand the dried finish (above). Later steps are buffing with steel wool and applying wax, which is buffed with a soft cloth (above right). The finished plaque (below right) makes an attractive wall decoration.

11. Apply an additional 10 coats of lacquer finish. Use procedure in step 9. Allow coats to cure for at least 48 hours. For better results, let the project cure several weeks.

12. Wet-sand with sanding block, using #400 sandpaper, until level and dull. Sand with grain, except edges.

13. Wet-sand with sanding block, using #600 sandpaper, until soft shine is achieved. Sand with grain except edges.

14. With #0000 steel wool, buff with the grain until desired shine is achieved.

15. Apply wax. Buff with soft cloth.

16. Measure, cut, and glue lining.

17. Install bracket for hanging.

Figure 25. The second project is an antiqued trunk-shaped box. This box has been trimmed with gold embossed braid and lined with velvet. A dark shade of antiquing was used.

ANTIQUE TRUNK BOX

Necessary supplies for this project are: (1) a trunk-shaped wood box; (2) a print (antique in character); (3) rust-color water-based paint; (4) gold embossed braid; (5) plasti-tak; (6) umber spray antique; (7) concealed hinges; (8) hobby knife; (9) scissors; (10) one package of wet sandpaper, including #220, #400, and #600; (11) spray sealer; (12) sanding block; (13) base paint brush; (14) finish brush; (15) glue; (16) brayer; (17) one quart of synthetic lacquer finish; (18) one pint of brush cleaner; (19) #0000 steel wool; (20) clear wax; and (21) velvet for lining.

Procedures

1. Examine wood for cracks or imperfections. If necessary, fill with wood putty. Allow wood putty to dry.

2. Sand wood with grain, using #220 sandpaper on sanding block.

3. With knife, cut notches for hinges in both box base and box lid.

4. Spray-seal wood with sealer. At proper drying intervals, spray and seal two additional coats.

5. Apply base paint to box base and box lid by brush. Allow paint to dry 30 minutes. Add additional coats sufficient to cover. Allow base paint to dry 12 hours.

6. Stir lacquer finish and apply one coat to painted wood with a brush. Allow finish coat one hour to dry.

7. Cut out print. Spray-seal print and gold braid trim with three coats of sealer. Use plasti-tak at box corners to hold box base and box lid together. Plan design.

8. Glue print and gold braid trim to wood. Top coat gold braid trim with glue. Sign with ink. Dry 12 hours.

9. Spray-seal print and signature with sealer.

10. Using the hobby knife, slit print and gold braid extending over box opening. Remove plasti-tak from corners of box.

11. Apply with brush six coats of lacquer finish over all painted and decorated surfaces. Allow one hour drying time between coats. Use flow-on method over decorated surfaces and brush-on method on edges of box. After last coat, allow to dry 24 hours.

12. Spray antique. Wipe for streaked effect to give desired shade of darkness. Allow antiquing to dry 24 hours.

13. Spray-seal entire antiqued area.

14. Apply 15 coats of lacquer finish, by brush, over all painted and decorated surfaces. Allow one hour drying time between coats. Use flow-on method over all painted and decorated surfaces, brush-on method on edges. After last coat, allow to dry 24 hours.

15. Wet-sand by hand, using #400 sandpaper, until surface is level and dull. Clean with water. Let dry.

16. Apply an additional 10 coats of lacquer finish. Use procedure in step 14. Allow coats to cure a minimum of 48 hours. If possible, let cure several weeks for best results.

17. Wet-sand with sanding block, using #400 sandpaper, until level and dull. Sand with grain, except edges.

18. Wet-sand with sanding block, using #600 sandpaper, until soft shine is achieved. Sand with grain, except edges.

19. Using #0000 steel wool, buff with grain until desired shine is achieved.

20. Apply wax. Buff with soft cloth.

21. Measure, cut, and glue lining in box base and box lid.

22. Install hinges on box base and box lid.

For Additional Reading

Harrower, Dorothy, **Decoupage: A Limitless World in Decoration,** M. Barrows, 1958.

Hukel, VIrginia, "Exquisite Decoupage Art," **Decorating and Craft Ideas Made Easy,** Oct. 1971.

Manning, Hiram, **Manning on Decoupage,** Hearthside, 1969.

Nimock, Patricia, **Decoupage,** Scribner, 1968.

Nimock, Patricia, "Tops In Tables," **Needles and Craft for the Creative Woman,** Spring/Summer, 1974.

Robertson, Joyce, "Under Cover of Glass," **Decorating and Craft Ideas Made Easy,** Mar. 1972.

Wing, Frances S., **The Complete Book of Decoupage,** Coward-McCann, 1965-70.

Figure 26. These boxes, each very different but handsome, suggest the many design possibilities in decoupage. The shape of the box, the color of the finish, and the prints are all factors in design.

Paper Crafts

Paper, one of the most versatile of the craft mediums, offers limitless opportunities for creativity and imagination.

Although the word "paper" is derived from papyrus, which is a plant used by the Egyptians as early as 2400 B.C. to make a paper-like material on which they wrote, it is not known when or by whom the process of paper-making was discovered. It is generally believed, however, to be of Asian origin. By 300 B.C. the Chinese, who attribute the discovery of paper-making to one of their ancient statesmen, were using papers made from silk wastes for painting and writing. Paper was also being used in Taiwan (Formosa) and Korea before the Christian Era.

Figure 1. The Japanese have put paper to many novel uses. Among the most familiar of these is the paper kite. (Courtesy, The Smithsonian Institution, Washington, D.C.)

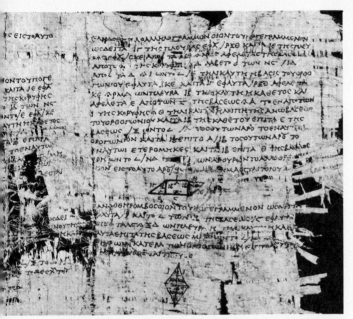

Figure 2. Papyrus is one of the most ancient forms of paper-like material. This Greek fragment (above) is inscribed with Euclidean geometry. (Courtesy, Chicago Natural History Museum.)

Throughout history almost every country has used paper in many ways other than writing or communication. The fine arts of painting, watercolor, and drawing, now usually done on canvas, were mostly produced on paper. In Mexico, where festivals have always been popular, paper was used for papier-mâché pinatas, banners, flags, and often even for costumes. The Japanese, famous for the artistic use of paper through *origami* and wood block prints, have long used paper in everyday life as well as for trimmings at festivals. The walls of many Japanese homes are built of thin translucent sheets of paper stretched across bamboo and wooden frames; Japanese kites in the form of a fish or large dragon are familiar sights. Indeed, there are similar special uses of paper for every country of the world.

The modern art of quilling was first known in the fifteenth century as rolled paper work. Later, in the seventeenth century, Italian nuns meticulously rolled small bits of paper around the quill end of a bird feather to use in decorating religious pieces of manuscript and ornamental plaques. Quilling spread through France, England, and then to colonial America as a craft which often replaced embroidery or tapestry work as a pastime.

Papier-mâché, the art of molding wastepaper,

was first introduced in France and Germany to use up paper left from newspapers, handbills, and posters. These ground-up papers were mixed with a paste and fashioned into such useful and decorative articles as toys, trays, frames for mirrors or pictures, and sometimes even furniture. Often, very old (200 years or more) and fine pieces of papier-mâché can be found in museums — objects made this way are more durable than might be imagined.

Paper is a significant creative craft material because of its versatility and adaptability. It can be twisted, cut, folded, laminated, lacquered, carved, ground-up, and sculpted. It is truly the most practical of all craft media due to its unusually low price and its availablity in a variety of sizes, shapes, and textures. There are coarse grades of paper, such as cardboard or press board, as well as very fine, expensive papers. Some papers have treated or coated surfaces to allow for special printing effects. Some are decorative, such as the very expensive and famous Japanese papers which have dried flowers, leaves, and butterflies pressed right into them. The type of paper used for paper craft depends upon the project. There are papers particularly suited to specific projects and each is easily obtained.

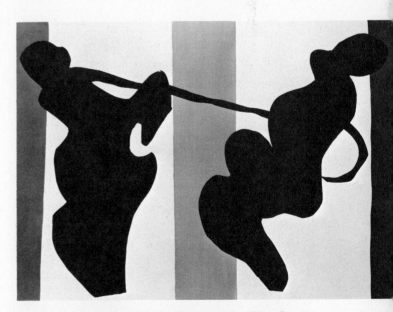

Figure 3. Henri Matisse's color stencil, "The Cowboy," demonstrates this artist's brilliant use of cut paper forms. (Courtesy, Collection, The Museum of Modern Art, New York. Gift of the Artist.)

Common Terms Used In Paper Crafts

Curl: to run paper over the straight side of a table, ruler, or edge of pair of scissors.

Expansion: the cutting and folding of paper to create expanded forms.

Grain: the direction in which the fibers of the paper run and in which the paper will roll the easiest.

Mash: the ground-up paper used in papier-mâché; can be sculpted and sanded.

Papier-Mâché: the art of working paper mixed with glue into forms and shapes.

Quill: to roll quilling paper into various shapes.

Quilling: the art of filigreed paper folding and rolling; openwork.

Score: to run across the paper with a blunt knife or dull scissors blade in order to break the top layer of the grain of the paper and achieve a crisp fold line.

Weight: the thickness of paper.

Basic Equipment And Supplies

The supplies necessary for paper crafts are easily acquired at crafts stores and often already on hand. A list of materials includes a variety of brushes for painting and applying glue; paper clips; a compass; polymer gloss medium; white craft glue; gesso, a glue and oil liquid; an X-acto knife for detailed work, a blade knife, and a dull kitchen knife for scoring; pencils; straight pins; a ruler with a metal edge; T-square; a stapler; scotch tape; and finally, of course, a variety of paper, including newspaper, medium-weight drawing paper, cardboard, colored tissue paper, quilling paper, waxed paper, and graph paper.

Basic Procedures

In order to facilitate the making of paper projects, it is best to learn at the outset some fundamental procedures in the manipulation of paper. Each of the techniques discussed here includes a small exercise to demonstrate its use, as well as to provide familiarity in working with paper. Because each new skill is based on a skill previously described, it will be to the reader's advantage to follow this section step-by-step. It would be best to use a medium-weight drawing paper for these projects; other types of paper can be used once the procedures are learned. Drawing paper can be bought in tablets of 25 or 50 sheets.

FOLDING

There are several ways to use folding as a tool in paper craft. Generally, unless the paper is quite thin, it first needs to be scored and then folded on the score mark. Therefore, draw a line where the fold is needed, then draw a dull knife or dull scissors along the line. Now erase the line and the paper should fold crisply where the score was made.

Straight Fold

As illustrated in the accompanying diagram, score and fold a 10" x 10" piece of paper (medium weight). This will produce the basic or accordion fold, which is used in most folded designs. It takes practice and patience because the paper can be

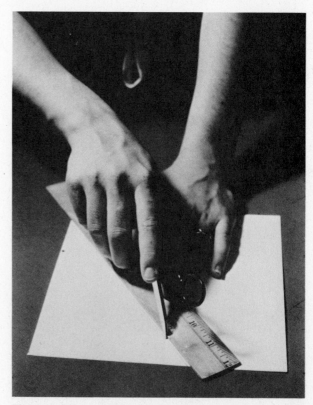

Figure 4. Use a ruler to draw a light line where a fold is needed. Then draw a dull knife or scissors along the line to score the paper for a crisp fold.

Figure 5. Accurate scoring is a necessity when preparing paper for the basic accordion fold.

easily crumpled. Do not try to bend the paper without scoring, or the paper will not form a crisp, even fold.

1. Draw the pattern onto the paper using a ruler and pencil. Make solid lines on one side and dotted lines on the other.

2. Score on the front of the sheet on the solid gray lines.

Figure 6. When the paper is properly scored and folded as shown, the accordion fold is neat and even.

3. Score on the back of the sheet on the dotted gray lines.

4. The paper should begin to crease itself into an accordion fold.

5. Bend the paper carefully without creasing anywhere except on a scored line.

Curved Fold

This fold is slightly harder because it is done working against the grain of the paper.

1. Scale and transfer the diagram illustrated to a sheet of 10" x 10" paper. (Place a sheet of tracing paper over the diagram and trace. Place the tracing over graph paper and count how many squares run across and down the tracing covers.) On the sheet of 10" x 10" paper, draw lightly the same graph but in a larger scale — e.g., one square equals 1/2" or 1". Then, redraw the pattern, extending the lines through the larger squares that correspond to the smaller squares. Again, draw solid lines on one side of the paper and dotted lines on the other side.

2. Carefully score the solid gray lines on the front side of the paper. Then score the dotted gray lines on the back side of the paper. The paper should begin to bend into a three-dimensional surface relief of curves.

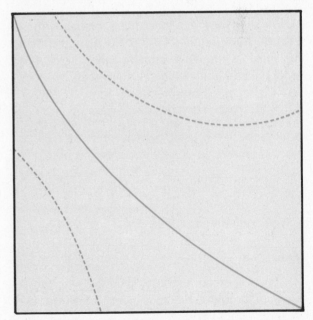

Figure 7. This curved fold pattern is worked against the grain of the paper. Make sure that solid lines are scored on the front side of the paper and dotted lines on the back side.

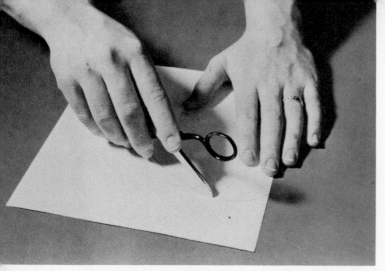

Figure 8. Hold paper securely while drawing the scissors across the curved fold lines (above). The completed fold (below) was carefully worked to avoid creases in areas other than those scored.

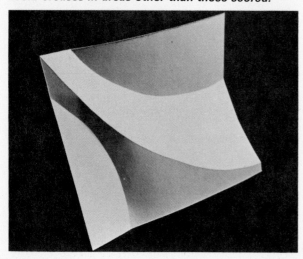

3. Practice with different sheets of paper to see exactly how much of a curve a particular paper will take without creasing in other areas; some papers "give" or stretch better than others.

CUTTING

Cutting is mainly used to create an outer edge and should always be done with some sort of padding underneath, such as several thicknesses of news-paper or a cutting board. Cutting may also be used for decorative slits or for expansion, which is a type of alternating cutting.

Expansion

To become accustomed to working with the pa-per, cut through a medium sheet of drawing paper several times with an X-acto knife. Work for a precise cut. If the edges of the cut are jagged or rough, either the blade is dull or the knife is being jerked through the paper. It is better to cut the

same place lightly two or three times to make the edges precise and crisp rather than press too hard with the knife, causing a rough, jagged cut.

1. On a sheet of scrap paper, with a ruler and pencil, lightly draw a line.

2. Put the ruler next to the line.

3. With the edge of the blade of the X-acto knife next to the metal edge of the ruler, cut precisely along the line.

4. On another scrap of paper, draw a curved line.

5. Without the ruler, practice cutting along curved lines with the knife.

6. Following the diagram, cut along the solid black line as evenly and as carefully as possible, being sure to cut all the way through the paper.

7. Pick up the piece of paper carefully in the center and gravity will pull it into shape, causing expansion.

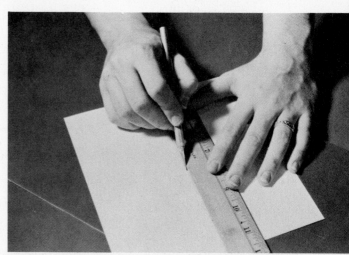

Figure 9. Draw a line on a piece of scrap paper and put the ruler next to the line. Cut along the line with an X-acto knife (above). Then draw a curved line and practice cutting without a ruler (below). Cutting surfaces should always be well padded.

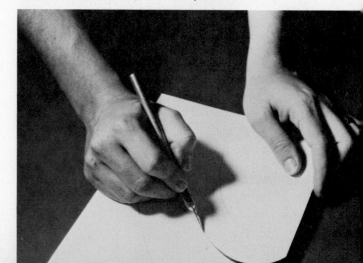

8. Trace the expansion pattern onto a 10″ x 10″ piece of paper.

9. Try more of the illustrated expansion diagrams. Cut along the solid black lines carefully and try a different type of expanded paper form each time.

Figure 10. The diagram (above) for a spiral fold should be carefully cut all the way through the paper along the solid black lines. When the paper is picked up in the center, it will fall into an interesting shape (below).

Cutting and Folding

After completing the expansion exercise, cutting should be much easier and it will be fairly simple to learn the process of cutting and folding. Familiar examples of this cutting procedure are Mexican folk art cutouts and lacy paper doilies. Because the paper is folded first, the resulting designs are almost always symmetrical.

To experiment with cutting and folding, take a piece of square paper and fold it once in half. (Practice cutting with the X-acto knife through folded scrap paper first.)

1. Transfer the pattern in one of the accompanying diagrams to the twice folded piece of paper.

2. Cut along the solid black lines, removing the negative or inner areas and leaving behind the outer form (the piece of paper is still held together).

3. Discard the small cut-out shapes and open the paper. The result will be the same design that was drawn onto the paper.

Figure 11. When paper is folded, cut designs are almost always symmetrical. This paper (below) was folded in half and the inner shapes were cut out.

Figure 12. These folded diagrams will make interesting patterns when the inner portions are cut out.

4. Experiment, using different folding methods, to create original patterns. For example, fold a sheet of paper three times and then in half once. Cut patterns as desired.

Cutting and Scoring

Creating a three-dimensional shape instead of a two-dimensional design with paper is most easily done by cutting and scoring. Each technique, when used alone, has its limits; but when combined, they produce numerous designs.

1. Transfer the diagram to a sheet of 10″ x 10″ paper, with a pencil.

2. Cut along the solid black lines.

3. Score on the front side along the solid gray lines.

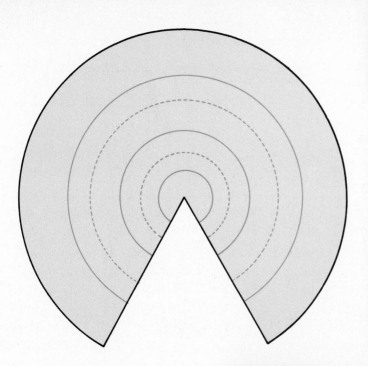

Figure 13. A three-dimensional shape may be made from this pattern (above). Cut along the black solid lines and score the gray and dotted lines (above right). Bend the scored lines, then overlap the edges and glue them together (right).

4. Score on the opposite side along the dotted gray lines.

5. Bend the shape along the scored lines carefully.

6. Bring edge A to edge B, creating a small three-dimensional relief sculpture.

7. Overlap these edges and glue them with small amounts of white craft glue (do not use too much). Several of these may be made and glued together. The diagrams offer other patterns with which to experiment.

BENDING AND CURLING

Bending and curling are primarily used to create small free-form sculptures. Working these two basic exercises will add to one's familiarity with the texture of paper and its ability to adapt to various shapes. Bending and curling are often used in making preliminary sculpture models in which the intended material, such as steel, would be too expensive with which to experiment. To do a bending test to check the direction of the grain, roll paper between hands to see which way it bends most easily — it will bend with the grain.

Bending

1. Using a 10" x 10" sheet of drawing paper and following the diagram, bend side A over to point C by curling or rolling the paper.

2. Staple the curl in place.

3. Bend side B under to point D and staple.

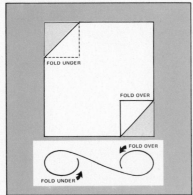

Figure 14. This is a diagram for a basic bend, a small free-form sculpture.

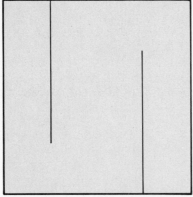

Figure 15. This diagram is for a bending and cutting exercise. Cut only the solid black lines and then bend the paper almost any way.

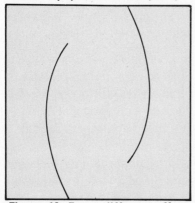

Figure 16. For a different effect, follow the curved cuts shown in this diagram.

Bending and Cutting

Bending by itself is somewhat limited until it is combined with cutting. Then, the possibilities of creating beautiful three-dimensional sculptures become limitless.

1. Transfer the diagram to a sheet of 10" x 10" paper. Use only straight cuts.

2. Cut along the solid black lines.

3. Bend these and staple into place either according to the diagram or at will.

4. With another 10" x 10" sheet of paper experiment with cutting and bending following the diagram, using only curved cuts. Notice the different effects. Now try the next exercise with straight and curved cuts and bending before scoring.

Additional Bending With Scoring

When scoring is added to bending and cutting,

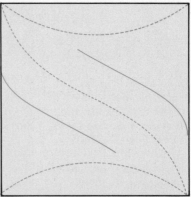

Figure 18. Another interesting design emerges as the pattern above is cut, scored, and bent.

Figure 17. These are two finished examples of cutting and bending patterns (below), created from two sheets of 10" by 10" paper.

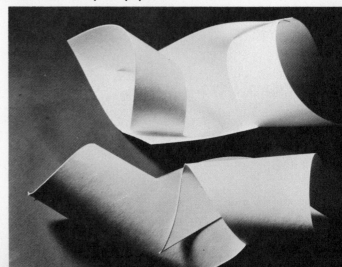

design or sculpture is further enhanced and expanded.

1. Trace the diagram onto a sheet of 10″ x 10″ paper.

2. Cut through the paper along the solid black lines, score along the front on the solid gray lines, and score on the opposite side along the dotted gray lines.

3. Bend the pieces indicated, letting the scored areas curve in and out naturally.

4. Staple where indicated. Try an original design — bending, scoring, and cutting. Then staple into place.

Curling

Curling the paper is almost the same as bending the paper, except that, in curling, the paper should retain its shape without glue or staples. There are many ways to curl paper — here are a few suggestions:

1. Roll a piece of paper 1″ wide and 3″ long tightly around a pencil. Release. Roll another piece of paper the same size around the fingers loosely, hold, then release. The difference is noticeable and will also depend on the type of paper used.

2. Pull a strip of paper over the edge of a table (only a table edge which is at a 90° angle will work), or pull the paper over the edge of a ruler. The paper will curl inward towards the side pulled over the table or ruler. Because one side of the paper has been stretched more than the other, the paper will curl. For extreme curling use the

Figure 19. These three paper forms are excellent examples of abstract designs. When bending and scoring, try to create original designs, letting the scored areas of paper curve in and out naturally.

Figure 20. When curling paper, pull it over a table or ruler or across a scissors blade (above). It may also be rolled around either the finger or a pencil (below).

edge of a scissors and pull the paper across the blade as on the ruler. Be cautious of the scissors' edges. Curling exercises are a good introduction to the art of quilling.

QUILLING

Quilling is decorative and very lacy. Each small piece is a strip of quilling paper (available at craft stores) 1/8″ wide rolled into a particular quilling shape and glued to the other pieces in a woven fashion.

Before beginning to quill, the basic rolls must be learned. Each roll is a variation on the first roll, which is called the *master* or *tight roll*. Take a strip of quilling paper and moisten one end. Bend one edge of the strip into a small fold. Insert the round end of a toothpick into the fold and begin wrapping or rolling the quilling paper around this end. Try to keep the paper tight while rolling it. By holding it as shown, the roll should remain aligned. The longer the strip of paper, the wider the roll will be. With a small amount of glue on the end of another toothpick, glue the loose end in place. Hold the roll until the glue is dry. Carefully remove the toothpick.

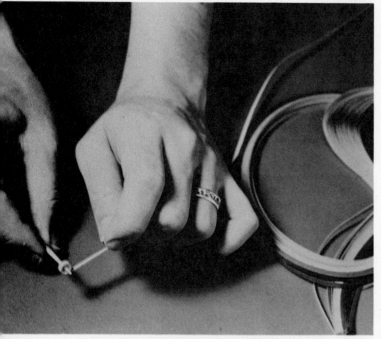

Figure 21. Begin decorative quilling by rolling a strip of quilling paper 1/8'' wide (above) into such shapes, as a master roll or tight roll (below).

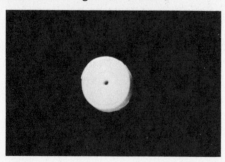

Loose Roll

Roll as for a tight roll, then let the roll unwind until the desired amount of looseness is achieved. Glue loose end as before.

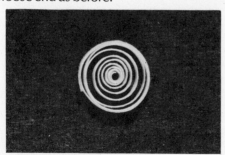

Teardrop or Leaf

Make a loose roll as above, gluing as before. Taper the glued end by pinching; leave the other end rounded.

Marquise

Make and glue a loose roll as before. Taper both the glued side and the opposite side into an eye shape, pinching it into a point.

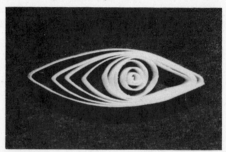

"S" Shape

In opposite directions, make a loose roll at each end of a strip of quill paper. Do not glue. Vary the tightness of the roll or the lengths between the rolls.

Scroll Shape

Loosely roll the ends of a strip of quilling paper towards the center. Distances and tightness can be varied.

"V" Shape

Pinch the center of a small strip of paper. Roll the ends out loosely — glue if desired.

Heart Shape

Pinch the center of a small strip of quilling paper and roll the ends to form a heart shape. Do not glue. After trying all of these basic rolls, try some of the combinations of rolls and scroll as indicated in the diagrams.

Lattice

Sometimes lattice is introduced into quilling to create lacy areas with an effect different from that of a roll. To make up lattice for special effects,

Figure 22. Lattice work objects (below) introduce an effect which is different from the usual roll design of quilling. The collar is useful as a support for the center of a quilling project.

place a piece of graph paper onto a foam board. Place a piece of translucent waxed paper over the piece of graph paper. Pin both to the foam board. Line strips of quilling paper flat onto the waxed paper, using the graph paper as a guide line. Pin ends of strips into place. Lay strips in the opposite direction, gluing with very small amounts of glue at each overlap.

Corners

Corner areas may be reinforced by putting several rolls together and then lining the edge with a strip of quilling paper, as illustrated in the diagram.

Collar

A collar is used to make the reinforcement for the center of a quilled frame. It is sometimes topped with a curled or braided rope. A braided rope is made by braiding three strips of quilling paper together and gluing the ends. This is then glued carefully to the top of the collar (see diagram). To top a collar with a curled rope, wind a piece of quilling paper around and up the length of a toothpick. Glue to top of collar for both decoration and added strength.

Quilling is usually done over a pattern, not in a free-form style. Once quilling is mastered, it is fun to experiment with original designs.

The following exercise is an introduction to the easiest method of working quills together.

1. Trace the pattern.

2. Place a sheet of translucent waxed paper over the pattern.

3. Pin both of these on a sheet of cardboard, or use another material in which pins may be inserted easily.

4. Make the first quill. In the illustration of the flower coaster, the first quill should be a marquise.

5. Place a pin in the center of the quill to hold it in place on the proper pattern.

6. Make a quill (in this case another marquise) which fits next to the first quill (see diagram).

7. Dot a small amount of white craft glue on the end of a toothpick and place a small amount where the first marquise contacts the second.

Figure 23. This elaborate pattern can be transferred to paper (below left) with the quilling pinned to the pattern (below right) for accuracy.

8. Pin the second piece into place, making sure the glue touches both areas.

9. Keep working until all the quills are glued into place.

10. Let dry and unpin. With a flat knife carefully slide the quills off, using the knife where glue is stuck to the waxed paper.

11. Move onto a piece of cardboard. Glue only small edge areas down (see diagram). Spray with acrylic clear spray for permanence and stiffness.

PAPIER-MÂCHÉ

Papier-mâché is the art of sculpting, molding, and pasting together wastepaper or the stripping and gluing of sheets of paper. Once the basics have been learned, almost any project can be crafted from papier-mâché: for example, rings and bracelets, toys, figurines, ornamental plaques, masks, and even simple furniture. In varied stages of drying, the paper may be carved, smoothed, or sculpted. When dry, it may be sanded, painted, and decorated in many possible ways. To learn to work with papier-mâché, a step-by-step procedure follows for making a coaster.

Strip Papier-Mâché

This process is used for major shape definition and under-strength in making any type of object. It is usually finished over with ground paper mash or is painted as is. The strips of paper are usually used over either heavy or corrugated cardboard or wire.

1. Cut a circle of corrugated cardboard the size for a coaster. Add about 1/4″ so that the layers of papier-mâché will not make the piece too small.

2. Cut a strip of corrugated cardboard 1/2″ wide and as long as the perimeter length (circumference) of the circle (see diagram).

3. Lay the circle flat. Run the piece of cardboard around the outside edge of the circle and tape the ends together with cellophane tape. Tape bottom to sides as shown in the diagram.

4. Tear sheets of newsprint in approximately 1/2″ strips (it is easiest and quickest to tear several sheets at a time by tearing them against the edge of a ruler).

5. With a wide brush, dampen one strip of paper with water. Coat the strip liberally with wheat or wallpaper paste. (Keep the brush, when not in use, in a jar or old container filled with water so that the paste will not harden. As after any project, clean the brush thoroughly with soap and water and hang it up to dry.) Wrap the strip around the sides of the coaster form (the cardboard shape) and bend the edges of the paper over the edges of the cardboard. Parts of the paper may be cut with scissors to make them fit more evenly over the form. With the brush and extra paste, work over the strip so that there are no air pockets and the paper flatly adheres.

6. Continue tearing and coating the strips, first with water, then with paste. Apply flatly to the cardboard form until there is a three-layer buildup of strips on the form.

7. Let the form dry overnight. (It will have a tendency to warp. To avoid this, place a rubber band around the edge of the coaster form to hold it in a circular shape until thoroughly dry.)

8. When the coaster is dry, a design may be painted on it with acrylic paints or poster paint. If using poster paint, apply two coats of clear lacquer for surface durability. The coaster may also be covered with paper mash.

Papier-Mâché Mash

This is ground up paper with stiffeners and glue added. It is used over a prepared surface such as the coaster described above. The mash may be purchased or it may be made at home. For the purposes of this project, it would be easier to buy the mash. It comes in one-pound packages in dry form.

1. For this project, use the coaster already made. Paint it with a thin coat of diluted glue (half water and half white craft glue).

2. Follow the instructions on the mash package for making it moist, pliable, and ready to use (prepare only a small amount at a time so that none will be wasted).

Figure 24. To use papier-mâché mash to finish a coaster, apply the mash (above) and blot it with a paper towel. Sand the dried coaster (below) until the surface is very smooth.

Figure 25. The entire coaster is painted with gesso (above) and, when dry, sanded again to a smooth surface. Acrylic paint is used for decoration (below) and a polymer will help to waterproof it.

3. Apply the mash with an old kitchen knife. Spread it evenly onto the sides and inside of the coaster. Do not cover the bottom of the coaster.

4. Blot the excess moisture with a paper towel to shorten the drying time.

5. Place the coaster on a tin pan in a 150° F oven with the door open. In about 20 minutes, the coaster should be almost dry.

6. Take it out and flatten or scrape along the surface of the mash with the kitchen knife to smooth out the unlevel areas — do as much of this as possible because it saves work later.

7. Allow the piece to dry overnight.

8. Smooth the dried coaster with sandpaper until the surface is uniform.

9. Paint the entire coaster except the bottom with gesso (a readily available water-based primer) and let it dry. The gesso will fill in those areas of the mash which are marred or have a texture. When the coaster is dry, *lightly* sand the surface again to make sure it is smooth.

10. Decorate the coaster with the pattern in the diagram or an original pattern. Use acrylic paint. Let it dry and then paint over the design with polymer gloss medium. The polymer will seal the surface and help to make the coaster waterproof. Coat it again with polymer and let dry.

11. Glue felt to the bottom and carefully trim the edges for an attractive finished effect.

Projects You Can Do

The following are useful and creative projects which will assist the beginner in understanding the many and varied effects that can be achieved with paper. The projects are easy to complete and are given in a step-by-step format. The first project is no harder than the last but it is imperative that the section "Basic Procedures" be reviewed before these projects are begun.

STAINED GLASS WINDOW

For this project the following items are necessary: (1) the materials described above, under "Basic Equipment and Supplies"; (2) a sheet of very heavy white poster board (see guidelines below regarding the size needed); (3) a variety of colors of tissue paper for the stained glass; (4) a can of white or black spray paint; and (5) a small jar of gloss acrylic medium.

To estimate the size of the window, measure the area of the window and frame to be covered and subtract 1/2" from the length and width. The window should not be placed where it might be exposed to extreme moisture.

Figure 26. This pattern will make a very effective paper stained glass window. It can be scaled to fit the measurements of any window.

Procedures

1. Plan a design of the window including desired colors on a separate sheet of paper. This may be an original design or one that is traced.

2. Scale the design to fit the area of the glass in the window.

3. Transfer or trace the design onto the front of the large piece of poster board in pencil.

4. With a matt knife, cut away the excess board from the edges so that it is the same size as the window measurements.

5. Again using a matt knife, cut precisely every area to be filled with the tissue paper. The area left after cutting should resemble the leaded areas of an actual stained glass window.

6. Spray the entire front and inner edges of this area with either white or black spray paint. This will insure a uniform front surface.

7. With an X-acto knife, cut out a piece of tissue paper to fit into the window. This will be glued from the back. Turn over the large cut-out design.

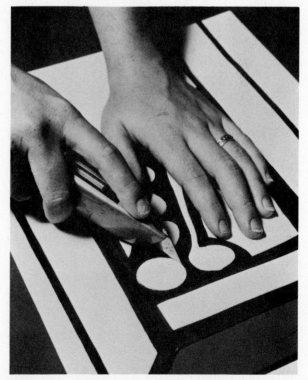

Figure 27. After tracing a design onto poster board, use a mat knife to cut away the excess board and the areas to be covered with tissue paper.

Figure 28. The tissue paper pieces are coated with gloss acrylic medium (above), which glues them to the poster board (below) and makes them translucent.

Lay the tissue paper over it and cut out a piece slightly larger than the area to be covered by that color.

8. (Practice this step first.) Lay the piece of tissue on some scrap paper and coat the front of it with gloss acrylic medium. While the piece of tissue is still wet, stretch it across the back of the major poster cut-out. The gloss medium will adhere the piece to the back of the poster board. Since tissue paper may bleed, try not to fold the tissue paper or get the bleed onto the hands while the tissue is still wet. Do not place this anywhere near the front of the window or it will transfer color onto the front. Let the piece of tissue dry and then trim away the excess edges.

9. Repeat this procedure with each additional area until the window is complete. Do not overlap colors. Let the window dry. The gloss medium should make the stained glass areas translucent. If there are places where the gloss medium on the piece of tissue is not sufficient to be transparent, repaint it from the back. Paint on the back color by color. Do not press hard with the brush while the tissue is wet because the fibers are weak and the tissue may tear.

10. Staple the window into place and touch up the staple marks. Do not glue the window into place or it will never come off. If the frame of the window is metal, tape the frame into place with double-faced tape.

The window should not be placed where it might be exposed to extreme moisture.

Figure 29. This stained glass window has been placed in a bedroom where the light filtered through the design creates a unique and pleasant effect.

PAPER-FOLDED SCULPTURAL HANGING LAMP

This sculpture should only be used as a mood lamp and not as a primary source for lighting a room. For fire safety and protection, use only a low watt light bulb in this lamp.

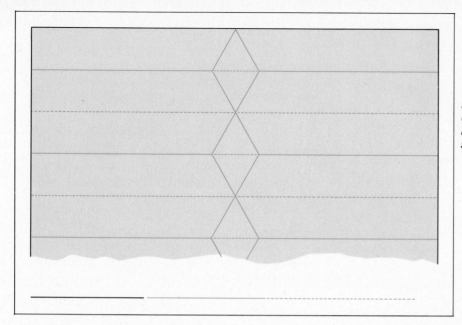

Figure 30. This is the basic diagram for a folded paper lantern. The lamp can be scaled to fit any area.

For this project, the following items are needed: a sheet of No. 2 white bristol paper or board or very heavy drawing paper, pencil, white craft glue, a paper punch, string or fishing line, clear spray varnish, shellac, and alcohol (or linseed oil).

Procedures

1. Transfer the diagram to the large sheet of paper. The measurements may be changed according to the desired size of the lamp.

Figure 31. For the paper lamp project, score and fold the lines (below). Use a paper punch (top right) to make holes for string (bottom right) that gathers the top and bottom of the lamp.

2. Score and fold on the lines indicated. Score on the solid gray lines on the front of the sheet. Score on the dotted gray lines on the back of the sheet. Fold the score lines carefully (do not fold anywhere except where the paper was scored).

3. With the paper punch, punch holes in the sides of the paper. These will then become the top and bottom of the lamp.

4. Referring to the diagram, bring side A to side B and glue carefully with white craft glue.

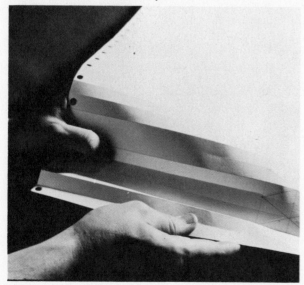

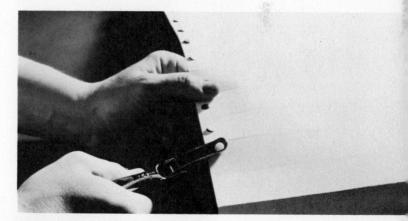

5. Running the fine string or fishing line through the punched holes, gather the top and bottom of the lamp as in the diagram.

6. To make the lamp translucent, paint it or coat it with a mixture of half shellac and half linseed oil or alcohol. Let dry (drying may require several days). Spray the lamp with clear spray varnish to provide durability. This should first be done to a small test strip of paper to make sure that it does not ruin the paper.

Either buy a lamp hanging fixture to use or make one. Never let the light bulb touch the lamp itself.

Figure 32. The finished sculptural lamp (above) makes a striking addition to any room.

TISSUE HOLDER

This project combines both quilling and papier-mâché. It may be used in a bedroom or bathroom.

Necessary supplies are: an empty tissue box, heavy corrugated cardboard, newspaper, wheat or wallpaper paste, cellophane tape, papier-mâché mash, papier-mâché tools, brush for mash, scissors, gesso, spray paint (optional), string, white craft glue, ruler and pencil, felt, acrylic paint, and sandpaper.

Procedures

1. Cut out the corrugated cardboard according to the illustration. The cardboard should be slightly larger than the tissue box — add 1/2" to each measurement.

2. Score along the fold lines as indicated.

3. Fold sides up and fasten with tape.

4. Check to see if tissue box fits loosely.

5. With a pad of newspaper under the work, begin dampening and coating layers of newspaper onto the box, alternating with water and wheat paste.

6. Cut a few sheets of newspaper large enough to completely wrap around the sides and bottom of the box.

7. Make sure to brush each time over the entire surface so that all air pockets are removed between the cardboard and the newspaper.

8. Cut pieces to finish the corners. Completely wrap the box with newspaper, inside and out.

9. Repeat until all areas of the box are covered with three coats of newspaper.

10. Cut a lid out of corrugated cardboard to fit the box. The dimensions of the lid should be slightly larger than the bottom of the box.

11. Carefully cut out an oval area from the center of the lid. (The center of the lid is easily determined by running diagonals from one corner to the opposite corner. Where the diagonals meet is the center.)

12. Make a rim 3/8" high that will run 1/4" inside the bow on the lid.

13. With paste and newspaper (which has been

ripped into strips), apply the rim to the bottom of the lid — use three coats of newspaper to secure it.

14. Put the lid on the box to make sure that it fits. Make any necessary alterations in the rim at this point because it is very difficult to change after it has dried.

15. Cut strips of newspaper as in the illustration to fit around the oval area of the lid. With other strips of newspaper, begin to cover the top and bottom of the lid with alternating layers of paste, water, and newsprint until the top, bottom, and oval edge have three coats of paper. Work around the rim on the bottom. It is a good idea to alternate the paper at the edge of the oval and the paper covering the top so there will be no bulging areas.

16. Let the pieces dry completely. To avoid warping, place small pieces of cardboard at the edges and corners of the box and then secure it tightly with string. Place the lid flat side down and weight it with small stones to keep it flat (do not place the stones on the rims).

17. Now make up 1 quart of paper mash.

18. Wet the surface of the *sides* of the holder and the *top* of the lid with a thin mixture of half glue and half water. Do not put the mash on the inside of the box, the bottom of the holder, or the bottom of the lid.

19. Press a layer of mash onto the top of the lid, along the edges of the oval cut-out and on the ends of the lid.

20. Blot excess moisture with a paper towel.

21. With a kitchen knife, apply mash to the sides of the holder; blot.

22. Put both the holder and the lid on an old tin pan and place into a 150° F oven to dry. Leave the pieces in for 20 minutes with the door open. This will remove most of the moisture but not all of it.

23. Remove both pieces from the oven. With the flat side of the kitchen knife, smooth over the lid and sides of the holder until as smooth as possible.

24. Let dry completely and sand first with coarse sandpaper, then medium, and then fine until the areas covered with mash are again as smooth as possible.

Figure 33. The newspaper covered cardboard box should have a matching top with either a rectangular or oval opening in the center. Be sure the pieces match before any further work is done.

Figure 34. The cover of the tissue holder (above) has a rim that is placed on the underside, 1/4" from the edges. This will insure a good fit. The overall size of the holder should be tested with a tissue box (below) before it is finished.

Figure 35. The completed tissue holder (above) combines both quilling and papier-mache work. It is not only attractive but very durable.

25. Dust the holder and top with a dry brush to remove excess sanding mash.

26. Give the holder and the top a coat of gesso and let dry. The gesso will fill in any rough, pitted areas and should dry in several hours if the coat is not too thick.

27. Sand lightly again to insure a slick surface.

28. Paint the inside of the holder and the bottom of the lid with a brush and acrylic paint of desired color.

29. Paint the outside of the holder and the top of the lid with the same color or a contrasting color.

30. Let dry and check to see if the tissue box still fits.

For Additional Reading

Johnston, Mary Grace, **Paper Sculpture,** Davis, 1952.

Johnson, Pauline, **Creating With Paper,** Univ. of Washington Press, 1967.

Kenny, Carla, and John B., **The Art of Papier-Mâché,** Chilton, 1968.

Ogawa, Hiroshi, **Forms of Paper,** Van Nostrand Reinhold, 1971.

Wallace, Maud, **Decorative Quilling,** Craft Course Pub., 1973.